Praise for *Pornified*

"A dire portrait of porn's influence on our lives."

—*Milwaukee Journal-Sentinel*

"A persuasive argument that today's pornography is not the *Playboy* centerfold or the *Deep Throat* of yesteryear. . . . Paul's remedy charts a sensible middle ground between restraints and free speech."

—*The Washington Post Book World*

"Pamela Paul convincingly and sometimes shockingly details the effects on men, women, and children of living in a 'pornified' world. Her book should be a wake-up call for parents and should change the way we view—and rationalize viewing—pornography today. As Paul makes clear, porn is not 'cool,' or 'liberating,' or basically benign. It is a poison eroding relationships between men and women and darkening our children's horizons."

—Judith Warner, author of *Perfect Madness*

"The great virtue of Pamela Paul's book is that it deals with pornography at the level of human experience. . . . A refreshing and utterly correct response."

—*Commentary*

"This is a quietly forceful book. It helps everyone—from libertarian to moralist—by offering a common ground from which to proceed: pornography is one more alienating product of a consumer culture, and in some ways a particularly lonely one. By definition it is selfish. That doesn't mean it needs to be banned; it does mean we need to think about what it's doing to each of us, and to our shared society."

—Bill McKibben, author of *Enough* and *The End of Nature*

"Confronts porn head-on."

—*The Boston Globe*

"Plenty to unnerve the knee-jerk 'free speech crowd' . . . A major water-cooler book."

—*Publishers Weekly*

"*Pornified* is rife with the tales of Americans experiencing a new level of sexual pathos, filled with snapshots of surreptitious lives: it is as compelling as it is troubling. A provocative book, sure to stir debate and reflection."

—Alissa Quart, author of *Branded: The Buying and Selling of Teenagers*

"Pamela Paul has written a brave and important book about the ubiquity of porn and how it shapes what we expect of women, sex, and human contact. It's enough to make defenders of an unbridled free market and even a few *Girls Gone Wild* fans think twice about the culture we're living in, and how we made it."

—Margaret Talbot, senior fellow, New America Foundation, and staff writer, *The New Yorker*

Pornified

Also by Pamela Paul

The Starter Marriage and the Future of Matrimony

Pornified

How Pornography Is Damaging Our Lives, Our Relationships, and Our Families

PAMELA PAUL

A Holt Paperback
Henry Holt and Company | New York

Holt Paperbacks
Henry Holt and Company, LLC
Publishers since 1866
175 Fifth Avenue
New York, New York 10010
www.henryholt.com

Distributed in Canada by H. B. Fenn and Company Ltd.

Library of Congress Cataloging-in-Publication Data

Paul, Pamela.
Pornified : how pornography is damaging our lives, our relationships, and our families / Pamela Paul.—1st ed.
p. cm.
Includes index.
ISBN-13: 978-0-8050-8132-9
ISBN-10: 0-8050-8132-1
1. Pornography—Social aspects—United States. 2. Popular culture—United States.
I. Title.
HQ472.UP38 2005
306.77'0973—dc22

2005041760

Henry Holt books are available for special promotions and premiums. For details contact: Director, Special Markets.

Originally published in hardcover in 2005 by Times Books

First Holt Paperbacks Edition 2006

Designed by Paula Russell Szafranski

Printed in the United States of America

3 5 7 9 10 8 6 4 2

For M.S.

Contents

Author's Note

Throughout the book, I have recorded and reported speech in the words of the individuals interviewed. I have chosen to use these individuals' slang, graphic descriptions, and vulgar language because they accurately reflect the way in which people think about and discuss pornography. The use of sexually explicit and crude language is part of the story of how pornography is changing our lives; to avoid such language in *Pornified* would give less than a full picture.

Pornified

Introduction: A Pornified World

What's a nice girl like you doing writing a book about porn?"

This was the first question editors asked when I initially proposed this book. And I was asked over and over again. Two months into my research, I was hunched over a worn paperback, making cramped notes in the margins, on a bench outside Independence Hall in Philadelphia. Out of the corner of my eye, I saw the well-dressed man seated next to me lean over and peer at the book cradled in my lap. "Why are you reading a book about pornography?" he asked in a gruff midwestern voice. His primly coiffed wife looked up. "A book about *what*?" she asked.

I had never discussed pornography with septuagenarians before. I saw myself through their eyes and wondered what they could possibly make of me, a young woman calmly flipping through a book on pornography in the middle of the day, smack out in public. "I'm writing a book about it," I said, somewhat abashed. "This is just research," I explained, realizing how defensive I sounded.

"Are there any girlie pictures in that book?" the man asked, squinting at the pages. I told him it was a collection of essays and he frowned.

"It's ruining this country," muttered his wife. "Just terrible. Pornography everywhere. Not like it was when we were young." She shifted in her seat and sighed, then suddenly became animated. "Do you remember your uncle Joe?" she asked her husband, nudging his side. "He had those special poker cards, with the naked girls, remember? That's what pornography was when we were young."

"Wolf cards," her husband responded with a slow smile, pleased at his recollection. "That's what they were called. Wolf cards."

"But it was so much tamer than what's out there today," his wife continued. "Nothing like what you have in *Playboy* or one of those magazines. We just didn't have that. Kids today are exposed to such awful things." She fingered her pearl necklace, staring at its clasp.

"So," her husband said, turning to me once again. "Pro or con?" I looked at him, confused, and he repeated, "Is it pro or con? Your book, I mean. What are you going to say about pornography?"

• • •

For most of my life, I gave little thought to pornography. It was not something I considered relevant to me, nor did I consider it—in the daunting spectrum of social, cultural, and political problems—a particularly pressing issue facing this country. Pornography had played a negligible role in my own life and, I assumed, had little effect on the lives of those important to me. Like many Americans, I believed pornography was no big deal. But on assignment to write about pornography for *Time* magazine, my eyes were blown wide open. During the weeks spent researching my article, I spoke with dozens of men and women about how profoundly pornography had affected their lives. I talked to male pornography users, female pornography fans and girlfriends of pornography fans, sex addicts and their wives, child psychologists and couples therapists.

One twenty-four-year-old woman from Baltimore confided, "I find that porn's prevalence is a serious hindrance to my comfort level in relationships. Whether it's porn DVDs and magazines lying around the house, countless porn files downloaded on their computers, or even trips to strip clubs, almost every guy I have dated—as well as my male friends—is very open about his interest in porn. As a result, my body image suffers tremendously. . . . I wonder if I am insecure or if the images I see guys ogle every day has done this to me." She later confessed that she felt unable to air her concerns to anyone: "A guy doesn't think you're cool if you complain about it. Ever since the Internet made it so easy to access, there's no longer any stigma to porn."

A thirty-eight-year-old woman from a Chicago suburb described her husband's addiction to pornography: "He would come home from work, slide food around his plate during dinner, play for maybe half an hour with the kids, and then go into his home office, shut the door, and surf Internet porn for hours. I knew—and he knew that I knew. I put a filter on his browser that would e-mail me every time a pornographic image was captured. . . . I continually confronted him on this. There were times I would be so angry I would cry and cry and tell him how much it hurt. . . . It got to the point where he stopped even making excuses. It was more or less 'I know you know and I don't really care. What are you going to do about it?' "

From the other side, from dozens of men, I heard about how something that once seemed fun was having unexpected side effects. A twenty-eight-year-old New Yorker wrote me an e-mail that said, "I used to view porn online, but I began to find it more difficult to stay aroused when having sex with a real woman. It's an interesting feedback loop, because I watched porn before I ever had sex, and in the old days, if I was having trouble staying aroused for other reasons (e.g., too drunk), I could visualize scenes from those movies and that would help. But later on, during a dry spell, I discovered i-porn, and the easiness of it made it easy to glut—to the point where now, even though the dry spell is over, real sex has now lost some of its magic. And that's sad."

Much of what I heard was not just news; it was revelatory. There was a story about pornography that had not yet been told, a story many Americans, male and female, don't realize is unfolding—in front of their eyes, inside their minds, on their family computer—at this very moment.

But instead of hearing these stories, we hear about the new craze for porn-star-penned memoirs and for the latest pornographic movies, TV shows, and Web sites. Still, no widespread public outcry. Men and women who came of age during the sixties, seventies, or eighties, or whose experience with pornography date to those eras, think of pornography in terms of gauzy centerfolds, outré sexuality, women's liberation, and the Hugh Hefner lifestyle. Back then, the lines between softcore and hardcore pornography were clear and distinguishable. Mainstream nudie magazines differed fundamentally from the tawdry interiors of adult stores and even from the pages of *Hustler* magazine. You could easily limit your consumption by selecting the desired publication. Likewise, the lines between the pro-pornography and the anti-pornography forces were distinct. To be for pornography was to stand in favor of civil liberties, sexual liberation, and science. Opposition to pornography was considered repressive, reactionary, and anti-sex. Dislike or disgust with obscenity could simply be reduced to some form of religious superstition, sexual shame, or fear.

Scroll back to the fifties, when pornography was relegated to dusty newsstand corners or to run-down adult theaters on the wrong side of town. Or even to the eighties, when pornography was surreptitiously obtained on videocassettes via mail-order catalogs or watched in the back rooms of video stores. People were ashamed of, or, at the very least, embarrassed by, the prospect of being caught looking at porn. It just plain wasn't considered nice to look at dirty pictures. (Of course, pornography's secretive nature contributed to its allure.) When confined to certain all-male circumstances—bachelor parties, army stints, auto garages, prep school dormitories—pornography gained a level of acceptability, but even then, it carried with it a tinge of embarrassment.

Today, pornography is so seamlessly integrated into popular culture that embarrassment or surreptitiousness is no longer part of the equation. How many eleven-year-old boys or girls would be ashamed or amazed to discover a copy of *Penthouse* or *Hustler* when the Internet regularly features full-motion pornographic banner ads, e-mail boxes overflow with messages marked XXX, and Christina Aguilera chants about the delights of being "dirty"? Would *Playboy* have the power to shock, scare, or confuse a preteen girl today? Would it even have the power to titillate a preteen boy, exposed to the "everything but" covers of men's magazines that bray from the local newsstand—magazines that would have once been considered softcore pornography but today have slipped into the mainstream media? Would it surprise in a world in which preteens read *CosmoGirl!* rather than *Young Miss* magazine? In a world where

Monica Lewinsky is yesterday's female headline rather than Mary Lou Retton? In a world in which sitcoms like *Friends* make regular unmasked references to pornography, a far cry from the occasionally ribald—but couched—humor of *Laverne & Shirley*?

The all-pornography, all-the-time mentality is everywhere in today's pornified culture—not just in cybersex and *Playboy* magazine. It's on *Maxim* magazine covers where even women who ostensibly want to be taken seriously as actresses pose like *Penthouse* pinups. It's in women's magazines where readers are urged to model themselves on strippers, articles explain how to work your sex moves after those displayed in pornos, and columnists counsel bored or dissatisfied young women to rent pornographic films with their lovers in order to "enliven" their sex lives. It's on VH-1 shows like *The 100 Hottest Hotties* where the female "experts"—arbiters in judging the world's sexiest people—are *Playboy* centerfolds (the male experts are pop stars and journalists), and on Victoria's Secret prime-time TV specials, which attracted a record nine million viewers in 2003. Softcore pornography has now become part and parcel of the mainstream media. The majority of men interviewed for this book did not consider *Playboy*—once the epitome of the genre—to even be pornography at all, because it doesn't depict actual sex acts. "True" pornography today is confined only to the hardcore.

Pop music is intimately connected with the pornography industry as today's pop stars embrace and exalt the joys of porn. Eminem, Kid Rock, Blink 182, Metallica, Everclear, and Bon Jovi have all featured porn performers in their music videos. Trying to keep up, Britney Spears, Lil' Kim, and Christina Aguilera emulate porn star moves in their videos and live concerts. Pornography has not only seeped into televised music videos; musicians have crossed over into the adult film industry. Rock musicians regularly date porn stars, cameo in their movies, and invite them backstage. *Rolling Stone,* hardly a staid publication, notes, "Until recently, public fraternizing with a porn star was pretty much a no-no; now it lends the musicians an aura of danger and intrigue."[1] Rap artists and hip-hop stars such as Snoop Dogg ("Snoop Dogg's Doggystyle"), Ice T ("Ice T's Pimpin'"), and Lil Jon & The East Side Boyz have all created pornographic videos. VH-1 offers a show called *Porn to Rock and Rap,* in which, its Web site breathlessly describes:

> The worlds of music and porn link together perfectly. In the rock world, porn stars are seen as trophies, adding a coolness factor to a rock star's image. In the rap world, porn is another way rap stars can be entrepreneurs and make their paper. The stars in each genre of music go about it differently, but they all have learned that porn and porn stars are a GOOD thing. We will examine the history of the marriage, the current slew of musicians involved, and get behind the scenes of this interesting arena.

According to a report by Black Entertainment Television, "The Making of Sex Hop," the link between hip-hop and pornography began a decade ago when DJ Yella of NWA made a pornographic film in 1994. "I set about to change things," Yella explained matter-of-factly to *Adult Video News*. "By putting my name on it and associating it with rap, I'm bringing porn to the mainstream."[2]

Pornography has not only gone mainstream—it's barely edgy. On the recent fiftieth anniversary of *Playboy,* Hugh Hefner, seventy-seven, was treated like an elder media statesman, with a front-page profile in the *New York Times* Arts section and a Christie's auction of his personal memorabilia. A coffee-table book of porn star portraits published in the fall of 2004 featured essays by literary luminaries from Salman Rushdie to A. M. Homes and was accompanied by a documentary special on HBO. A wave of porn-infused fare is putting pornography on a par with family entertainment. Mainstream cable channels like HBO offer up series such as *G-String Divas* and *Cathouse*. A reality show hosted by porn star and California gubernatorial candidate Mary Carey, *Can You Be a Porn Star?,* launched on Time Warner's InDemand in 2004. On Bravo, a reality show called *Private Stars* features five men locked in a house with five porn actresses. The men are judged on sexual performance with the winner awarded a contract by a producer of pornographic films; the show crossed the Atlantic after a successful run in Europe and the U.K.[3]

Pornography is taking on Hollywood, too. In Regency Pictures' 2004 film *The Girl Next Door,* a love story unfolds between a teenage boy and his porn star neighbor played by Elisha Cuthbert, who played a teenager herself on the hit Fox TV series *24.* The film celebrates pornography—its producers, its fans, and its very existence—even as it portrays its starlet as eager to escape the shame and degradation of the industry. Stars keep signing up for Hollywood's take on porn, keen to replicate the indie cool of the 1997 film *Boogie Nights.* Jeff Bridges recently joined an ensemble cast for the indie comedy *Moguls,* about a small town banding together to make a porn film—an update of *The Full Monty*? As Brian Grazer, whose 2005 documentary *Inside Deep Throat* looks at the first pornographic film to move into the mainstream, explains, "We're experiencing in a much grander fashion porno chic. I think it's now entering the mainstream in a much more pervasive way than the fad surrounding *Deep Throat.* If you're going to spend the time or money to make a movie and you want it to be sexually charged, you're forced to go further because we've become somewhat sexually desensitized. Every poster and television ad, you get on the Internet and it's clogged on pornography. I think if a filmmaker wants to have impact or shock you—and that's what movies have to do—you have to find original images that shock."[4]

Meanwhile, pornographers have crossed over into the mainstream media. Hugh Hefner recently appeared in commercials for fast-food chain Carl's Jr. Jenna Jameson, the porn star who reportedly earned more than a million dollars in 2002, wrote a bestselling book entitled *How to Make Love Like a Porn Star* with former *New York Times* reporter Neil Strauss. In addition to her own Web site, Jameson makes regular TV appearances and writhes in music videos, and has appeared in Hollywood films such as *Analyze That* and—surprise, surprise—*Private Parts,* a Howard Stern vehicle. Ron Jeremy, the star of more than 1,800 X-rated films, has become a recognizable brand outside the X-rated film aisle. He starred in the WB reality show *The Surreal Life* and in his own documentary film, *Porn Star—The Legend of Ron Jeremy,* and has cameoed in mainstream films such as *The Rules of Attraction, Detroit Rock City,* and *Killing Zoe.* These days, Jeremy tours shopping malls and makes regular appearances on the university lecture circuit, where he is typically met by thousands of adoring fans, many of them teenagers charmed by his retro-cool "Starsky and Hutch" style. He also shows up at wet T-shirt contests, rock concerts, and other live and televised entertainment events. Kids love him. In May 2004, the ex–porn star was treated to a VIP pass at Disney World in Orlando, where he was mobbed by "clean-cut dads and moms and their kids [who] took turns snapping pictures with him all day," according to local reports.[5]

While pornography has seeped into mainstream culture, the images that remain confined to the porn world have become increasingly intense. Old school defenders of pornography may not be familiar with the direction in which Internet and DVD-era pornography has gone. They might not understand the infinite possibilities offered by online pornography and the intoxicating effects of the anonymity, accessibility, and affordability of the Internet. They have most likely not watched recent hardcore videos, such as *Gag Factor 15*, the latest in a popular series of pornographic movies in which the action takes place in a room full of men in head scarves and masks holding photos of torture from Abu Ghraib. They probably haven't heard the sound track of such a film, in which one man screams nonsensically in what is supposed to be Arabic while another translates, "We will do to your women what you have done to our men—you degraded our people, now we'll degrade yours. The streets will spill over with spit!" They probably have not continued to watch as the film shows the men standing over a woman dressed in military clothes and dog tags shouting, "I was only following orders!" Or seen the penultimate move where one of the "Arab" men brandishes a sword and threatens to slice off the girl's head before the film's true climax, multiple oral sex scenes in which the girl is shown to choke on genitalia and semen.[6]

Pornography itself has changed radically over the last twenty years, but outdated ideas about pornography have gone unchallenged and so-called eternal truths have been perpetuated without protest. Back in the seventies and eighties, pornography was a topic of much discussion. Both men and women debated its merits and harms, its legality and morality, its inevitability and its outcomes, but by the late nineties, the debate quieted down. In Christian corners and enclaves of the social Right, outcry occasionally emerges and is ignored by the mainstream as so many Puritans in search of the next Salem. Elsewhere, when talking about pornography today, one hears complacencies and certainties such as:

- "Porn is harmless; it's just looking at pictures. What's wrong with fantasy?"
- "If we women want to be naked and be proud of our bodies, what's the problem? We're in control, and it's our choice."
- "All men look at porn. It's human nature—men are biologically programmed to be visually stimulated."
- "If you believe in civil liberties and freedom of the press, you've got to be in favor of porn."
- "Women are objectified everywhere—advertisements, movies, fashion magazines. Pornography is no different—and there's nothing that can be done about it anyway."
- "Only scumbags use pornography. Who cares what a bunch of lowlifes do?"

We hear these arguments all the time. We hear them from men who do not view pornography themselves and from women who would be appalled to find out their boyfriends watch pay-per-view porn in hotels while traveling on business. We hear them from parents who would shudder to know their ten-year-old sons are clicking on Internet porn when they're allegedly doing homework.

Americans are nonetheless confident they already know everything there is to know about pornography. After all, pornography has been around in one form or another for as long as "the oldest profession" has been in working order. Men have always looked at pictures of naked ladies. Women have in turn often tried to sneak a peek at naked men (albeit somewhat more of a challenge). And couples have looked at other naked couples doing things they may or may not have wanted to do—or wondered what they were missing if they didn't.

It's difficult, therefore, to approach a subject like pornography from a fresh perspective. Both men and women have so many preconceptions: a person is either for pornography or against it, a prude or a player, a religious fanatic or a radical feminist, Larry Flynt or Andrea Dworkin. There is no middle ground on the playing field of consumers and abstainers, civil libertarians and Comstockian curmudgeons. Yet framing the debate in terms of distorted polarities ignores the vast middle ground where pornography plays a significant and growing role. One need not be a prude or a religious zealot to experience revulsion at the sight of certain pornography, just as one need not be a depraved pervert or a lefty activist to use pornography.

The fact is, none of the current assumptions reflect how pornography really affects people and their relationships—and to continue to abide by them would mean ignoring an issue that is transforming most Americans' lives. Instead of relying on political posturing and abstract arguments, I have sought answers to some simple questions: Who uses pornography and why? What do men see in it? Are more women indulging? How does pornography affect people? Will looking at online pornography at age nine affect boys and girls when they reach sexual maturity? What is the impact of a pornified culture on relationships and on society as a whole?

Countless other books have treated the supply side—the subject of pornography itself: the images and the industry, the players and the played with, the production values and profitability. This book will leave that subject alone. Only when it is relevant will I dwell on the particulars of pornography itself. Instead, this book discusses the demand—who uses pornography and how—and why it matters even to those who do not use pornography. This story is about how pornography's growth, ubiquity, and acceptance are affecting American society, told through the words and lives of the people who know it best: pornography consumers. To find out the private stories that people suspect but never hear, experience but never talk about, I interviewed more than a hundred people (approximately 80 percent male) about the role pornography plays in their lives. Perhaps surprisingly, men were quite willing to open up about a subject they rarely get to discuss seriously and at length. Both men and women were often relieved to have the opportunity to explore issues that are usually swept under the bedsheets.

While the scope of such qualitative research can never claim to be fully representative of all Americans, the people interviewed were expressly chosen to provide a broad spectrum. They ranged in age from twenty-one to fifty-nine; most were in their twenties and thirties. They were heterosexual (a whole other book could be written about gay pornography, an opportunity I leave to others). The men and women interviewed were otherwise diverse—ethnically, geographically, socioeconomically. They were from a variety of backgrounds and religions, educations, and occupations. No "profile" of the pornography user emerged because pornography cuts across all swathes of society.

In addition, I commissioned the first nationally representative poll of Americans to deal primarily with pornography. Unlike other polls referred to in this book, many of which were online surveys, this poll actually reflects what the spectrum of Americans think; the poll is weighted demographically and geographically to represent the actual ethnic, age, and socioeconomic composition of America. It's the first poll to ask many important questions, such as: Does pornography improve the sex lives of those who look at it? Is using pornography cheating? Do you believe all men look at pornography? How does pornography affect the children who view it? This poll, conducted by Harris Interactive, will be referred to throughout the book as the *Pornified*/Harris poll.

My point is not to outline a comprehensive overview of pornography users in America but to use individual stories to illustrate key themes and trends, and back them up with solid quantitative data. The comments of one interviewee were often repeated by multiple interviewees, but rather than reiterate exhaustively what I heard, I chose to highlight prevalent themes through a sampling of individual stories that were typical or representative. Few subjects are more private than sexuality, and pornography in particular is a sensitive topic. For this reason all of my interviewees have been given pseudonyms and any identifying characteristics have been obscured in the pages that follow; their words are rendered just as they spoke them.

I will show, through real-life experiences and evidence, how and why all of us—men and women, users and nonusers, advocates and foes—must rethink the way we approach pornography. The pornification of American culture is not only reshaping entertainment, advertising, fashion, and popular culture, but it is fundamentally changing the lives of more Americans, in more ways, than ever before. We are living in a pornified culture and we have no idea what this means for ourselves, our relationships, and our society.

1

A Guy Thing: Why Men Look at Porn

If dominant wisdom holds true, then all men look at pornography. In an essay in *Glamour* magazine entitled, "Why Nice Guys Like Online Porn," the anonymous author "Jake" claims, "The world is made up of two different kinds of guys: those who are turned on by porn and those who are really, *really* turned on by porn. If a guy tells you he's impervious to smut, the truth is: for reasons moral, religious or masochistic he has chosen never to look at it; he is afraid of his own sexuality; or he's lying."[1] Like Jake, most men who look at pornography believe that every man—liberal, conservative, uptight, married, or religious—looks at pornography. And nearly every man in America probably has at some point.

But is it true that all men look at pornography, at least occasionally, throughout their lives? Ethan, a twenty-seven-year-old music executive, is a typical porn consumer. When asked his opinion on pornography, he immediately says with a laugh, "I love porn. I think it's fantastic." He started looking at it in seventh grade, when he stumbled across a stack of magazines belonging to a friend's divorced father. After that, he turned to pornography regularly, beginning with print, upgrading to video and then

DVD, and ultimately going dot-com, especially after getting broadband at home. These days, Ethan logs on every day for about twenty minutes, when he's bored at work, or feels like goofing around. He and a group of about ten guys—"a bunch of lecherous friends in the industry"—will e-mail one another good porn gathered during their Internet forays. Funny Web sites, really hot girls, celebrity porn, sick stuff. The strangest things can be found when you're surfing. Working in the music business—not a traditional corporate environment, he emphasizes—it's no big deal to have porn playing on your computer. Once, a female colleague walked into Ethan's office and noticed explicit pornography beaming out from his screen. "I said, 'Check it out!' and she laughed," he recalls. "She thought it was pretty amusing." At home, he pops in a pornographic DVD about three times a week. Every morning, he listens to Howard Stern; he particularly enjoys when porn stars are on the show. For Ethan, pornography is a natural part of life. Men, he explains, are visual beasts and overtly sexual people. They're built for porn.

Reliable figures are hard to come by, as many people are reluctant to admit to their usage even with the anonymity of a phone or online survey. But some statistics give an inkling. Discretion notwithstanding, pornography is demonstrably a popular pastime. In an online survey of 10,543 Americans by the Kinsey Institute, only 3 percent of respondents said they had never looked at pornography.* Only 20 percent of respondents said they had looked at pornography before but hadn't looked at least once in the past month. That leaves 77 percent of respondents looking at pornography at least once in any given thirty-day period. Of these, 58 percent said they looked at least once a week and 19 percent looked at least once every day. When they do look, they frequently spend a lot of time. One quarter of those who looked in the past month had spent at least six hours doing so. A number of polls have looked specifically at Internet pornography. A nationally representative Zogby poll in 2000 reported that 32 percent of men and 11 percent of women said they had

*This Kinsey poll was a voluntary online survey whose results are interesting and valid, but not nationally representative. The results do not reflect the population of the United States, but are more likely to represent Internet users interested in talking to the Kinsey Institute about pornography.

visited a sexually oriented Web site.* Younger Americans were more likely to visit such sites: 37 percent of eighteen- to twenty-four-year-olds compared with 22 percent of thirty-five- to fifty-four-year-olds. Of those who visited such sexually oriented Web sites, nearly half were in committed relationships.

Women frequently ask, What *is* it men like so much about porn? I know lots of guys are into porn, some men say, but I don't understand the appeal. Only those who look at pornography understand their reasons for doing so, and at first, many of them have a hard time giving an answer. But when offered an opportunity to think it over, nearly all open up and divulge the appeal—how and why they started looking, the ways they respond to different kinds of pornography, the physical and emotional benefits they derive from it, and how it makes them feel. Most have never had the chance to freely discuss what lies behind their pornography preferences, and it's only while talking about it that many begin to learn the answers themselves.

For Ethan, pornography is all about seeing what he would like to do in real life—not about abstract fantasy. Because he's "in touch" with his sexuality, Ethan knows what he likes. Mostly, it's young women, between the ages of eighteen and twenty, blondes. "I'm a big fan of the schoolgirl look and the thigh-high stockings, which I guess go hand in hand," he says. He likes his women to be athletic—not too skinny. He's an "ass man" when it comes right down to it. "Oh and Jenna," he says. "Love Jenna." He pauses and adds, "Jenna Jameson, obviously."

Woman-on-woman porn, one of Jameson's specialties, is something he'd love to experience live. He also seeks out depictions of oral sex, especially "cum shots." The charm of pornography is its depiction of women who are over-the-top enthusiastic about sex. "Women in porn tend to act like sex is earth-shattering, even though in reality, sex isn't like that all the time. Unfortunately . . ." he adds, with a chuckle. Like other men who enjoy pornography, Ethan not only seeks enjoyment from pornography, he allows pornography to open up new worlds to him, teaching him about

*While this Zogby poll is old, particularly in terms of Internet time, it is nationally representative and therefore methodologically more valid than an online poll such as the Kinsey Institute's.

sex and his response to it, providing him with the means for sexual release, a way to fantasize about sexual opportunities he cannot enjoy in real life, and a safe and friendly arena for self-validation. Mostly, however, Ethan discusses pornography the way most men do: it's fun.

And more men seem to be having a good time of it. There has been an explosion in online sexual activity. A 2004 poll of 15,246 men and women conducted by MSNBC.com and *Elle* magazine documented that three-fourths of men said they had viewed or downloaded erotic films and videos from the Internet.* (Forty-one percent of women did as well.) One in five men had watched or sexually interacted with someone on a live webcam. Three in ten admitted they go online with the intention of "cheating on their girlfriends or wives," be it via pornography, online dating, or sex chat rooms. But not everyone said they looked at porn. In the same poll, the one in five men who said they abstain from Internet pornography expressed the following reasons for their disinterest: one third said they had no need to seek out women on the Web—they already had a fulfilling sex life; one in four felt that using Internet pornography would make them feel disloyal to their partner; an additional one in four said Internet pornography violated their moral beliefs; and pragmatism ruled the remaining 27 percent who said that Internet pornography clogged their computer with too many pop-ups and cookies. It wasn't worth the hassle.

Several companies track pornography usage online, avoiding the potential for underreporting characteristic of self-reported polls. Each month, Nielsen Net//Ratings tracks usage; for example, in October 2003, one in four Internet users accessed an adult Web site, spending an average of seventy-four minutes per month—and that doesn't include time spent on amateur sites. (Nielsen admits they are capturing only a fraction of actual pornography consumption.) According to comScore, an Internet traffic measuring service, 70 percent of eighteen- to twenty-four-year-old men visit a pornographic site in a typical month—about 39 percent more than the average user. These young men comprise about one-fourth of all visitors to pornography online.[2] The numbers for those in their twenties

*Like the Kinsey poll, this poll was a voluntary online survey whose results are interesting and valid, but not nationally representative. The results likely represent the readers of *Elle* magazine and the users of the MSBNC.com Web site.

and thirties run nearly as high: 66 percent of all men between the ages of eighteen and thirty-four look at Internet pornography every month.

Learning to Like Pornography

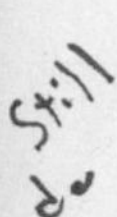

Most men clearly remember the first time they saw pornography. For boys on the cusp of puberty, porn is a rite of passage, an entree into adulthood, and a peep into the world of women. In the pre-Internet days, at least, boys often passed around pornography at summer camp and circulated it in the locker room during junior high. It was handed down from uncle to nephew, older brother to younger, father to son, usually around the time a boy hit the age of eleven or twelve. Whether that first glimpse delights or disgusts, most men are quickly socialized to look at pornography as teenagers.

For men now in their thirties, the initiation came through the pages of a magazine. "Whoa, cool, boobies!" recalls one thirty-three-year-old man of finding his first stack of *Penthouse* in a friend's attic when he was twelve. "We immediately split them up. I hung on to my precious copy for quite a while." Another man, now thirty-five, reminisces, "I used to go to my older cousin's house when I was nine. He had these very explicit magazines, the hardest core you can imagine. I thought, 'Eww, nasty!' But soon I got into some pretty rough, wild bondage stuff myself." For those in their twenties, the earliest experience increasingly occurs online. One twenty-year-old undergraduate student, a physics major at a large university in upstate New York, remembers first encountering pornography when he was fifteen. "It was online, on the family computer. I discovered some great stuff right away—group sex, bondage, voyeurism, exhibitionism. And so many women—white, Asian, Hispanic. I was able to learn what 'my type' is by looking around online—thin women with C- or D-sized breasts and long dark hair. Porn gave me a sense of what's out there and exposed me to the kind of stuff I enjoy in real life. It was eye-opening, a real education."

Pornography is frequently the first place boys learn about sex and gain an understanding of their own sexuality, whims, preferences, and predilections—their desires filtered and informed by whatever the pornography they watch has to offer. As adolescents, many boys learn through pornography to direct their sexual feelings toward the opposite sex, to explain the source of their desires and the means to satisfy them—lessons traditionally supplemented by sex education, parental guidance, peer conversation, and real-life experience. Whether mediated by outside sources or not, the pornography lesson is nothing if not straightforward; most is geared toward the adolescent mind: simple, primal, hormone-driven, results-oriented, a winnable game. Pornography depicts sex as an easy process that provides a welcome refuge from the tangle of sexual politics teenagers encounter in the real world.

Growing up in Alabama, Sandeep got turned on to porn in the most all-American of ways: in the Boy Scouts. He was twelve years old when one camping trip turned out to be a lot more interesting than prior outings. He quickly learned there were other ways to track down porn—at summer camp, from other boys in junior high. It wasn't difficult when you knew what you were looking for. Then Sandeep went to college, enrolling at an Ivy League university. Suddenly, pornography wasn't so cool anymore. Even owning the *Sports Illustrated* swimsuit edition was considered a sign of Neanderthal man in the early nineties. "Pornography seemed really gauche at the time," Sandeep recalls. "I think I even began to see it that way myself." He laughs. "What a ridiculous Ivory Tower way of looking at things!"

After his porn-free interlude in the Ivy League, Sandeep returned to the South to attend a large state university medical school and snapped back to his old habits. The med school was quite conservative, and as a consequence, professors made an effort to get students to understand that there were many sexual proclivities beyond "married missionary sex." Sandeep was shocked by how little some of his classmates knew. During sexual behavior class, the professors showed the students a wide range of sex videos. "For doctors," Sandeep explains, "it's important to know what people can do." Sandeep, of course, had picked up his lessons already.

During his post medical school residency, Sandeep worked one-hundred-plus hours a week. For those three years, he masturbated all the time. "It must have been the stress." He didn't get out much. The nurses weren't interested in the young residents and he didn't have much of a sex life, let alone a romantic life, with the exception of an intermittent long-distance girlfriend. Instead, he was looking at porn movies almost every day. His tastes veered from "vanilla porn"—good old-fashioned naked girls—to more fetishistic bondage and leather fare. For a while, he had a cable descrambler and watched the Spice channel every night; later, when his cable luck ran out, he rented videos from a store down the block. Nervous about maintaining his privacy, he scoped out the store first, renting only mainstream movies before getting up the nerve to visit the back room. "I just felt kind of weird," he says. "I don't want some stranger knowing about me and my sexual proclivities." On the safer side, Sandeep kept a stash of pornographic magazines on hand, usually *Penthouse,* but magazines no longer always satisfied him, especially compared with film.

Today, Sandeep works as a surgeon at a hospital in Texas. He usually rents porn videos when he has a day off and not a lot to do. He's also found new options for seeing women stripped down. Among surgeons at the hospital, it's common to gather after work at one of the local strip clubs. In Texas, Sandeep says, a lot of business gets done this way. In order not to discriminate, his group at the hospital is always careful to invite female surgeons along. "As a young surgeon, you're not going to pass up the opportunity to hang out with the older guys after work," Sandeep explains. "You have to play this game for people to remember who you are." So far, nobody has objected to the strip club meetings, not even the surgeons' spouses. "They understand who they're married to," Sandeep explains. "They know this is what goes on." Most of the surgeons who attend are married; most have been married more than once.

Pornography can provide quite an education. In the Kinsey Institute poll, 86 percent of respondents believed pornography can educate people and 68 percent believed it can lead to more open attitudes about (one's own) sexuality. Many men, particularly those younger and less experienced, use pornography to figure out what women want and expect from sex. In fact, studies show that men learn from and emulate what they see in pornography; experts refer to this as *exemplification theory*: "Each and every sexual act portrayed in pornography is treated as an exemplar of sexuality. . . . Thus, to the extent that pornography shows almost all women screaming ecstatically when anally penetrated, for instance, exemplification theory projects the generalization that almost all women outside of pornography will do likewise."[3] In other words, men learn that what goes in porn, goes in the real world.

While some of those lessons might be basic and informative insights into the mechanics of sex, that learning extends as well to ideas such as: all women really want sex all the time, multiple women are better than one woman, women usually want what men want. Men who watch pornography collect other nuggets of wisdom, too: what to say; how to say it. As the anonymous writer Jake explained in *Glamour* magazine, "The most acceptable and most common word for [a man's penis], which rhymes with rock, is what they use in porno movies, so most men have been brainwashed into thinking it's sexy."[4] For many, pornography almost becomes equated with sex.

Learning to Dislike Pornography

Of course, some men dislike pornography or simply don't find it interesting enough to bother. For Pete, a thirty-one year-old writer in New York, pornography never caught on. It's not as if he hasn't been exposed to pornography. When he was thirteen, he caught late-night glimpses of sexploitation B films on cable outlets such as Showtime showcasing naked breasts and the occasional zip-by full-frontal nudity, but steered clear of actual sex acts. He would see the passing magazine, though nothing more graphic than *Penthouse*. A couple of times when he was traveling, he watched a porn movie in his hotel. None of it did anything for him.

Pete is neither in favor of pornography nor opposed to it—he simply doesn't pursue it. He has never even looked at pornography online, though he uses the Internet on a daily basis. "I wouldn't know where to start," he claims; the truth is, he has never bothered. Strip clubs make him uneasy. "I once went to one for a bachelor party and I left after ten minutes," he says. "It seemed kind of pathetic from both ends of the spectrum—for both the men and the women. There's this whole charade where the guys are trying to pretend to themselves that the women are really interested in them and that they're not just paid to act that way, and the women are trying to pretend that the men don't disgust them. There's something incredibly lonely and sad about it."

Three years ago, a girlfriend suggested they watch a video of what she thought of as female-friendly porn. Pete assumed that, like many women, she figured all guys were into threesomes, the film's theme, and that he would want to watch one on video or would think she was hip for being open to his fantasies. Pete didn't take her up on it. "It would have made me uncomfortable," he says. "I don't want to watch other people having sex when I'm with a woman who I want to have sex with. The idea just isn't appealing."

Classically handsome, Pete has never been short of girlfriends and never felt the need for pornography. Even if he didn't easily capture female attention, he doubts he would turn to it for refuge. True, he's attracted to many of the women, but so much of what he sees he finds downright unappealing, even repugnant and upsetting. For example, he doesn't like anything where there's a power dynamic or it looks like a degrading experience for one of the participants. "There seems to be a whole realm of pornography dedicated to the idea of humiliation and power, subservience and punishment—and that just does not appeal to me at all."

When asked what kind of man dislikes pornography, most men fall back on the easy—but easily proven false—supposition that only pious men might not look at pornography because their religion counsels them against it. Religious men, of course, look at pornography, too. "At least half of the men in Christian churches struggle with pornography at some level," says Jonathan Daugherty, founder of Be Broken Ministries in San Antonio. "It's become the leading factor in divorce." According to a 2000 survey of clergy members conducted by *Christianity Today* and *Leadership* magazines, about 40 percent of clergy acknowledge visiting sexually explicit Web sites.[5] Another poll, conducted by Pastors.com in 2002, found that 50 percent of pastors admitted to viewing pornography in the previous year.[6] And a 2000 survey by Focus on the Family found that 18 percent of those who call themselves born-again Christians admit to visiting porn sites.[7] According to Henry Rogers, a corporate chaplain who studies pornography, between 40 and 70 percent of evangelical Christian men say they struggle with pornography.[8] It's not necessarily the pious who abstain.

The idea that a man simply doesn't find pornography exciting rarely enters the picture; the notion that a man might not like the way pornography affects him or the role it plays is rarer still. And the concept that men other than Bible Belters, Orthodox Jews, or fundamentalist Muslims might have moral reservations about pornography—whether because they're married, feminist, progressive, or conservative—strikes men who love pornography as unlikely. Nearly every user interviewed for this book found it hard to imagine a man who didn't look for reasons other than sexual repression or religion.

Men who like pornography don't seem to understand men who don't, and vice versa. Each group suspects the other, in its own way, of being somehow sexually subversive. "How is it that so many of you thirty- and forty- and fifty-year-olds are quite prepared to invest hours and hours and countless dollars in pornography?" wrote TV writer Burt Prelutsky (*M.A.S.H.*, *Rhoda*, *Dragnet*) in a recent *Los Angeles Times* column. "Call it a hobby, a pastime or an addiction, but I'm begging that golf doesn't even run a close second." He concludes, "I just never considered sex a spectator sport."[9]

Not every man discusses pornography with his circle of acquaintances or even his closest buddies. For many, consumption remains a private matter, assumed but rarely outlined to others, at least not after the raucous tumult of hoots and exchanges during adolescence. Perhaps, as a consequence, men who don't like pornography aren't as rare as fans think, or even as unusual as guys who don't like it suppose they are. In the *Pornified*/Harris poll, only 27 percent of Americans agreed with the statement "All men look at pornography." Men were only slightly more likely to agree than women—31 percent versus 23 percent. And men most likely to agree were between the ages of eighteen and twenty-four, not only the age at which men most often look at pornography, but also the generation most exposed to pornography via the latest technological wave.

Ian, a thirty-five-year-old New Yorker, sometimes feels like a freak for *not* being into pornography. Working in the often sex-obsessed music industry, he feels as if his disinterest requires an explanation, even a defense. "I'm probably the odd one out," he says. "In a strange way, I'm mildly ashamed to be the guy who *really* has read *Playboy* for the articles." As a teenager in boarding school, a filthy dog-eared copy of the magazine periodically made its way around the dormitory. Ian would pick it up for the record reviews. "I have a distinct memory of reading the review for a live Hall and Oates album, but I can't remember a single woman or pictorial image," he says. "And I don't even like Hall and Oates." The first porn movie Ian saw was *Caligula,* the mainstream Hollywood film to which *Penthouse*'s Bob Guccione added several graphic sex scenes. One of Ian's friends rented the fiasco of a film ("The most controversial film of the twentieth century!") in the early days of the VCR. Ten-year-old Ian recalls being bored by the sex and enthralled by the violence. That the adult film industry pumps out 11,000 films a year baffles him. Don't people get bored of the same old thing? he wonders. It's not that Ian is a prude. He likes to party, enjoys a night out drinking, and is open to sexual experimentation.

Over the course of his thirty-five years, Ian has seen about five pornos, either in group settings or because he needed to view them for work. Part of the problem with pornography, he thinks, is the way such movies are made. A film buff, Ian appreciates good filmmaking: compelling characters, tight scripts, original dialogue. "But in porn, there *is* no narrative," Ian says. "They're not concerned about whether the Swedish plumber actually fixes the washing machine. The outcome is always inevitable." Nor does Ian find pornography arousing. "In heterosexual pornography, there's a lot of footage of men's penises," he explains. "There's not a heterosexual man on the planet that would rent those movies if they were called something like 'This Guy's Cock' and yet that's what you're seeing." There's no way around it, either—in order to show a blow job, you have to show a man's genitals. "I'm just not interested in seeing some guy's hairy ass," he says simply.

Even the way pornography portrays women strikes Ian as unappealing. "There's this kind of David Cronenberg aspect to it; it's almost gynecological," he says. "A woman standing around naked is fine; it can be quite nice. But in pornography, they'll have the woman splaying her legs, and basically showing you her interior. These women seem to be almost trying to disgorge their intestines through their vaginas. I don't see why that's any sexier than looking at a woman's spleen. It makes me squeamish.

"Sometimes, I flip the question around in my head," Ian says. "I ask, Why *would* men be interested in this? Doesn't it strike them as peculiar that they're spending half their time watching some guy naked? I don't understand it. But nor do I understand why so many men will go out in the freezing cold on a Saturday night to watch a sports team lose." Ian ties his disinterest in spectator sports to his disinterest in porn. "When it comes down to it, I'd rather be having sex or playing football than watching either of them be done by other people. I don't need some idiot from *Penthouse* to map out my fantasies for me. I have a pretty vivid interior life." For example, he gets turned on by passages in novels, not even especially sexual stories, just ones that evoke erotic ideas. He likes to watch certain female news anchors. Tabloid shots of celebrities caught naked sometimes strike him as titillating. "I find odd things to be pornographic in my own way," he says.

Popular men's magazines like *Maxim* and *FHM*, which Ian considers unequivocally pornographic, offend him above all other forms of pornography. "I think they are far, far more damaging. Because even though *Hustler* is a hugely offensive magazine and I can understand why women would want to shut it down, it at least, generally speaking, depicts women in a realistic fashion." But in *Maxim*, the women are "savagely airbrushed"—people just don't look like that, Ian explains. "I read an interview with [Hollywood starlet] Jessica Alba in which she talked about how degrading it was to do one of those photo shoots, how she was in absolute tears, but her publicist made her do it, because that's what seventeen-year-old actresses are expected to do for their careers these days. But I don't get aroused by it. I find it so fucking vacant."

Ian has trouble believing that as many men are into pornography as most people seem to think. "I know it's supposed to be a huge percentage of men," he says. "But when do people do this? It seems odd to me that porn is supposed to be such a huge part of men's lives and yet it leaves no trace whatsoever. Personally, I never hear any of my friends talking about pornography or see them watching it. I haven't been invited to see porn or had someone put on a video in my presence since I was twenty-two. Nobody in my weekly poker game ever mentions it. For all I know, *nobody* I know watches pornography." In fact, if one of his friends were to stick a porn DVD into the player in a group setting, Ian thinks it would be regarded as weird. But it's hard to imagine, since pornography generally passes as an unspoken issue.

So Why *Do* Men Like Porn?

Except among teenagers and college-age men, for the most part, pornography isn't a subject of debate or everyday conversation. Among men, there seems to be a lack of judgment about pornography, except, that is, to condemn those who judge *other* people's usage. The consensus is that pornography is just "a guy thing." It may be biological or it may be cultural, but most agree that it plays a part in nearly all men's lives.

In a pornified world, pornography has become seamlessly woven into the wake-up routine, the workday Internet break, and the bedtime ritual. It's part of revving up in the morning and relaxing at the end of the day. It's a prelude to sex or an alternative to sex. As an accompaniment to masturbation alone, pornography exerts a powerful pull. Ethan, for example, masturbates to porn "all the time" when he's at home; he has to abstain while he's at work, for obvious reasons. "How can you even ask what pornography is for?" laughs Christopher, a twenty-five-year-old who works as a customer service representative in a suburb of Dallas. "Isn't it obvious?" For Christopher, pornography is about sexual gratification, pure and simple. "It's cheaper than a date with dinner and a movie." And, the bonus is, while he's looking for the right pornography to masturbate to, he can find out what turns him on and what doesn't. It's easier and less risky to try things out by himself than with a partner, whom he would be afraid of scaring off with some kind of new activity.

Growing up in rural north Texas, it was hard for Christopher to get his hands on pornography. In a town with only 1,000 inhabitants and dry laws still on the books, there wasn't much pornography for sale at the local convenience store. Occasionally, he landed some magazines, but it wasn't until the Internet that Christopher's consumption took off. Luckily, he discovered "the wonders of online porn" early; online at age ten, he was pulling pornography off binary newsgroups and early Web sites back in 1995. "I can remember the days when porn really was openly available on the Internet," he recalls nostalgically. "There were no warning screens ever. You would just go to Penthouse.com, and *bam!*—naked people."

"There's nothing wrong with sexual pleasure," he explains. "I enjoy watching other people have sex and porn is about seeing other people healthily enjoying themselves." For Christopher, who hasn't had a girlfriend in four years, pornography offers a sexual release. When he was having sex a lot, he didn't need to look as much; but his dating life, he admits, is "not that great." Granted, he hasn't been looking his best lately. Being sedentary at his customer service job doesn't help. He finds himself eating a lot of junk food and could stand to lose twenty pounds or so. Because he's picky, it's been a good while since Christopher has found a woman worth his time. "The egotistical reason is that I'm quite a bit more intelligent than most people," he explains. "My interests are broad, and I don't have an interest in stupid things like sports or fashion. I like to focus on higher philosophical things and world politics. Not many people can converse on those levels."

As a teenager in the nineties, Christopher visited professional sites adorned with airbrushed, *Playboy*-model types. He has since moved away from that, but likes to keep an open mind, cycling through a wide range of Web sites, depending on his mood. "Like when you're going to a store—do you want vanilla, strawberry, or chocolate ice cream? I'll sit down at the computer and say, 'Hmm, I feel like Asian girls tonight.'" As long as the women fall somewhere between Calista Flockhart and Camryn Manheim ("I'm not into fat-chick porn"), Christopher is satisfied. It's like plucking just the right product from the shelf.

Because his energy starts low in the morning and builds over the course of the day, Christopher has what he calls his daily "session" at night, sitting down at the computer before bedtime. Inevitably, after twenty to sixty minutes of surfing, Christopher finds what it is he's looking for. "I masturbate pretty much every time," he says. "Once in a while, I'll just be bored and go search online objectively, thinking, 'Hmm, that's interesting,' but generally, when I pull up porn it's with one objective in mind: getting off."

For most men, pornography is precisely that: an easy way to get off. Men generally masturbate while they're looking at pornography, or immediately after, unless they're at work. In the online Kinsey Institute poll, 72 percent of respondents said they used pornography to masturbate or achieve physical release. An additional 69 percent used pornography to sexually arouse themselves and/or others. In a 2001 MSNBC.com poll, three-quarters of online users said they masturbated while looking at sexual content online: 30 percent said they do so sometimes, 20 percent said often, and 9 percent said all the time. Not a single man who looked at pornography interviewed for this book did so without masturbating at least some of the time.

For Zach, a twenty-three-year-old unemployed Web site developer, pornography comes down to two things: getting off and relieving boredom. "Women see pornography a lot differently than men do," Zach explains. "They think that if a guy is looking at pornography, then that's the way he wants women to look and act. That guys have some kind of emotional attachment to it." But according to Zach, guys use pornography as a visual aid. "We see porn the way women view vibrators—it's a quick way to get off and get on with your day." Often he'll go online first thing in the morning, always with the goal of masturbating. "This may creep you out, but that's what it's for," he says. "I don't think there's a time when I've looked at porn and haven't masturbated. And I think most guys would say that." For Zach, jerking off online has become "a habit." He goes online for pornography every couple of days for about twenty minutes. Or sometimes only five. "Sounds pretty bad," he says sheepishly. "But sometimes, that's all it takes."

Pornography just isn't that big a deal, Zach insists. "It's like scratching an itch." He would never go out and buy a magazine or rent a movie. Since Zach and his friends grew up with the Internet, pornography was never about print or video. It's too big a hassle. You have to spend money. Somebody could find it lying around. Zach doesn't even like to go to the trouble of downloading video images; it takes up too much bandwidth and isn't worth the effort. Generally, he prefers *Playboy*-style images rather than hardcore raunch. "I've come across things I really don't like, some of it disturbing. Japanese anime often has rape scenes in it, like tentacle rape [a Japanese specialty that shows women being raped by monsters with numerous tentacles]," Zach says. "I saw a picture of a guy holding his ass half a foot open. It surprises me that people can get off on this stuff."

No matter what men choose to look at, masturbating to pornography isn't merely something men do when they lack for anything else. Contrary to expectation or myth, not every man who uses pornography is lonely or depressed. Many of the men interviewed for this book have full lives and committed relationships. Those who are married or monogamously attached admit to using pornography either when their girlfriends or wives aren't around or when their partner isn't in the mood. But they also use pornography when they're not in the mood to have sex with their partners—when women aren't into what they want at that particular moment, do not look their best, or come across as cranky or difficult. They may simply feel the urge to be with someone else altogether.

Men Need Variety

Even if a man is in a relationship and has an exciting sex life with a willing partner, many men say it's important to feel they're free to enjoy other women, to act as if they could spread their seed, willy-nilly, among multiple willing partners. And pornography is a world in which promiscuity—often anonymous, usually ephemeral, ultimately superficial—is the norm. Sociologist Michael Kimmel has found that male sexual fantasies have become increasingly shaped by the standards of porn. Two-thirds of male fantasies feature more than one woman, almost always strangers or near-strangers. When talking about their fantasies, men typically describe women's physical attributes (i.e., "There's this tall blond woman with . . .") and not their other qualities or their relationship to the man himself. The focus is on a woman (or, increasingly, multiple women) serving a man's sexual pleasure.

Pornography allows all men—single or committed—to enjoy the fantasy of endless variety. "Look," says Ethan, the recently married music exec, "most men are enthusiastic about sex and want to have it with different women, but they're married or in a monogamous relationship. Pornography is an outlet to release sexual energies when they're not in the mood to engage in these activities with their wives or girlfriends. And it's better than the alternative—cheating." Indeed, that's exactly how Ethan, who has been married for seven months, views pornography's role in his own life. Porn has absolutely nothing whatsoever to do with his wife, he explains. Pornography provides the vicarious thrill of other women without the threat of actually being with one. He can live out sexual situations, such as multiple women or girl-on-girl voyeurism, that he'd still like to experience but can't because he is committed to his marital vows. So far, Ethan hasn't cheated on his wife, though he cheated in earlier relationships. It's different this time, Ethan insists, and porn helps.

When he married Candace after five years of dating, Ethan made it clear he had no intention to stop or even cut down on his pornography consumption. Candace has been accommodating, even buying Ethan his first porn DVD, *Emotions of Jenna Jameson,* when she got him a DVD player. "She'll even watch it with me," Ethan says proudly. "Not that it turns her on—she's not attracted to women. But she likes that it turns me on." Still, Candace doesn't understand the appeal. She once asked Ethan why he liked to watch it so much. "But we didn't have a heavy discussion or argument about it," he says. "She thinks it's silly, but she's fine with it." If she had complained or asked him to stop, that would have been totally uncool with him. If Candace threatened to divorce him over it, he would stop, though it would raise serious questions for him about their relationship. "Any attempt by her to exert too much control over who I am and what I do with my time would be a total infringement on my freedoms as a husband," he explains. "If she asked me to stop using porn, I'd tell her she's out of her mind."

The fact is, Candace, a tall and athletic brunette, doesn't know how often Ethan looks at pornography. Ethan figures she probably thinks he looks at it a couple of times a week and that it's best to leave her with that impression. Like many men, he obscures the reality in order, he believes, to protect his partner. "I don't think she would understand," he says. "She would probably think I was perverted and oversexed if she knew just how much I looked at it every day." But then, Ethan would consider her feelings to be irrational; he considers pornography part of being a normal guy.

Men like Ethan often justify their pornographic needs with loosely understood "evolutionary psychology" theories. Men need variety, they say, presenting their own versions of Kiplingesque "just so stories," arguing that science proves that in order to effectively promote his genes, man has evolved to seek—even require—a large number of female consorts. Looking at lots of women naked is merely a remnant of this Cro-Magnon legacy. It's only natural. Fidelity and commitment are unnatural, while ogling and bedding multiple women are part of man's biological imperative. Such theories often characterize men as aggressive and insatiable and women as mere tools for reproduction, a view, not surprisingly, espoused by many social conservatives who see women's social role as taming the male beast. This antediluvian vision of the sexes also conveniently matches pornography's palate, which rests on the idea that men need not only a Miss January, but a Miss February and a Miss March as well, a tendency expanded online to include whatever particular sexual proclivity a man wants at any given moment.

I'm Only Looking

With all the pornographic variety available, particularly on the Internet, it's not surprising that men find themselves "just browsing," checking out what's out there. There's very little to prevent a guy from doing so—he can always click on to another page if someone walks in or delete his browser history. Thirty-five-year-old Gabe, who works in Houston's oil and gas industry, likes looking at pornography so much he's made it into a bit of a sideline. At his office, which is 98 percent male, all the men look at pornography during the day. It's not a big deal. Some watch streaming videos; others scroll through naked poses or read erotic stories. Pornography is so acceptable that Gabe doesn't need to worry about putting his job in jeopardy. Everyone's computer screen is easily visible in the large shared room where they all work, and Gabe assumes that his boss has probably looked over Gabe's shoulder and seen what he's up to. Gabe doesn't even bother cleaning the file cache on his work computer.

Pornography has climbed out of the bedroom and slinked into the workplace for many men like Gabe. One 2004 survey by Web-filtering company Cerberian found that 75 percent of people have accidentally visited a pornographic site while at work; 15 percent have done so more than ten times. Forty percent say they've seen their coworkers surfing pornography on the job.[10] Peeking at pornography during office hours isn't *always* an accident. In another 2004 survey by the Employment

Law Alliance, one in four workers say they or their coworkers visit pornographic Web sites or engage in sex talk or other sexually oriented Internet activities on their work computers during office hours. Twelve percent admitted that either they or a coworker have forwarded sexually explicit e-mail content to others in the office. Men were about twice as likely as women to pursue such activities. They were also more likely to report being aware of other coworkers' use of sexually explicit material online.[11]

But Gabe probably looks more often than most of the other guys in the office—he guesses they spend about one-fourth the time cruising porn he does—because he spends about twenty hours a week working as an amateur "aggregator." When Gabe first went online in the late 1990s, he was immediately hooked, enjoying the search for the best sites, the hottest women, the most exciting images. He loved being able to track down high-quality material and realized he had a knack for it. So Gabe offered his services as a cyber-sleuth to several pornography portals. He now works freelance for three different sites, scoping out the best links and downloadable videos. The pay is minimal, but Gabe thinks he has a sharp eye and good taste, and he likes when his suggestions prove popular with his Internet audience.

Many men in fact consider pornography to be just another form of media entertainment, something to consume without consequence. It's like flipping channels on television or strolling through a sports equipment store—checking out what products and information are available. Part of the interest in pornography is the adventure of investigating the netherworlds of pornographic titillation. Why not click the remote control just to find out what's featured in that pay-per-view feature *Naughty Amateur Home Videos: Stripped to Thrill*? In the Kinsey Institute poll, 54 percent of respondents said they view pornography out of curiosity, and they figured others did the same: 87 percent believed other people used pornography out of curiosity, too. In the 2001 MSNBC.com poll, 81 percent of men pursued online sexual activities for "distraction." Pornography can be a voyeuristic journey, a glimpse into other people's lives, the X-rated version of *Us* magazine—images to absorb and discard like any other entertainment trifle.

William, a thirty-five-year-old legal clerk from Missouri, masturbates only about half the time; otherwise he's just "cruising porn," as he puts it. Often he's at work, so it's not as if he can just reach into his pants in the middle of a law office. Mostly, he likes to check out the women and get a sense of what's out there. "Men are culturally programmed to like porn," he explains. "We're raised with women objectified in our culture. You're just exposed to women as"—he pauses—"not necessarily as sex objects, but as sexual in nature." It has nothing to do with biology, according to William, it's just sheer entertainment, part and parcel of the American male culture.

In 1982, during his freshman year of high school, one of William's friends popped in a video at a party—the first time William saw sex in motion. He was excited—and freaked out. Watching with the guys was part of the problem. William doesn't like pornography to be so out in the open; he didn't want to witness other men masturbate. It's all well and good to enjoy porn on your own turf, but William has never rented a video himself or visited an adult theater because it gives him the creeps. "Pornography has always been a private thing for me," he explains. "It seems really seedy to go to one of those theaters or stores."

Nonetheless, when William left home to join the navy, he began frequenting strip clubs, which were popular with his navy buddies. A few times a month he would pay for lap dances. But now that he's out of the service and working as a legal clerk, he's stopped going. On a recent St. Patrick's Day, some friends suggested visiting a strip club after an evening of barhopping. But the others were all in their twenties, and William felt "too old for that shit." He couldn't carouse all night with strippers when he had to work the next day. He went home. These days, William's pornographic adventures are confined to the computer. He browses for about ten or fifteen minutes before moving on to another form of online infotainment, celebrity gossip, the news.

Nearly everyone likes to look at pretty pictures; men and women enjoy admiring a beautiful woman, the curve of her body, the expression in her eyes. Artful photography, elegant poses, atmospheric lighting—they're pleasing, whether they're in a Hollywood movie or a softcore magazine. Men profess that in this way pornography is often about appreciation, discovering and beholding beauty. But pornography isn't just pretty pictures, and what men look at when they watch pornography reveals much more about them than just their aesthetics. What they look for, men say, is often about what they wish they could experience in real life. It's about legitimizing their desires as well as masking their deepest fears and dislikes. For example, woman-on-woman pornography, with luscious lipstick lesbians squealing and oozing femininity while they grope each other, bares only a faint resemblance to real lesbian sex, an activity from which men in the real world are clearly excluded. Pornography allows men to get in on the game and to change the rules in the process. Woman-on-woman pornography also has the advantage that it does not feature men; for men uncomfortable watching other men naked, girlie action is particularly appealing.

In other ways, pornography reveals men's insecurities with their own sexuality. Psychologists point out that much of what is portrayed in pornography assuages men's fear of and disgust with their own semen; they need to see women revel in it and adore it in order to allay their own feelings of unattractiveness and discomfort. Many male performers in pornography are notoriously unattractive; this, too, feeds into men's fears and hidden desires. If the men were anything other than pathetic, unattractive, wooden, and stupid, they could pose a competitive threat to the men who are watching. The viewer instead can imagine himself as "better" than his pornographic counterpart, and thus can imagine inserting himself into the scene. After all, if a female porn star would stoop to this lunk, then surely she would be eager to be with him. (Ironically, some men find male porn actors so fake and unappealing as to be "degrading" and insulting to men.) Pornography literally creates the man's world as he would ideally have it, free of exclusion, discomfort, stressful competition, and rejection.

The Power of Pornography

Walking down the street, a man has permission to look at a girl but not to look too hard. In the office, he can notice a woman but must look her in the eye—not her cleavage. In a bar, he can glance at a woman to signal interest, but not lasciviously run his gaze over her entire body. In so many ways, a man's ability to observe is restricted by social norms that demand men not treat women as sexual objects, no matter how provocatively tight her jeans. But in the porn world, none of those restrictions apply. Men can look at whatever women they want in whatever way they choose for as long as they desire to do so.

Walking down the street, a woman has the ability to look the other way or to sneer at the man who passes by her. In the office, she can write a more effective business plan than her male coworker or outperform him in a board meeting. In a bar, she can refuse to give a guy her phone number or brush off his attempts at conversation. But in the porn world, she has none of these options. She may retain the power to reject a man by the very nature of her femininity, but in pornography she chooses not to reject. In porn, she treats a man the way he wants to be treated, relieving him of the fears that plague everyday male-female interaction. In the porn world, men retain the power and the control. It's an incredibly seductive fantasy.

Jacob, a lanky thirty-three-year old journalist, has mixed feelings about pornography. He has spent quite a bit of time, more than most guys, mulling over the causes and implications of men's fascination with pornography. For Jacob, the arguments of evolutionary psychologists are powerful and convincing. Men are biologically programmed to reduce women to something that exists only for their sexual pleasure. This is a natural impulse to which all men succumb, he believes. However, *natural* does not mean *moral*. Even though it's natural, as Jacob puts it, to "fuck as many women as possible" in order to "spread the seed," that doesn't make it right. But it's hard to argue with biology and history. "Look at the Bible," he says. "That's the way men lived back then. These urges are very basic."

According to Jacob, if men weren't looking at the images of pornography to release those urges, they could very well "be out raping Girl Scouts." In place of such real-world acting out, pornography gives men a sense of power, an aura of sexual power in particular, that can be exercised in a fantasy world without real-world implications. "Powerless people tend to think a lot about power," Jacob explains. "A lot of sex is wrapped up in power and a lot of porn is a fantasy about power." The combination is intensely alluring, especially when real-world relationships leave one feeling insecure and out of control.

That's what compelled Jacob toward porn in the first place. His heaviest pornography period took place after college, when he was living in Washington, D.C., where dates were scarce. "When I watched a ton of porn, and was subscribing to *Playboy* and watching videos, I was feeling very cut off from my sexual power," Jacob says. "I even questioned whether it existed. I think a lot of men experience this sad paradox of pursuing this ideal of having power from a position of powerlessness. And sadly, that behavior then deflates that power or pushes them even further away from it." If a man is getting a sense of validation and power over women by looking at pornography, he's not actually out in the real world getting real women. If he were, he would feel sexually powerful and wouldn't need to go searching for power through pornography. It's a vicious cycle. And for Jacob, who has enjoyed pornography, a real conundrum.

Pornography has traditionally been the province of males, a place where, despite the recent incursion of women into the industry, men dominate production and consumption, often learning to appreciate pornography in the presence of male friends, colleagues, and family members. Pornography is a kind of male utopia that men are keen to protect:

> Let me tell you boys, the Mommies are coming for our Internet. We've been beaten by them into submission about drinking, smoking, speeding and just about every other fun guy's activity. . . .
>
> Then along comes a beacon of light . . . the Internet. And it features . . . pictures of girls wearing things that our wives won't wear anymore and doing things that our wives won't do anymore. Yes, this harmless activity can be done in the safety of our own homes . . . and costs far less than a night at the local gentleman's club (so it doesn't drain the family budget).
>
> Sound good? Absolutely not! The objective of Mommydom is to control every aspect of a guy's life.
>
> —*"Bob" on MarriedtoMommy.com*

Perhaps in a world where women have gained near-equal footing and sometimes surpassed their male counterparts in some traditionally male arenas—higher education, professional graduate schools, certain industries—pornography offers a safe haven where men can still dominate, undisturbed. Outside, life has become "feminized"—it's a world of Oprah, therapy, parenting, work/life balance, and yoga. Inside the porn fantasy world, men are most definitely on top. David Marcus, a San Jose, California–based psychologist who specializes in treating men who use pornography excessively, says use has risen in part because of the tremendous stress men are under. "More is being asked of men emotionally these days," he explains. "Many men are still providers and they're still in the workforce, where the skills required often demand a kind of calculating callousness. The workplace is more competitive and there are fewer jobs. It's tough out there. But at home, the kind of behavior that works in the workplace is simply unacceptable. Men say they have chronic anxiety as a result of those two clashing worlds. They feel like they're mastering neither home nor work and that, overall, they're not in control. So they go online to look at pornography. It's a place where they can get release from that stress. Voyeurism offers a certain kind of control."

Not surprisingly, workplace incidents revolving around pornography and power abound. In 2004, forty-three employees in Kentucky's state transportation department were suspended or fired for viewing pornography on their office computers. A twenty-four-hour monitor found that 212 computers were used to view pornography on a given day.[12] In 2002, a computer-abuse sweep at the Virginia Department of Transportation found that seventeen employees were accessing the Internet on their computers for more than two hours daily to look at pornography online; fifteen were subsequently fired and two resigned.[13] At a freight services company in Minnesota in 2002, female employees accused their male colleagues of using office e-mail to disseminate pornography in ways easily visible to women in the office, creating a hostile work atmosphere.[14] In February 2004, an audit manager at the University of Texas Health Science Center in Houston resigned after fifteen investigations documenting employee visits to pornographic Web sites in the workplace resulted in only four terminations. In her most recent investigation, ten male employees were found viewing pornography; eight of them were visiting teen pornography sites. Frustrated, the manager, Cynthia Davis, explained that it was "disturbing" that one of the employees, a pediatric dentist, was logging on every morning to visit sites with graphic depictions of sex with young teenagers and then seeing child patients later in the day.[15]

It's easy for men to feel more powerful and in control when they look at pornography. Women who pose for pornography must be stupid, many men say. Or addicted to drugs. Something has to be with wrong with them; otherwise they wouldn't sell themselves in order to get strangers off. It's only natural for men to feel superior to women who are mere fodder for their fantasies. Sandeep, the trauma surgeon, would never seriously date a porn star, because he would never date someone he wasn't willing to marry. "I wouldn't want to have to face my mother!" he exclaims, laughing. "I mean, shit! God, she would freak out! She would say, 'This woman has sex on camera for all the world to see—what are you thinking?' " Sandeep can't see how any of the women in porn could possibly be capable of having a normal relationship, at least not the kind of relationship he'd want. "I think all of them have had some kind of sexual trauma, if not abuse, then some seriously shitty boyfriends in high school." The strippers he knows from the Houston strip club scene are all "relatively messed up people"—whether that's the type of person drawn to stripping or because of how stripping affects people, he's not sure. Either way, he isn't interested. Nor would he ever want a daughter of his to land in that world. "I would do everything I could to discourage my daughter from posing in *Playboy,*" he says. "I'd tell her there are other ways of looking good and making money while keeping your clothes on. The only people it opens doors for are those for whom there are few doors to open. You don't fulfill yourself by posing nude."

Pornography is not only a place where men can exert control over their own lives; it's a place to validate one's maleness. Online pornography, with its message boards and chat rooms, is particularly adept at creating a place where men can enjoy pornography in an all-male arena. As sociologists Michael Barron and Michael Kimmel explain, "Internet news groups are the closest things to the all-male locker room that exist in the pornographic world: a world, in a sense, entirely without women, a world in which men control absolutely all facets of the scene and in which women do not insert themselves as corporeal beings, even in the highly stylized forms offered by magazines or videos."[16] An atmosphere of posturing and competition pervades such chat rooms. By commenting on women as a group, men keep women at a distance, parading their masculinity and proving their potency to one another, and to themselves, like roosters strutting their stuff in a barnyard competition.

"Bjoobies!! I love dem Asian features," exclaims one man in a bulletin board of responses to a series of online photos showing a half-Asian, half-Caucasian woman, dubbed "Kitana," frolicking naked in a bathtub. "Dammit," writes another man. "I thought it was Kitana Baker . . . oh well this chick is still decent enough. She has a weird midriff though." He's not alone in his opinion. "Looks like she's had a few too many sandwiches!!!" exclaims another viewer. "Or she needs to stick to light beer!! She has no waistline—goes straight down from her shoulders!!!" A third man chimes in, "She does nuthin 4 me. Maybe the fugliness, I don't know." A man who calls himself "Drexel" agrees. He writes:

> I'm confused. Whose idea of beauty are we subject to? What are the qualifications needed to get one's boobies on [this site]? The reason I ask, is that there doesn't seem to be anything extraordinary about this particular young lady. No shocking hair color, exceptional beauty, fancy outfit, giant boobs, etc, etc, that separate her from any other bathing booty. She's fine, I'd hit it and all but, I'm sure I could find 50 more interesting versions within a few keystrokes.

Then there are the dissenters. "I'd hit it! I'd hit it! I'd hit it! I'd hit it! I'd hit it! I'd hit it! I'd hit it! I'd hit it!" writes a man who goes by Root Boy Another Kitana fan adds, "I'd slice it," while someone named Mr. Guy notes, "Ahhhh, dammit, is that a wedding band I see on her finger? I don't wanna have to share."

Another Web site, another forum: a blonde peels off her white bustier, French-cut bikini, and garters in a frame-by-frame montage, ending with her legs spread wide. She poses from the front, and now from the back, squatting, lying down, smiling. "I dunno, man, her face is screwy. . . . The eyes/eyebrow combination is off one way or another," writes one observer. "What's up with the beaver rash?" asks a second. "Nice granny panties," sneers a third, the self-proclaimed I Dig Chicks. Yet another viewer piles on: "This chick's boobies are weird. How come her nipples aren't somewhat centered within her areolas? I don't think I've ever seen that before." Nobody seems to like the blonde very much: "Call it nitpicking," writes a man who calls himself Half Mast Trousers, "but I've got a problem with those stringy inner-thigh tendons that seem to show up on a lot of these anorexic-type models. I like to see that little connecting tendon part just sort of peek out on either side of the spread cooter and disappear into some decent thigh meat." When one man complains that the others are being unduly harsh, a debate breaks out on the board. "Any skank who appears naked on the Internet automatically gains immunity from criticism?" replies a poster. "I've seen plenty of nasty meat [online] that I wouldn't touch with a ten foot pole. . . . Actually, now that I think of it, you're right, from now on I'll commence heaping praise on every used up skanky butterface implant ridden ho-bag that gets posted here."

This isn't quite the aesthetic appreciation that men make pornography viewing out to be, nor does it seem to be about men loving women. Comments in such porn forums generally fall into two categories: whether the viewer would have sex with the woman depicted or not and whether the image inspired him to masturbate, accompanied by a dissection of the woman's attributes that turned him on. The prettiness of her face, the curve of her ass, whether she's been too airbrushed or not airbrushed enough. Women become objects to be praised, scorned, and sized up according to the degree to which they appeal to men. Such banter and debate might sound harmless, but it solidifies certain attitudes about the ease of judging a woman's merit solely on the basis of her appearance.

Not all pornography is so controversial. Some images meet with near universal approval. A brunette with long hair, wearing a white men's shirt, dripping wet as she climbs out of a pool, solicits a cacophony of praise and enthusiasm. "When she gets out of the pool I'll be glad to dry her off with my tongue," writes a man who calls himself Eat More Possum. "That has to be one of the hottest chicks I've ever seen," seconds

Cubansaltyballs. "I wish her career would fall apart so she would be forced to become a stripper . . . like all the ex-adult film chicks that are strippers here in Vegas." The men seem to like this one and even to wish that she weren't merely a feature of pornography, but a real woman they could somehow insert into their own lives. "I'd do 'er," writes a third guy on the board. "I'd eat her out, that's for sure. She could suck my knob anytime. I would even lick her ass. Yes, I would. I'd lick her from her ass to her clit. Until she came multiple times, then I'd make love with her. All night if she wanted. Then I'd cuddle her." But most of the commentary sticks closely to form: "Sweet lord," writes Buckshot. "Them breasts are either natural or an excellent set of implants. The first pic, where she's sitting down pushing them together with her arms. So innocent . . . I'll be back in minute."

Porn Is Easy, Porn Is Safe

Compared with the ease of masturbating to women in pornography, sex with real women involves a lot of effort, and often time and money to boot. Real women may get angry when men gape, gawk, and get hard at inappropriate times. In pornography, the women demand it; sexual arousal and gratification are the whole point. The contrast between the demands of sexual conquest with real women and the instant gratification of pornography are seductive enough to win over many men, at least some of the time. A man can have his cake without the calories. "I don't see how any male who likes porn can think actual sex is better, at least if it involves all the crap that comes with having a real live female in your life," complains Frank in an online message board discussion about the prevalence of pornography.[17]

Men say that women underestimate the fear they, and men's desire to have sex with them, inspire. In the real world, women hold a power: the power to judge and to rebuff, spurning a guy's desire and making him feel inadequate and unwanted. The rejected male, particularly during his teenage years when he is most apt to discover porn, is constantly subjected to humiliation and frustration. Each rejection gets tucked away into the private place where men mull over their excessive body hair and insufficient paychecks; where pride is swallowed and humbleness dwells, accumulating the emotional debris of ongoing denial and frustrated desire. And this becomes the emotional impetus that brings them to pornography and the ineffable release of masturbation.

In the face of what appears to be such intimidating control by women, many men experience frustration and even anger. Austin, a twenty-nine-year-old musician from Chicago, is one of several men who described the experience of "The Street Dilemma." Walking down the street, he says, you see all these girls you want to have sex with. "And it makes you angry in a way. Not violently angry, but just pissed off. It pains us every time we see another woman we can't have sex with. You want to see all these women naked and you know you never will. It's really frustrating." Guys talk about this sort of thing with friends, Austin explains. "You'll say to your friend, God, I saw this really hot woman walk by today and I was just like, 'Fuck!' " Sure you might get to see one woman, but the point is you can't get every one. There's always another woman who will walk by and torment you. It makes life seem incredibly unfair: all temptation, with little reward. First you're single and you can't get the women you really want; then you're married and you're tied to one woman for the rest of your life.

The appeal of voyeuristic pornography like *Girls Gone Wild,* a franchise of videos featuring young women—mostly college girls on spring break—drunkenly baring their breasts to cheering crowds, is to capture all those missed opportunities. "*GGW* gives you all the breasts of all the girls you never get to see," Austin explains. "You would never get to see every shape of breast in your lifetime in real life, but now you can." Austin, who has never had a serious girlfriend but would like to get married someday ("If you asked me at a party, I'd probably say something like 'If it happens, it happens,' but in secret, I think it would be really romantic to get married. I've thought about my imaginary wedding and what I might say in my vows"), says pornography relieves the stress of not having a girlfriend. When he feels horny he starts to worry: "Why don't I have a girlfriend? When will I get one? When is my life going to come together?" Austin says that "masturbating to porn brings all that into perspective. I realize that my horniness got mixed into a lot of emotions, and once I have that release, it dissipates. It definitely relieves insecurity."

Robert Jensen, a journalism professor at the University of Texas at Austin who studies pornography, says it appeals to men because it delivers without requiring any effort. Most men, Jensen says, use pornography as a means to sexual release without the typical real-life requirement of love and affection.[18] In other words, pornography explicitly offers men the option of sex without risk, without vulnerability, without the potential to be hurt. Psychotherapist David Marcus attributes the appeal to men's fear of experiencing emotions; pornography offers a vacuum in which such emotions are unnecessary. "Many men tend to be cut off from their emotions and overly reliant on the rational. They're very logical people and they have trouble doing well with emotions. Pornography is the perfect outlet." Zach, the twenty-three-year-old Web site developer, has a theory: most guys who are really into pornography are probably shy and don't date much. He thinks they're intimidated by real women and have a hard time relating to the opposite sex. Internet nerds are probably more into pornography than most guys; they tend to be social rejects or shut-ins. "Come to think of it," Zach admits, "I'm probably describing myself." Zach's sexual experience has been fairly limited. He hasn't had a relationship for more than a year and, while he can discuss his porn habits freely, is loathe to admit how long it's been since he had sex. "It's pretty pathetic," he says ruefully. "I have trouble making friends and getting dates. I move around a lot for work and it's hard to maintain relationships." It's not always easy to move from acquaintanceship to intimacy.

The beauty of pornography is that there are never any hiccups in courtship. Nobody fails to get an erection, the woman doesn't have trouble achieving orgasm, nobody fears their gut looks too big or they're sweating too much or they can't catch their breath. If a man tries to take a woman from behind or tie her up or asks her to spank him or ejaculates on her body, the woman doesn't wince or object or ask questions. In pornography, no one needs to make pillow talk. There's no expectation that a man will tell a woman he loves her, or to get up and make her breakfast. Nobody gets genital warts or heaven forbid the AIDS virus. Nobody gets pregnant or wants to get married or tries to pin down a date for next weekend.

And porn can serve as a refuge. The desire to use pornography may stem directly from trouble in a man's relationship and contributes to it as well. Take a regular guy with no previous sexual problems. He'll be fine with his partner early in the relationship, as he is falling in love, but then finds himself experiencing some performance trouble: difficulty maintaining erections and control. He starts to feel a certain amount of anxiety in his sexual relationship with his partner. Worries about what kind of man he is. So he begins masturbating to pornography or ups the amount he's already been viewing. It's easy. Nobody is asking, "Honey, what's wrong? Are you okay?" There's no need to confront anything even remotely unpleasant. There's no one else to satisfy. And that's a huge relief. He feels more virile, more sexually potent. He can get used to this—and he does. Now, when and if he turns to be with his partner, sex is even *more* difficult than it was before. She's tough by comparison. And pornography certainly didn't help matters; he didn't learn how to please her or how to communicate better with her. His sexual dysfunction worsens.

Thus, pornography can be too safe, too easy. For Sandeep, the surgeon in Houston, pornography is often all he needs, satisfying the desire to have sex rather than stimulating it. It's been a while since Sandeep has had a serious girlfriend. Occasionally, he'll get depressed about not being married yet—thirty-one already and so many of his friends wed!—though he has come close to asking three different women he dated. Part of the problem is he's busy with work—so busy that "luckily" he's often forced to put the pornography away. There just isn't the time, and it may well be for the best. "God forbid I sat around spanking off to porn all the time. It's all about fantasy and you can't just live in fantasy all the time or you lose perspective on reality."

It helps for Sandeep to get out into the real world, to interact with real women and either "score" or be rejected. "You've got to have that visceral experience one way or other or you just lose the ability to interact normally with women you'd otherwise want to go out with, or at least be in a sexual situation for real," he says. Fortunately, Sandeep gets the real thing fairly regularly—having succeeded in his profession and created a full social life for himself in Houston, he's managed to have about fifty or sixty sexual partners in his thirty-one years. Not all the sex has been great, but when the real thing fails to satisfy, Sandeep conjures up images from pornography in his head. "There are times when I've been so utterly bored while having sex with a woman, I'll think of porn to hasten things along."

Still, he admits, "I've found myself feeling like I'd rather just spank off to porn instead of going out. Usually, it's related to having been rejected by a woman in real life. When I have some kind of emotional investment in a woman, being rejected by her leads to a lack of confidence." Pornography becomes a cause and a symptom. If Sandeep gets down or worries that he's not going to be successful asking a woman out, he'll just sit home and watch porn. It helps with the physical frustration of not having the real woman, even if not with the emotional component. Yet, over time, pornography can build his frustration. "If I don't go out and have real sex, it feels like I'm going to burst," Sandeep says. "I've actually thought using pornography might have a negative effect on how I cope emotionally," he says. "But I can't really see it. I *do* know it's not positive though." Sometimes pornography serves as a warning. "If I'm looking like eight or ten times a day, I realize I need to do something to build my confidence level back up," he says. "I'll go to the gym or go out and eventually find some woman who seems eager to talk to me. That's always the first step to getting laid and feeling better about myself."

I Can Get a Porn Star

In the meantime, pornography makes a lot of men feel a lot better about themselves, even if only on a short-term basis. Divorced, with two kids and no college degree, William, the thirty-five-year-old legal clerk, sees himself as unlikely to attract the kinds of women portrayed in pornography. At five feet seven and 170 pounds, he's a little overweight ("I've got a spare tire going on"). He doesn't have any illusions about why pornography works for him. "I'm looking at women I don't have a shot with," he explains. "The fantasy is that I could actually get them." It's a convenient ego boost.

Unlike women in real life, the girls in pornography seem willing to share themselves with a man. At least in William's experience, real women aren't nearly as into sex. Of course, the porn star is a conscious if elaborate fantasy, requiring several leaps of faith. The first leap is believing—if only for a fleeting moment—that the woman in pornography wants the viewer. Even if only in a corner of the brain where reason doesn't enter and imagination dictates all, a man needs to suspend disbelief (*No, she's not just an image, No, it's not just because she's getting paid*) in order to believe she sees something in him others haven't seen before. It's the same corner of the brain where adolescent girls fantasize that members of their favorite band would actually date them rather than the supermodels they're photographed with. If she just shuts her eyes she can reach a place where it doesn't matter that she's only fourteen and he's thirty-two, that she spends her days at a suburban high school and he lives in London, that she has never met him and likely never will. The fantasy is pure irrationality, but it can feel very real.

In the porn fantasy, a guy is no longer the tech geek nobody liked in junior high school or the awkward college student lacking in social skills. In his mind's eye—despite a paucity of dates and a sexual history confined to the girl from math class—he has always gotten the woman he wants. She gives him that essential validation that everyone, man and woman, craves. He tells himself it's a fantasy, that she's just an image and the real woman behind it may hate men, or be addicted to cocaine, or be dating the cameraman. But he can close his mind to those inconvenient facts, if only for fifteen minutes.

The women in pornography exist in order to please men, and are therefore willing to do anything. They will dominate or act submissive. They can play dumb or talk back, moan quietly or scream, cry in anger or in pleasure. They will accommodate whatever a man wants them to do, be it anal sex, double penetration, or multiple orgasms. The porn star is always responsive; she would never complain about a man being late or taking too long to come. Her hair never gets trapped under his elbow and her thighs never tire. She's easily aroused, naturally and consistently orgasmic, and malleable. She is what he wants her to be. She's a cheerleader, a nurse, a dominatrix, a nymphomaniac, a virgin, a teenager, your best friend's mother. She is every woman who was ever out of your league. She's the girl next door, the prom queen, the hot teacher, the supermodel, the celebrity. She is every woman who ever did the rejecting. She used to be a lesbian, she used to be frigid, she used to be afraid of sex. She is every woman who cannot be had. Now she loves sex, she can't get enough of it; she can't get enough of sex with *you*. She is every woman who *should* appreciate you. The women in pornography are undiscriminating—it doesn't matter what you look like, if you've got bad breath or can't keep an erection. She certainly doesn't care about occupation, reputation, or history. Each encounter begins anew, meeting as welcome strangers and parting with gratitude.

Of all the requirements for enjoyable pornography, men most commonly cite the appearance of a woman's reciprocal pleasure as key. She has to *seem* as if she's having fun; she should be smiling, welcoming, and at ease, and she should make the viewer feel that she's doing what she does because she wants to—not because she's being paid. Even when the sex acts depicted are clearly made to look nonconsensual or painful, most men (there are exceptions) insist that she not seem *too* distraught by the appearance. It should at least be clear—if she's crying or wincing—that she's only acting. "The women in porn tend to act as though the sex act is earth shattering every time, even though realistically speaking, it's not like that all the time," Ethan says. "But it's still fantastic—that enthusiasm really appeals to me." Asked if his wife is enthusiastic about sex, he says in a lackluster voice, "Yeah, I guess so." But he goes on to say, "The women in pornography are just different, though, and that's the appeal. I like the whole innocence vibe of young girls. The tautness of youth, tighter and clearer skin, the bright faces." His wife, Candace, is already twenty-nine years old, a good decade past his ideal.

It's Just a Fantasy

Of course, pornography should be put into perspective, fans insist. "It's not like I would ever date a porn star seriously," Ethan explains. "They're not the kind of women you could bring home to your mother. My mom would go out of her mind seeing me date a slut, a girl with no moral compass whatsoever. Plus, I'm a pretty jealous lover like most guys. If I knew she was going to be off with some guy making a porn movie, that would drive me crazy."

Ethan will be sure to talk to his own children someday about pornography. "I would make sure my son understands that these women are objectified and treated in ways on video or film that no human being in real life should ever be treated," he says. His daughter, he hopes, won't see pornography until high school. "I would teach my daughter that acting the way women do in pornography is not the way to please a man in real life. I would make sure she understood that the value of a person stems from within." He will tell his daughter that when boys look at her that way, they're objectifying her; they're seeing her as a piece of meat. She shouldn't abide by that. *She* should be the one to dictate how they see her so they don't value her purely for sex. If Ethan's kids found out that he looks at porn, he would be sure to explain that he loves their mother for many other reasons beyond the physical. That he doesn't see their mommy as just a disposable outlet for his sexuality.

Candace, after all, is nothing like the women in pornography. By and large, Ethan explains, women in porn are treated like receptacles for men. They're not in a position of control. Weaker men than he might be inclined to be affected by such images. Perhaps some men, those who would be predisposed to view women in a certain negative light, might have their ideas reinforced by pornography. The key, in Ethan's mind, is recognizing the fantasy. It's different from the way women are portrayed elsewhere in the media. After all, in a commercial advertisement, the situation is kept in the realm of reality. "We know we're seeing a car that we don't really need, but we see the car in an environment we can relate to. In porno, the situations are so far outside the norm. No man is going to answer the door and find a woman there in a Girl Scout outfit, ready to have sex. Most men—at least the smarter ones—can tell porn is pure fantasy."

Of course, fantasies still matter, Ethan allows. If a guy were looking at violent rape porn, that would be different. "His fantasy could become a reality," Ethan explains. But what about Ethan fantasizing through pornography about being with another woman—couldn't that become a reality, too? "Yes, but my adultery fantasy is less harmful. If it came true, it would be horrible for me and for my wife, but it would be much more horrible if some guy who looked at rape porn's fantasy came true."

Yet even Ethan has trouble keeping it all in perspective. Ethan could even see himself becoming addicted to pornography since "it's just so pleasurable to look at and there's so much of it out there." He loves being able to admire a new girl every day, never having to see the same girl twice. "I've noticed that I find myself thinking more sexually about women I see on the street after I've had a prolonged exposure to porn," he admits. "I'm not sure if it's because I've been in a monogamous relationship for so long and so I'm inclined to really check out other women, or if it's because I've seen so much porn."

Some men fail to distinguish between fantasy and reality, or slip slowly into failure. It's not difficult, considering that women in pornography are equated with sexual pleasure, yet men continue to get sexual pleasure with women in real life, too. How can the women really be so different, and who will hold men to seeing that difference? And for men who don't have much contact with women, the women in pornography become all he knows. At least that's what thirty-five-year-old Gabe thinks. A couple of guys living in Houston who Gabe first met online have a "porn problem." Both are in their twenties, both are overweight, both live in the Houston area, and neither leaves his house very often. Gabe describes them as social outcasts who spend all their time online, twenty-four hours a day, looking at porn. "I have no idea why they're like this," Gabe says. "I don't think either of them has ever had a girlfriend or been with a real woman sexually. They never learned to interact with people." In Gabe's experience, it's hard to pull them away from their porn, and whenever he convinces them to go out, they're chomping at the bit to get back home. "I guess if you look at something every day for two or three years, it becomes part of your daily routine and starts to affect you."

But doesn't Gabe look on a daily basis? Hasn't he been spending twenty hours a week with it for the past five years? "Yeah, I guess I use porn as much as they do, but I don't do it to masturbate," he explains. "I go online for fun. It's just kind of snowballed into a hobby." Besides, Gabe is careful. "There have been times when I thought I shouldn't look at it so much," he admits. He'll give himself a thirty-six-hour break when he won't go anywhere near the Internet. For the past two or three years, he's tried to provide himself a break every few weeks, to get his focus back on reality. Plus, his girlfriend of eight months doesn't like him looking—not that she knows how often he does or that he provides links to Web sites for money—but when she's seen him looking at porn, she's made comments. "Why do you have to look at other women?" she'll ask, or "Are you done yet?" He tells her he doesn't *have* to look at other women, but that it kills time.

There have been periods when Gabe spent so much time with pornography that he wasn't doing any work at all in the office. He wasn't going out. He wasn't spending as much time with his two kids from his first marriage. Every night he would go home straight from work and go on the Internet. One week, he stayed online 24/7. At the end of seven days, he was exhausted. Then, after meeting the two porn shut-ins, Gabe got worried. "I thought to myself, 'Oh hell, this is what you could turn into,'" he recalls. "I made the decision right then and there. I thought you've got to shut it down, at least every once in a while. I've got to focus on my real life."

2

How We Got Here: Life in the Porn Lane

When did pornography start to insinuate itself so thoroughly into people's everyday lives? When did porn become so ubiquitous and why? The chicken-and-egg conundrum pops up: Is pornography's enormous growth propelled by increasing demand or does the growth of available pornography in the marketplace spur people on? The answer is likely a bit of both. For suppliers, technology has created new and profitable means of distribution. For users, increased distribution means pornography is available in ways never before: cheaply or freely, with anonymity and unlimited access. Moreover, given the growing consumption—online, in homes, on TVs, beamed into cell phones, watched in cars, forwarded via e-mail—the rest of our culture has scrambled to catch up, if only to catch our attention. America has porn on the brain. For any kind of media or entertainment to grab our attention away from pornography, it's got to be good, sexy, hot, exciting, dangerous, illicit, fun, titillating, new, more, more. . . .

We're only beginning to recognize the implications of the growth in pornography and the pornified society's impact on the individuals who live in it. We're only starting to grasp the extent to which the technology revolution of the past two decades has transformed the way in which pornography is produced and consumed. Those who argue that pornography has been with us since cavemen first drew fornicating women on earthen walls ignore the vast discrepancies between a world in which pornography was glimpsed on the sly, where naked girls were glanced at on the faces of nudie poker cards, and today's culture, in which pornography is omnipresent, accepted, and glorified, and on an incessant advance. Furthermore, poet David Mura notes:

> Attributing pornography's growth to demand by individuals ignores what we know by experience: if one walks down the street and sees ten images of women as sexual objects, one may certainly be able to reject those images; yet it is also true that one will have to expend a greater amount of energy rejecting these images than if one saw only five or two or none at all. Assuming that human beings have only a limited amount of energy, it is obvious that the more images there are, the harder it will be for the individual to resist them; one must, after all, expend energy on other activities too. . . . The greater the frequency of such images, the greater the likelihood that they will overwhelm people's resistance. This fact is known, of course, by all those involved in advertising and the media, and is readily accepted by most consumers—except when it comes to pornography.[1]

Our resistance is already down. Pornography has proliferated and the market is scrambling to stay abreast, unaware and unquestioning. More men consume more pornography at ever younger ages; women accommodate and attempt to keep up. How people use pornography, how they feel about it, the ways in which it works in their lives, sexual and otherwise, are rapidly transforming. The ups and downs, the coming and going, the staying online, and the occasionally agonizing ecstasy of it all—whichever way one uses it, and whether or not one ignores it, pornography is powerful stuff. And there's more to it than just fun and fantasy. To understand why requires a look at how the pornified culture evolved and where it's taking us.

"It's Just a Healthy Fantasy"

Dave can't imagine anyone having a problem with his interest in porn. He first saw pornography when he was ten years old, back in 1980. The U.S. Olympic hockey team had just beaten the Soviets at Lake Placid and Ronald Reagan was the new president. Paul McCartney was busted for pot possession and the owners of the famed disco nightclub Studio 54 were sentenced to prison for tax evasion. The hit musical *Grease* closed on Broadway, the Police topped the charts, and Tom Wolfe's *The Right Stuff* dominated the bestseller list. It was the year of *The Empire Strikes Back* and *Ordinary People*.

But at that time, Dave was more captivated by the private world he found hidden away in his father's closet: the latest issues of *Penthouse*, *Playboy*, and *Hustler*. Even at that age, Dave was far from a sexual innocent. He recalls finding a copy of Nancy Friday's collected female fantasies a couple of years earlier and flipping through his parents' *The Joy of Sex*, fascinating to a prepubescent boy. But this was his first encounter with pornography. And he liked it right off the bat. Soon thereafter, the family got its first VCR. In follow-up forays into his parents' bedroom, Dave discovered a stash of porn videos tucked amid his father's videotapes. He began to sneak peaks at films like *Behind the Green Door* and *Taboo* when his parents weren't around. He never told them about what he found and he was never caught. "I don't think it caused me any harm," he says of his age-ten encounter with pornography.

Given his father's supply, Dave never had to stray far if he got the urge for porn. Indeed, he only had to buy magazines for himself on one occasion, and that wasn't until years after he left his childhood home in Ohio. Pornography was readily available around the dormitory at his Ivy League university, too. Occasionally, someone would rent a porn flick and the guys would hang out at a "porn video party," popping in a videocassette when a group gathered. It was all fairly casual.

But after graduation there were no longer videos lying around and nobody to pop in a cassette and no father's closet through which to pilfer. Dave purchased his first and last pornography at a dingy adult storefront shop in Manhattan, after he moved to the city to take a job in finance. He chose a plastic-wrapped packet of three high-quality glossy magazines that displayed a photograph of two women having sex with two men on the cover. On the flip side was a photo of a woman sucking on an ejaculating penis. Dave paid for the shrink-wrapped package, got home, and opened it up to find similar hardcore images inside. He flipped through his new trove of pictures and masturbated. Whenever the urge struck again, he would pull out the packet. That single batch of photographs lasted the next four years.

All guys look at porn, Dave says. Those who don't look are just afraid of getting caught. Or maybe, he theorizes, they're the kinds of people who have made a conscious decision not to look at pornography because they're really religious or really uptight. After all, there's no way pornography would not appeal to all guys. "I think it's natural for men to be curious and interested in sex, same as women," Dave says. "And porn is an easy way of sating that craving for sex."

Dave estimates that at least one-third of women look at pornography, too, a trend he embraces. "I'm a feminist," he explains. "I'm more feminist than many of my female friends. I fully believe in the empowerment of women and equal rights and access—politically, economically, and in every other sphere." In an ideal world, he says, men and women would be treated equally and would have the same or similar approaches to both sex and pornography. In reality, however, "by nature and by nurture" as he puts it, "men think about pornography differently, just as they think about sex differently."

Sexuality is not demeaning to women, Dave is keen to point out. "If you define porn as images of people having sex, that's not demeaning. It's sexual, but it's not sexist." Just because a woman is depicted in a sexual way doesn't make it sexist—if a man can be depicted similarly. "My definition of feminism is equal treatment. That's why I always switch the situation around in my head: I answer the question 'Is it acceptable for a man to look at objectified sexual images of a woman?' by asking myself, 'Is it acceptable for a woman to look at objectified sexual images of a man?' and my answer to both is yes—as long as the viewer understands the difference between fantasy and reality." Feminism, according to Dave's definition, has taken women to a healthier place sexually. "I'm encouraged to see women challenging the stud/slut hypocrisy by conquering lots of men and to see women establishing a skin magazine that depicts sexual images of men for women. Some might complain I'm making women 'sink' to the 'low' level of men, but what's good for the goose is good for the gander. If the way men and women are treating each other becomes unpleasant in an equal way, then they'll realize it and change their ways."

Playboy, he concedes, portrays a lot of sexist imagery and ideas. "There's text in there about women being out to get money from men, and that's a very sexist notion," he says. "And I guess the whole idea that women are playthings for men has a sexist tone." But most guys don't think about those things when they're looking at *Playboy*. Or maybe they do a little bit. "It's true there's a subtext," he concedes. "Just like when kids see violence on movies on or TV." Dave sighs and tries out the analogy. "If your kids are watching violence on TV and you're not sitting down with them as a parent and talking to them about what's fantasy and what's reality, then they could have a problem differentiating the two." Images of violence are okay if people think about it critically and recognize that it's a fantasy, he explains. Of course, some people don't think critically, and some kids will go out and shoot up other kids at school. But, Dave concludes, while a sexual image has some element of humiliation, if you stop and think about it and recognize it's just a fantasy, then it can be dealt with in a healthy way.

The Supply: Porn Inc.

How far pornography has traveled—something that used to be considered seedy and hidden is now considered a healthy exercise in fantasy. As Larry Flynt put it in a 2004 editorial in the *Los Angeles Times*, "The adult film industry in Southern California is not being run by a bunch of dirty old men in the back room of some sleazy warehouse. Today, in the state of California, XXX entertainment is a $9 billion to $14 billion business run with the same kind of thought and attention to detail that you'd find at GE, Mattel, or Tribune Co."[2] Pornography has the technological revolution of the past twenty years to thank for much of its transformation. Whether pornography drives the adoption of technology in the entertainment world or technology spreads porn, a symbiotic relationship exists and expands pornography's reach with each new upgrade.

Back in 1973, there were fewer than a thousand adult theaters across the country. During the 1980s, Betamax and the VHS marked the first great leap forward. No longer did a guy have to skulk down to the seedy porno theater, hoping he didn't bump into his ex-girlfriend, wife, or mother—or, God forbid, his boss. Now he could watch pornography in the comfort of his own home. According to the trade publication *Adult Video News*, in 1986 one in every five videocassettes belonged to the adult category, and 1,500 new adult movies hit the market each year;[3] between 1985 and 1992, the business expanded from $75 million to $490 million.[4] Today, one in four American adults admit to having seen an X-rated movie in the past year, and $4 billion a year is spent on video pornography in the United States—more than on football, baseball, or basketball. Americans rent upward of 800 million pornographic videos and DVDs per year (about one in five of all rented movies), and pornography far outpaces Hollywood's slate of 400 feature films with 11,000 pornos produced annually. Total annual revenue estimates for the adult film industry alone run from $5 billion to $10 billion.[5] Not surprisingly, Columbia House—purveyor of "12 CDs for a penny" mail-order clubs—is launching Hush, a pornographic video club to sell through direct mail and the Internet in conjunction with Playboy Entertainment.[6]

The adult film industry is so successful—and attractive to new entrants—partly due to the high profit margins. Selling sex is cheap. Most pornographic films cost between $5,000 and $10,000 to make, a pittance compared with the $150 million budgets of Hollywood blockbusters. Even the highest-quality smut films, like some of those aired on the Playboy Channel, cost only $100,000, a fraction of the cost for an indie film festival effort.

Pornography is an extremely profitable endeavor not only for the producers but for cable operators and satellite television as well. Pornographic programming now accounts for 25 to 30 percent of all pay-per-view revenue, about $1 billion in total per year.[7] Whereas companies like Comcast and EchoStar have to pay CNN and Showtime for their content with the money they raise from subscriber fees, content from

Playboy and other adult channels is provided free, and only a small fraction of the profits from cable subscribers—between 5 and 20 percent—goes to the adult entertainment supplier. In 2002, Comcast reportedly made $50 million off pornographic programming.[8] Analysts estimate that AT&T Broadband probably makes between $8 million and $20 million per month on adult entertainment.[9] "These companies very much keep it below the radar screen," explains Michael Goodman, a cable and satellite TV analyst with the Yankee Group in Boston. "But when push comes to shove, adult content can be the difference between making money and losing it. And right now, there's an awful lot of money being made on it."[10]

Television pornography also pays off big in the travel industry for chains such as Holiday Inn, Marriott, Hyatt, Hilton, and Sheraton. Given that half of all hotel guests order pornographic pay-per-view movies, the industry is hot for porn. Such films on pay-per-view comprise 80 percent of in room entertainment revenue and 70 percent of total in-room revenue. Hotels keep from 5 to 10 percent of the revenue for each $8.95 movie a guest orders (with the remainder going to companies such as LodgeNet or On Command, which provides the programming).[11]

With so many producers, programmers, and distributors in on the game, the variety of pornographic fare has proliferated. Just as cable subscribers now have their Discovery Adventure Channel and their HBO Zone, pornography fans can choose between Spice Platinum and Hot Zone. Programming has become increasingly raunchy over time. In its early days, cable showed what's known as "hard R" or "soft X" material, but today, vaginal penetration and anal sex are common elements in adult programming. The harder the fare, the more expensive to watch; viewers are encouraged to trade up.[12]

The envelope is constantly pushed open wider. In 1998, Playboy bought Spice Entertainment, which consisted of two channels, Spice, which was more explicit than the Playboy Channel, and Hot Spice, its even more explicit cousin. Back then, Playboy distanced itself from the purchase, allowing Vivid Video to control Hot Spice with the option to buy it back, but such skittishness is now passé. Recently, the company rebought Hot Spice with no compunction. They also sought to upgrade their flagship channel. After conducting focus groups in 2004 that overwhelmingly found users eager for more explicit content, Playboy TV launched a cross-channel advertising campaign to battle the "misperception" that Playboy TV was softer than other networks. The new campaign, featuring the tagline "Up for Anything," aims to appeal to "young men's attitude about being free with the things they want to do and being a little edgy at times as well," explained the company's vice president of marketing.[13] Entertainment analyst Dennis McAlpine, of Auerbach, Pollak & Richardson, an investment brokerage house, says most cable operators still don't want to cross the threshold from "acceptable adult programming," which he says includes penetration, anal sex, oral sex, group sex, and lesbian and gay sex, to "pornography." But isn't anal sex considered pornography? As McAlpine sees it, such material "used to be called pornography, but a lot of that has become socially acceptable now. So it has moved away from pornography. Or, looked at another way, a line of what is acceptable and what is unacceptable has moved a lot more to the explicit side."[14] The door to the free marketplace of porn has swung wide open indeed.

"People Shouldn't Be Treated This Way in Real Life"

Dave prefers a world in which openness prevails. "I think censorship is always a bad solution because whatever is disapproved of just becomes more sought after, becoming the forbidden fruit. Moreover, government disapproval of certain speech or images creates implied government support or approval of other forms of speech and images, which can create a form of state-sponsored bigotry and sexism. Rather than censorship, I want a world where people discuss their values with their children and loved ones," he explains.

Dave plans to extend these values to his own family one day. "If I found out that my daughter or son were looking at pornography then I would sit them down and talk to them about how they felt about what they were seeing," he says. "I would tell them about how I feel about it. And make sure they knew that what they were looking at was just a fantasy—that what they saw people doing in porn is not how people should act in real life. If my son or daughter watched a porn movie that depicted a woman being brutalized sexually by a man (or a man being brutalized sexually by a woman), I would want to have a conversation with him or her, saying, 'The way he or she was brutalized was horrible and wrong. I understand if you were aroused by it, as long as you understand that it is imaginary and not the way people should be treated in the real world.' " If his daughter were to tell him she had decided to pose for a pornographic magazine or act in a porn movie, Dave says he wouldn't oppose it outright. "But I would tell her to think long and hard because whatever she does would be out there in the public eye forever. If your attitude changes later on, there's nothing you can do. It's like getting a tattoo."

Dave hopes to be married someday and have kids. He's just waiting for the right woman to come along. He has certain standards. If, for example, a woman Dave were dating asked him to stop looking at pornography, that would be a dealbreaker. Or rather, he goes on to explain, it would be if she were "very closed-minded" and had a narrow definition of erotica. What if she told him she were opposed to pornography on ideological grounds or she found pornography derogatory toward women? "I guess it would open us into a larger discussion," he hedges. He hopes it won't be an issue. He hopes he and his future wife will enjoy pornography together.

"I've heard people say that looking at pornography could be considered cheating," Dave says, "but it strikes me as silly." Cheating is an emotional betrayal, not a physical one. "If a married man were to spend a night in deep, heartfelt conversation with a woman who was not his wife, that's probably more a case of cheating than for him to have meaningless sex with some prostitute." Ascribing emotional meaning to pornography strikes him as a stretch.

Over the course of his thirty-four years, Dave has had a total of eighteen sexual partners. He and his last serious girlfriend—a woman he dated for six months—broke up about seven months ago. Some of Dave's girlfriends have known that he looks at pornography. "Sharing my porn with a girlfriend is a very intimate thing," he explains. Usually he keeps his favorite Web sites to himself. "I've only done it with a couple of girlfriends I really trusted. I was opening up to them. Both were interested in seeing the porn that I had and we looked at it together.

Both women said that they liked it, and I liked that they liked it. With the others, I never told them, and the subject never came up." The woman Dave is dating now is one of those he's opened up to. They've been seeing each other for a few months, and Dave thinks it could become serious. "It was pillow talk," he recalls dreamily. "She wanted to know about what I liked and disliked." She's seen some of the Web sites Dave likes to visit. They haven't watched an actual pornographic movie together yet, however. "I think that would be . . . a pretty serious step," Dave says hesitantly.

Not all their fantasies line up. The new girlfriend has confessed her interest in seeing pornography that depicts anal and group sex. "She's wanted to have anal sex, but I can't do that, I'm not comfortable with it at all." She's also discussed her rape fantasies with Dave, told him how she fantasizes about getting beaten, about women being beaten in general, and about getting raped herself. "Of course, she knows and I know that that doesn't mean she wants to be raped," Dave says. "She knows it's wrong. It's just a daydream." Pornography that depicts rape scenes isn't a turn-on for Dave personally, but he understands why it might be appealing to some people, "as long as they can clearly identify what's reality and what's fantasy." In other ways, he and his new girlfriend are remarkably compatible. "She likes sex rough, she likes it to hurt—even in real life," he says appreciatively. He can get into that.

The Supply: Porn.com

According to a major study of pornography across various media, with each iteration in technological advancement, pornography has become increasingly violent and nonconsensual. For example, in one study, a random selection of pornographic material, 25 percent of pornographic magazines showed some form of violence, ranging from verbal aggression to torture and mutilation, compared with 27 percent of pornographic videos. Usenet groups on the Internet depicted violence 42 percent of the time.[15] "We might expect that just as individual consumers of pornography tend to tire of a certain level of explicitness and need more, so, too, would the market, acting as an individual," noted the study's authors. "The more pornography is consumed at one level, the less arousing this material becomes, as the consumer becomes used to—satiated with—the material. This satiation leads the consumer to seek out newer, more explicit, and more violent forms of sexual material that will again arouse him/her."[16] The authors then concluded that as new pornographic technologies emerged, pornography would become increasingly violent—both to satisfy earlier, upgraded demand and to bring the viewer to the next level. That research was conducted in the late 1990s, still the early days in Internet time.

Doubtless, the Internet has been a major driving force—perhaps the greatest force ever—behind the proliferation of porn. The kickoff may have been with a certain inadvertent combination of professionalism, celebrity, and amateurism: the landmark pornographic home video featuring Pamela Anderson and then-husband Tommy Lee, which is credited with bringing more users online than any other single event. Pornography has not only brought in new subscribers, it helped pioneer online payment systems, encouraged the use of streaming media, and sped the adoption of broadband. Pornography pushed the usage of Usenet and then peer-to-peer sharing networks like Kazaa, Brokester, and Bit Torrent as users learned to download, copy, and pass along their porn.

In turn, the Internet's impact on pornography is practically a category unto itself. The Internet has thoroughly internationalized the world of pornography so that to speak of international borders with regard to production and tastes is increasingly meaningless. Americans consume Japanese *manga* (cartoon) pornography and gaze at nude photos of Dutch women. Russian women are virtually exported around the world, complicating the dimensions of international sex trafficking. Child pornography is pumped into Australia from across the globe. Men in Canada can visit the brothels of Bangkok from the comfort of their home offices. The impact on market growth is astounding. You can pump out one statistic after another; the bulging numbers are almost mind-numbing. According to the Internet content filtering company N2H2, there are 260 million pages of pornography online, an increase of 1,800 percent since 1998. In April 2004, Websense, a provider of employee Internet management software, revealed that the number of pornography Web sites in their URL database had grown seventeenfold in four years, from 88,000 in 2000 to nearly 1.6 million in 2004.[17]

Since the dawn in the 1980s of Usenet, a popular bulletin board service among techies and academics, pornography has been one of the most widely traded commodities online, becoming increasingly popular as the graphics capacity of computer software allowed. A 2001 federal study found more than 25,000 pornography files on file-sharing programs.[18] Today, on peer-to-peer networks like Kazaa, 73 percent of all movie searches are for pornography (24 percent of all image searches were for child pornography specifically).[19] And an estimated 22 million children regularly use these peer-to-peer networks. The amount of free pornography traded keeps rising. Another study, conducted by Big Champagne, a Los Angeles–based measurement firm, found that in March 2004, 51 percent of all video files being shared on peer-to-peer networks were pornographic, up from 42 percent in September 2003.[20]

Fueled by a combination of access, anonymity, and affordability, the Internet has propelled pornography consumption—bringing in new viewers (including children), encouraging more use from existing fans, escalating consumers from softcore to harder-core material, and propelling some over the edge into sexual compulsivity. Type "XXX" into Google and 106 million pages arise, up from 76 million six months ago. A 2004 study found that pornographic sites are visited three times more often than Google, Yahoo!, and MSN Search combined.[21] Pornography even has its own Googlesque search engine, Booble.com ("Play with our boobles!"), which attracts more than a million visitors a day.[22] Academics and psychologists have generated an entire field of cybersex sociology. The Computer Addiction Center at McLean Hospital has identified cyberaddiction, a syndrome often tied to pornography, and titles such as *Infidelity on the Internet: Virtual Relationships and Real Betrayal* and *Cybersex Exposed: Simple Fantasy or Obsession*? have hit bookstores in recent years.

"Here's Where Things Changed"

Around 1996, Dave, who often uses a computer for work, started to look at pornography online. He began by viewing still photos and then—especially after he got broadband at home about four years ago—started watching video clips. Nowadays, it's almost all always video. "And it's always free—I've never paid for anything."

"I guess, well, here's where things changed," he begins, a bit hesitant. First he was happy looking at magazines, which he kept around for a long time. So when he started with Internet porn, he also started with still photos, usually of naked women. But soon he discovered moving images, and once he saw what was available, his interest was piqued. "I found that I wanted to see actual sex acts, hardcore stuff, and especially group sex," he says. It was always available, with so much more to be uncovered. The Internet offered endless exploration, voyeurism, and discovery.

Dave calls his preferences in terms of sex acts carnal: *vivid, direct, hardcore* are words he uses to describe the close-up images he enjoys. "The idea of anal and oral and vaginal sex all at the same time is very appealing to me." His main focus is group sex. "I especially like multiple guys on one woman or multiple women on one guy," he says. Dave was surprised to find out how much he likes "the money shot"—ejaculation images, which usually show the man ejaculating outside of a woman's body. The Japanese style of pornography called *bukkake,* which typically features images of young Japanese women being ejaculated on by multiple men, and usually depicts the woman as upset or even crying, is surprisingly exciting. "I had never seen that before the Internet," he confesses. "I guess there's a slippery slope from naked women to something like bukkake."

Look, he points out, it's not like the images he likes to watch in pornography are necessarily things he would like to pursue in the real world. "It's a turn-on for me to see group sex, but I've never done it in real life," Dave explains. "If the conditions were right, I'd be open, but I'm highly skeptical that it would work out. In the real world, there are personal dynamics. It would probably end up being awkward or uncomfortable or result in some kind of relationship disaster." The appeal is the fantasy. "It's the complete carnality of it, the sensory overload. It's just one hundred percent physical."

A moment of silence passes. "I guess you could read into it as a psychologist that there's some issue I have personally about getting too emotionally involved with women," he says thoughtfully. "I've been accused of that by friends, ex-girlfriends. They say I'm reluctant to open up. But I don't think porn is what makes me that way, or that my being that way drives my involvement with porn. I think it's just that I'm a guy who is interested in and curious about seeing images of group sex."

Recently, Dave has come across what he calls "disturbingly brutal images" of women and men with very large penises. His intense excitement surprised him. "Basically, the men are having sex with these women's faces and the women are gagging on cum and on the dicks and they're slobbering because it's multiple guys, one right after the other," he describes. "And these images are on sites where you know what you're getting because the Web sites have names like Fuckerface and CockBrutality and Meatholes." Dave lets out an abrupt laugh. "I know objectively that it's horrid, but I have to admit that some of the images have been real sexual turn-ons.

"This is going to sound ridiculous," he warns. "But I do prefer images where she's lying on her back with her head bent back toward the floor and the guy is inserting his penis down her throat." He also likes it when she's getting stimulated at the same time and giving oral sex simultaneously. "I like the concept of pleasure and torture at the same time," he explains. "I like the idea that her throat is just being used to get this guy off." By comparison, a "pure image" of a guy "just getting off" while a woman closes her eyes and opens her mouth is "kind of boring." It somehow seems too . . . plain. "But if the woman is having sex with one guy while the others are getting off on her, coming all over her—on her face, her breasts, her body—that's really good."

Still, his enjoyment bothers him in a way. "I know a lot of this violates the dignity of a woman," he says. "When I realized how sexually turned on I was by stuff like bukkake, what I would do is force myself to stop and separate things in my head. I would make myself think, 'Yes, that was an enjoyable fantasy, but no, that is not the way I want to be with anyone.' I wish more people stopped and thought about it that way."

The Supply: Porn Everywhere

Having conquered home and office, porn tech marches forward, now at a healthy sixty-miles-per-hour clip. The latest option is "dirty driving." With built-in DVD players as the latest SUV accoutrement of choice, people can watch pornographic videos in the comfort and semiprivacy (depending on the tint of their car windows) of their automobiles. The number of cars equipped with DVD players and the number of passengers who use those players for pornographic purposes are unknown, because most people install players after they purchase their car. But entertainment systems are now available in 381 car models; nearly half of all buyers of the Nissan Quest minivan in 2004 said they want the DVD system.[23] Such cars can be driven down highways and rural interstates where, increasingly, porn "superstores" are sprouting, to take advantage of low real estate costs and high profit margins, under banners like Lion's Den Adult Superstore and X-Mart Adult SuperCenter—brightly lit and well-stocked emporiums just like their PG-rated mass retailer counterparts.

For those who would rather chat on the phone during their drives, the purveyors of porn have just the solution: cell-phone pornography. As of spring 2004, some fifty companies, carried by major telecom firms such as Vodafone and Hutchison, already provide such services in Europe. Cell-phone pornography in western Europe is estimated to reach $1.5 billion in 2005—about 5 percent of the total mobile data market.[24] America is scrambling to catch up. A certain amount of adult material, mostly text-based stories or simple drawings, has been available via cell phone in the United States since the late 1990s. Now, with more cell phones featuring color display screens, digital cameras, and Web browsers, technology firms are offering more sophisticated ways to provide pornographic content. XTCMobile.com, for example, can transmit video clips of two to four minutes, pornographic screensavers, and "sexy" games, along with specialized rings that simulate groaning or moaning (you pick!)—all for $7.99 a month. "Turn me on—turn-on your phone" coaxes the company's Web site, amid pulsing red animation and photos of porn stars. The company launched three phone channels in the spring of 2004. Another adult entertainment company, VTX, offers PocketJoy, a device for downloading pornographic images to cell phones.

Pornography companies also use wireless cell-phone technology as a venue for advertising and promotion, using cells to announce adult films and Web sites, as well as related goods and services. Altogether, wireless pornography is expected to generate anywhere between $1 billion and

$6.5 billion by 2007, according to telecom analysts.[25] Technological advances occur every day. Next on the horizon are personal media centers, a Microsoft product that will allow people to download and watch videos from mobile video devices. Pornography is increasingly available on a range of mobile devices; just in time for holiday 2004, Playboy.com launched "iBod," free pornography pics, for use on Apple's iPod photo device. Altogether, The Yankee Group consulting firm estimates that the wireless pornography market will be worth $90 million within four years, with 500,000 consumers in the United States and 8 million users worldwide by 2008.[26]

Fueled by technological expansion over the past twenty years, the pornography business is raking in big bucks. The industry boasts its own annual trade show and trade publication; it employs lobbyists, lawyers, accountants, marketers, Internet gurus, and industry analysts. Pornography businesses trade on the NASDAQ and the New York Stock Exchange. Though estimates vary widely, in part a function of the still-clandestine nature and slippery business practices rampant in the industry, total annual revenues are likely $10 billion a year, and may be as high as $20 billion in America alone. (One reason it's hard to pin down numbers is because the industry includes so many underground and private companies and because publicly held companies such as AT&T and Time Warner, which have substantial investments in pornography through their cable businesses, don't break out their adult business figures.)

Pornography empires keep expanding their purview. Back in 1972, Larry Flynt entered the industry with the small-time launch of *Hustler* magazine, a hardcore expansion into full-body nudity and up-close genitalia shots, because, as Flynt put it disdainfully, "*Playboy* and *Penthouse* were parading their pornography as art with the air-brushing and the soft lens."[27] Today, Flynt's domain extends from print (six magazines including *Hustler*, *Beaver Hunt,* and *Barely Legal*) to film (three production companies that create approximately forty new titles a month), to Hustler retail stores, which include coffee bars and tasteful wooden details reminiscent of Borders bookstores. In 2004, Flynt opened his ninth strip club, the Hustler Club in New York City, and announced plans to expand his brand to television with Hustler TV On Demand. Perched atop his multimedia throne, Flynt is reportedly worth more than $750 million.

The Hustler Club empire is only one of many new "entertainment venues" for live pornography. Nationwide, the strip club business is flourishing. No longer are such clubs the shady front offices of mobsters; farewell to the mom-and-pop strip joint. The newest clubs belong to branded chains: the Penthouse Executive Club, for example, which in New York City cost $10 million to construct and features a chef who once worked at famed restaurants Le Cirque and Daniel.[28] At these upscale clubs, businessmen gather after their workday, couples come in for mutual titillation, and people throw bachelor and bachelorette parties to celebrate impending marriages. Playboy Enterprises recently announced plans to revive the Playboy Clubs, the last of which closed in 1986. Soon, grown women will be "Bunny dipping" in their ears and tails in order to serve male customers drinks.

Multimedia conglomerates pop up all the time to fill in niche and growing categories. For example, Vivid Entertainment, a company boasting about $150 million in annual revenue, has marketed itself as high-quality pornography, with so-called Vivid Girls positioned to offer extra cachet compared with run-of-the-mill porn performers.[29] The company claims double-digit growth in the past five years.[30] New Frontier Media, Inc., with $43 million in annual revenues, operates a subscription/pay-per-view television unit and distributes branded programming through cable and direct broadcast satellite TV. Their Internet group sells content to monthly subscribers through its broadband Web site, partners with third-party gatekeepers for distribution, and wholesales content to other Web sites. New Frontier, traded on the NASDAQ, saw its stock price shoot up 775 percent between 2003 and 2004.

"You're Like a Gambler"

With so many choices, Dave still has his limits. He doesn't like bisexuality, gay porn, or bestiality, for example. Even within the types of pornography he likes, some moves are overkill. "Every once in a while there'll be something like a clip where a guy slaps the woman's face while she's giving him a blow job or in the process of having sex with her," he says.

"That just kills my arousal." Dave prefers it when the woman looks as if she's enjoying herself in some way. He also finds it titillating to see the table turned. "I have been turned on by images of a woman subjugating a guy and lording it over him. I admit I've never seen images where it's totally flipped around, where a woman is using a guy and tying him down and having sex with him and peeing on him afterward."

He always looks at Internet pornography at home—there's no way he would look at it at his financial firm, where Internet use is monitored assiduously. He started off looking two to three times per week, then got up to five or six times weekly. Because he's a self-professed cheapskate and doesn't want to pay for anything, Dave will often spend large amounts of time scrolling through images until he finds something to turn him on. "There's a lot of flipping back and forth trying to separate the wheat from the chaff. You'll find something good and then 'Oh, no, he's slapping her!' and something that was a turn-on gets cut short. It's a rocky road." But the challenge, the chase, is part of the enjoyment. "There's a fluttery feeling in your stomach because you know you're getting away with something illicit," he explains. "It's like gambling, like a gambling addiction trigger; you'll see something that's pretty exciting and titillating and you want to find more of that, you really want more of that, you keep hunting. You want to find something like that, but even more so. You're like a gambler, just playing one more hand until you win."

After Dave finds what he's looking for and gets off, he dumps his computer cache—"I guess I just don't like to leave a trail of where I've been or what I was looking at"—and goes to bed. "I feel like, yeah, that was a release, but I don't know, maybe not the best thing," he explains. "Like eating a bag of potato chips." Somehow you always consume too much. In Dave's world, masturbation and computers may as well be wired together. For the past six months he hasn't masturbated without looking at Internet porn. More than a few times, Dave has spent well over two hours at the computer, masturbating two or three times per sitting. On those occasions he feels "pretty ridiculous."

As a result, Dave has experimented with "restricting" or "reining in" his use of online pornography. There was a time when he limited himself to weeknights only, because, as he puts it, "If I looked on weekends there was no reason to keep me from staying up until all hours with it." Lately, he's tried to keep himself to two times a week because he's in a relationship. "To avoid dulling my sexual response too much," he explains. "I'd rather save any pent-up energy and excitement for the real thing than let it all dissipate through masturbation." Sometimes, while he's having sex with a woman, Dave will start thinking about pornography—things he's seen, things he's liked, things that turn him on. He'll conjure up the images voluntarily, to maintain and enhance his arousal. Or the images will just pop up in his head spontaneously. Dave doesn't tell his partner what he's thinking about.

Porn in America

Today, pornography is not only planted in people's psyches; it's everywhere in our culture. It's difficult to conceive of a twelve-year-old making it through elementary school and into junior high without having seen pornography; he would likely be less than shocked by an encounter with a softcore magazine. Certainly not in the post–Paris Hilton, post–Janet Jackson era. It's hard to imagine how, just ten years ago, Paris Hilton, the (possibly unwitting) star of her own Internet porn clip, would have survived being thrust into cyberspace and forwarded with exponential speed. But Paris's foray into pornography pushed her further up the pecking order from B-list It Girl celebrity into one of the year's most promising stars. Her Fox reality show reaped record ratings. She landed the cover of *Elle* magazine and frolicked on the cover of *Maxim*. *FHM* named her the most eligible woman in the world. She even won coveted roles in mainstream Hollywood movies and penned a bestselling autobiography. Some tongues may have wagged, and naysayers may have called her newfound success a flash in the pan. But Hilton was proof that being a porn star means being a star.

By comparison, Janet Jackson didn't have it quite so good. During Super Bowl 2004's halftime show, a duet by Janet Jackson and Justin Timberlake infamously resulted in what was later termed a "wardrobe malfunction." As Timberlake sang the words, "I'm gonna get you naked by the end of this song," he tore away Jackson's bustier and revealed her nipple, adorned with a large metallic piercing in the shape of a sunburst.

Across America, viewers gaped at one another dumbfounded. "Did we just see that!?" The next day, eager to review the proceedings or take in what they'd missed, Americans went straight to the Internet. Janet Jackson's breast quickly became the most searched-for image in online history, setting records on Yahoo!, where it accounted for nearly 20 percent of all searches.[31]

The fallout was immediate. A nationwide poll taken after Jackson's unveiling found that 56 percent of Americans thought the episode was disrespectful.[32] Of course, the objections were sparked not just by Jackson's nudity. People complained about the hypocrisy of a culture that implicitly endorses such behavior. About a culture that condemns the woman while letting the man, Justin Timberlake (and the men watching happily at home), largely off the hook. About a corporate media system that prefers to reap profits than to set standards. Moreover, Jackson's breast wasn't merely exposed, it was forcefully revealed in a mock-violent display, yet another nod to the way pornography has redefined our sexual terrain. But while Jackson's defenders tried to condemn the outraged as modern-day Puritans, anyone with open eyes, no matter their political stripes, can see that Janet's flap was far from an isolated incident.

In fact, a glimpse at the surrounding culture makes the Janet Jackson episode seem startling for its controversy. What else was going on in the mainstream media that week? That very same night, *Women: Stories of Passion: Grip Till It Hurts* was showing on one of Showtime's extended channels (albeit at 1 A.M. rather than prime time). Elsewhere on cable, ETV was airing Howard Stern's program, which features explicit conversations with female porn stars. With the click of a button, pay-per-view fare that night included such wholesome grist as *Horny Girls Next Door* and *Oral Majority*. Meanwhile, in the world of print, the laddie magazines—*Maxim*, *FHM*, and *Stuff*—all featured women in pornographic poses, only their nipples and crotches covered by lingerie, bikinis, and strategically placed hands. The famed *Sports Illustrated* "swimsuit issue" hit newsstands (reaching triple the number of readers for the average copy depicting fully clothed male athletes).[33] And this issue featured fewer swimsuits than ever: one-fourth of the photographs depicted women who were topless or naked, though some were adorned with "body paint." In a special offering, the fortieth-anniversary issue even included a nude "centerfold." Now where did they get that idea? In its February 2004 issue, *Playboy* gloated,

> Not since suburban couples lined up to see *Deep Throat* in 1973 has the mainstream so embraced pornography. . . . Adult-film queen Jenna Jameson sexed up a sanitized Times Square on a five-story billboard and graced a *New York* magazine cover proclaiming porn's ubiquity. It's been 17 years since the end of Traci Lords's XXX career, but fans lined up for her to sign her hump-and-tell autobiography. And when starlet Mary Carey leaped into California's 135-candidate gubernatorial race, she came in 10th. In one online survey, two-thirds of HR professionals said they had found porn on employees' computers.[34]

Playboy had reason to be pleased with the revolution it started fifty years ago. Given the current acceptability of pornography in mainstream culture, those who like it can assume its use is perfectly natural, just a way to enhance good old-fashioned masturbation. Something one would never need to worry about because normal guys—not just sex addicts, not just child-molesting perverts—look at pornography. They have wives and careers and families and reputations. They would never mistreat women or cheat on their girlfriends. For them, porn is a pleasure, porn is a hoot, porn is even healthy. Watching pornography with a partner can even be a form of sexual enhancement—the equivalent of a vibrator or *The Joy of Sex*.

Meanwhile, those who have never been into it, or have watched only occasionally for kicks, or haven't seen it since giggling over a lame softcore video (the one with the stripper nurse! the one with the strawberries!) while in college, can assume that pornography has nothing to do with them. Figure that boys will be boys, pornography is harmless, and women will just never understand. If they don't like porn, they can shut their eyes to it, delete their junk mail, unsubscribe to cable, and tune out. Live a porn-free life and assume their husbands don't look at it, that their boyfriends look only occasionally, that their kids can be protected from pornography before puberty.

But these people would be wrong. More people look at pornography—on a regular and increasing basis—than most of them, especially women, realize. Perhaps it's your brother, your best friend, your cousin, your boyfriend, or your son ordering pay-per-view porn every night. Perhaps it's your colleague or your boss checking out online anal sex between meetings. Maybe there's a reason your husband clears his Internet history after a night surfing the Web. Even fans themselves may be left in the dark. Those who consume pornography may be looking at more of it for reasons they don't know or don't understand. It may be affecting them in ways they aren't even aware.

"I Was Worried"

In early 2004, Dave went to the doctor to check if he had erectile dysfunction because he had lost his erection while having sex with a new partner he was very attracted to. The doctor told him it was just a passing psychological thing. "I wanted to double-check. I was worried that seeing a lot of porn had worn down my sexual response and numbed me. That it contributed to whatever uneasiness or lack of arousal I had.

"I felt like it was getting too out of control," Dave said in the spring of 2004. Already, he has seen a certain amount of desensitization. "I've definitely noticed that naked images that used to arouse me don't anymore, so I had to move on. I found that I was getting numb to basic images. I needed to keep progressing to more explicit stuff." At the same time, Dave found he was less aroused by real women. "But that could just be that I'm getting older."

For most of his adult life Dave has had a hard time achieving orgasm during sex. While he would come quickly during masturbation, it would take at least half an hour during intercourse. "Frankly, we usually wrap it up by me taking things into my own hands, just masturbating to end things. But that has nothing to do with porn. It's been like that since I was twenty. I think it's because I've been masturbating since I was five years old." Nonetheless, Dave feels he risks becoming compulsive. "I can easily see how I could become addicted to porn, if I didn't exert some control. Because there's a certain rush that you get. And I find myself thinking, I could get that rush again if I go on just a bit longer, if

I can find more of the same thing. I've noticed that I can just mentally tune everything else out while doing it."

Thus, the "restrictions." He's decided to hold himself back and "nip this thing in the bud." It's been three or four months since Dave decided to cut back and he's "more or less" stuck to his plan. Oh, sure, sometimes he ends up looking on the weekends, after already having his twice-a-week fill. When he does allow himself to look at pornography he tends to binge, and to look a lot longer than he used to. Since cutting back, he hasn't noticed a dramatic increase in his sex drive. But he feels a bit more in control. He's gaining a better sense of balance, moderation, variety. He hopes over time he may notice a change in his sex life, unless it's just a sign that, at thirty-four, his libido is winding down. In the meantime he's strengthening his resolve and working it out on his own. It's just a question of mind over matter, a challenge of self-control. Dave hasn't mentioned his cutback plan to his girlfriend, or, in fact, to anybody. Dave doesn't even like to think about it.

3

Me and My Porn: How Pornography Affects Men

Pornography, some say, has no effect on those who use it. According to the "neutralists," which include sex therapists and male writers on sexuality, people who dismiss the media and its impact, and others not particularly aware of pornography's contemporary parameters, porn is just a form of entertainment, neither positive nor negative, and ultimately inconsequential. Pornography, they claim with a shrug, is mere fantasy. It helps men masturbate, sure, but it's men who are doing the masturbating, not pornography making them do so. Once that's done, they can file it away under the bed and move on.

But to argue that pornography has no effect on the people who consume it would be like arguing that the multibillion-dollar advertising business is all for naught, that people aren't influenced by what they see, read, or hear, and that all media are inconsequential. To argue that pornography has no effect would make it kind of pointless. After all, pornography is explicitly created with the intention not only to entertain but to enhance sexual experience. Even fans contradict such assertions. They look because it feels good; sometimes it relaxes and other times it excites, and sometimes it accomplishes both in fine form. Pornography makes them feel better about themselves; it's a pick-me-up or a sustaining force in an otherwise dry or unsatisfactory sexual landscape. As with advertising, responses to pornography may not always be rational, but they are nonetheless extraordinarily powerful.

Others argue that pornography is far from neutral: it's good for you. Proponents—industry insiders, pro-porn feminists, certain sex and couples therapists, legal defenders of the industry, sex scribes—assign an array of benefits to pornography: It helps people overcome sexual inhibitions, particularly sex-related guilt, enhances insufficient libido, and teaches a wider repertoire of sexual activities, which then leads to greater sexual fulfillment.[1] Pornography makes people more comfortable with their own sexuality. It lifts the veil of religious repression and ideologically induced guilt. It helps people work up a sexual appetite and teaches them to sate it once they're in the mood. Sex therapists sometimes suggest to their clients that they look at pornography together. Adding some spice could be the kick tired couples need.

Common sense might lead one to imagine that pornography promotes positive sexuality, but this just isn't the case. To date, according to two University of Alabama researchers, professor of communications Jennings Bryant and professor of psychology Dolf Zillmann, authors of several groundbreaking studies on pornography, "no rigorous research demonstrations of desirable effects can be reported and beneficial effects of pornography consumption remain a matter of contention and conjecture."[2] Indeed, social science has had a difficult time *scientifically* proving that pornography affects men either positively *or* negatively; that old saw "causation" makes it difficult to prove definitively whether a particular kind of man is likely to use pornography, or whether pornography turns someone into a particular kind of man. Though scientific proof remains out of reach, men who use pornography attribute to it a broad array of effects. They've seen what it can do.

The first time Rajiv saw naked women was in porn, the first time he saw people having sex was in porn, the first time he masturbated—a "late bloomer" at age sixteen—was while looking at pornography. "The visual aspect of porn has definitely had an impact on my sexual development," says the twenty-eight-year-old New Yorker. "All of my first sexual experiences were with pornographic movies."

That's the only action he could get for a long time. Rajiv was a shy and dorky kid. He didn't date much in high school, and at college, a prestigious East Coast university, he didn't meet his first girlfriend or lose his virginity until his junior year, when he was twenty-one. During the sexless years of high school, he would watch movies like *Emmanuelle* on Saturday nights, starting at the age of twelve or thirteen. In high school, his best friends discovered a porn video called *Very Dirty Dancing*, and Rajiv made a copy, which he would masturbate to when alone. At college, however, he lived porn-free. He didn't have a TV or VCR. It never occurred to him to look for pornography on his laptop. And going out to buy magazines seemed pointless; after his early exposure to movies in high school, photographs were a pale substitute. "Print is so much less immersive and real," he explains. "What's the point?"

Besides, Rajiv was happy with his college girlfriend. Well past his dork years, he had grown to be a slim, thoughtful-looking man, with large expressive eyes and the dark coloring of his half–South Asian heritage. He had no trouble attracting women, and his girlfriend seemed to appreciate him. Rajiv didn't even masturbate much while they were dating. There was no need. Once in a while they would watch a porn movie together—when traveling, ordering it in their hotel room for kicks. It was more for him than for her, but she didn't seem to mind. Pornography was no big deal, never even a topic of conversation. And he didn't look at it when his girlfriend wasn't around. The couple stayed together for nearly five years.

It wasn't until after their breakup that Rajiv picked up pornography again. This was back in January 2002. One night, almost as a lark, he decided to subscribe to the Playboy Channel. Mostly, it was "silly softcore stuff," though occasionally they carried the more explicit movies that Rajiv enjoyed. But after a while he grew bored and canceled the service. In any case, paying was no longer necessary. Rajiv had collected in his head enough scenes and images that he could summon them on demand. Some of those images had been there since high school, dating back to *Very Dirty Dancing*, but Rajiv now had more to choose from. There was, for example, the movie where a busty blonde who still lives at home with her parents is caught having sex with some guy. Her parents are concerned because they think she's too young. They bring the girl to a doctor, who, finding her attractive, asks her to undress. While he's examining her, she starts to moan. It's clear she wants to have sex with him. So the doctor says, "I'm going to try this novel treatment on you." She says, "Please do," and they have sex.

Scenarios like this turned Rajiv on so much that they enhanced his real sex life. For example, when he was dating his college girlfriend, if he was having a hard time ejaculating because he had too much to drink or was tired, he would think of this scene, or a similar one. He never had a problem getting or maintaining an erection—but ejaculating within a reasonable amount of time was difficult. At these times, pornography helped him along.

The Rush

Excited is one of the first words that come to mind when men describe how they feel while looking at pornography. The physical act of masturbation alone is enough to fuel the experience. When a man looks at pornography and masturbates, he undergoes all the giddy physical sensations of sexual release. Adrenaline rushes through his veins. His brain releases dopamine, serotonin, and oxytocin—all powerful neurotransmitters associated with feelings of pleasure. Testosterone surges. It's a potent high. There's also the thrill of the hunt. And the surge of voyeuristic pleasure in observing and fantasizing once the sought-after object is found.

Tyler, a part-time computer science undergrad student and Web developer, lived out his entire adolescence in the age of the Internet. From the moment he hit puberty, pornography has been online. His first peek at hardcore was when a friend showed Tyler his older brother's online cache. "He had a thing for cum shots," Tyler recalls. That was back in the fifth grade, when Tyler was living on a military base in California. These days Tyler goes on the Internet at least once a day to masturbate, always at night, and then sometimes in the morning if he doesn't have an early class. "I'm very focused when I get into porn mode," he says. "It's like I experience this rush, this whoosh of excitement that drives me on." Once online, he'll plow through Web sites quickly. Click, click, click, download, and move on. "I throw a lot of sites out because they're not good enough, not wild enough, not crazy enough," Tyler continues. "I'm always looking for the right site. Finding it is part of the fun."

Female friends are amazed by Tyler's involvement with pornography. They'll say to him, "Wow, you look at Internet porn once or twice a day!" But he doesn't understand the fuss. "If you look at polls online, it's more often a couple times a week for most people," he explains, and then adds sheepishly, "Once a day *is* a little much. But it's definitely not compulsive because it's not like I don't do other things, like go to school or go to work." It's just so available. "Your partner in porn never says no. And if you've broken up with your girlfriend or if you're in a bad relationship, that can be a huge help." But it does seem to leave him wanting more. Like gambling, you get hooked on an unattainable fantasy, "because when you're done with the porn, there's still no woman right there with you, so you just want to keep going with it. And going. I guess that can lead to compulsion."

In the fall of 2003, one of Rajiv's friends mentioned a pornography blog called Fleshbot, which offers links to a myriad of Web sites. He decided to check it out. His dating life had dried up completely, work was slow, and sitting at the computer at least made Rajiv feel as if he was doing something. Online pornography was a completely different ball game from the movies he had watched intermittently since college. With movies, there was always a beginning and an end. In the online world, pornography was "an odyssey." He was captivated. "Online porn is an infinite exploration," he says. "There's this sense that not only could I discover all these new and interesting things, but that I could always be able to find exactly what I wanted."

For Rajiv, that meant women who looked different from the women in porn movies. Those women had seemed a bit too fake, too altered by surgery and implants. But on the Internet, image galleries offered visitors a choice between porn stars, teens, voyeurism, and other targeted tastes. Rajiv discovered the genre of "average girls"—women who looked like someone he might meet and have sex with, the occasional pimple, oversized thigh and all. "They seemed more real, and that was exciting to me," Rajiv explains. The Average Girls always looked cheerful and happy to have sex. They seemed friendly and realistic and, above all, enthusiastic—ideally, the way women acted in real life.

"I don't want a woman who is submissive and lets me be the boss," he says. "I want a woman who is as into it as I am and I want to be able to please her." With porn, Rajiv fancied himself the "stud who can please women" and that was part of the enjoyment. "I respect women and the idea of porn that degrades women repulses me. Porn where it's all about the guy, and the woman is just a sex object, isn't appealing to me at all," he says. "I like sex to be egalitarian." Pornography had become a lot more interesting online.

In a landmark experiment conducted twenty-five years ago—still one of the most thorough, balanced, and powerful studies on pornography—Jennings Bryant and Dolf Zillmann showed just how watching pornography alters viewers' perceptions of sexuality.[3] Eighty college students at a large northeastern college were divided into four test groups. Three groups were shown a variety of short films over a six-week period and asked to evaluate the films for their production values. The first test group, deemed the "massive exposure" group, was shown six explicitly sexual films per viewing session, about forty-eight minutes of exposure each week, or about thirty-six films over the course of the experiment. The second, "intermediate exposure" group was shown three erotic movies and three nonerotic movies per session, eighteen erotic films in all, or about two hours and twenty-four minutes of pornography over the six-week period. The third, "no exposure" group was limited to nonpornographic fare, asked to watch thirty-six regular movies, containing no sexually explicit content. Finally, the fourth group, the control, was shown no films whatsoever during the six-week period, which took place between 1979 and 1980.

The erotic films that subjects watched were far tamer than much of today's hardcore fare. All sexual acts portrayed were heterosexual and consensual. The films' sexual activities were confined to oral, anal, and vaginal sex, and none involved coercion or the deliberate infliction or reception of pain. The nonpornographic films were entirely devoid of sexual references or behavior.

Three weeks passed. At the next session, members of all four groups were asked to estimate the prevalence of certain sexual behaviors in America. Their opinions were solicited on everything from the percentage of sexually active adults to the percentage of Americans performing particular sexual acts. Without exception, the more pornography the subjects had viewed over the six-week period, the more likely they were to believe others to be sexually active and adventurous. For example, the "massive exposure" group believed on average that 67 percent of Americans engaged in oral sex (a fairly close approximation of the norm), compared with the 34 percent of those who had not been shown any pornography three weeks earlier. Those who had viewed "massive" amounts of pornography believed that more than twice as many adults had anal intercourse than did those who viewed no porn (29 percent versus 12 percent). The same applied for less common sexual practices. The massive exposure group believed that three in ten Americans engaged in group sex, compared with slightly more than one in ten estimated by the no exposure group. Pornography viewers also estimated that roughly twice as many people engaged in sadomasochism and bestiality; according to their assumptions, 15 percent of Americans practiced S&M and 12 percent had sex with animals—gross overestimations of actual sexual practices, according to all available data.

See the Girl, Play with Her

Harrison, a graphic designer who studied art in college, believes men are inherently visual and this drives their approach to porn. "If you want to call it superficial, fine," he says. "But for men, the visual experience of sex is very important, which is why men get drawn into pornography." Women, Harrison believes, are more sensual; they require a full sensory experience, and are more likely to be aroused by the look-touch-talk-hear of flirting than by watching porn. In fact, Harrison postulates, for men the equivalent of flirting is looking at pornography. When a woman is flirting with a guy, she's enjoying the fantasy that this guy really likes her; when a man looks at porn, he's fantasizing that the woman he's looking at really likes him.

The porn star is a blank slate on which each observer can graft his own recipe for reciprocal lust and pleasure. Beyond that, there's a certain vagueness to the women portrayed; she is literally the "object" of whatever kind of affection a man wants to bestow. Zach, the twenty-three-year-old unemployed Web site developer, checks out women online every couple of days. He'll flip through pictures, rarely lingering on one girl for more than fifteen or twenty seconds. "For me, the girls in porn aren't any specific girl—they're just a girlish image," he explains. "You enjoy it, but you don't get attached to it."

Like most men who use pornography, Zach says it has no effect on the way he views women in real life. The idea is laughable to him. "The women are completely different from the women in the real world—and they have *nothing* to do with each other." Unlike advertising, pornography doesn't change men's minds, he says. Here's the difference: Advertising is trying to influence you. Porn isn't. Advertising pulls a lot of dirty tricks, whereas porn is straightforward. Moreover, advertising is in people's faces, whether they want to see it or not. With pornography, on the other hand, people can decide whether they want to view it. They're prepared for it. Because people choose to see pornography and it's only showing something people already know exists, it can't in Zach's view possibly change their minds. "The kinds of men who are affected by porn already have something wrong with them," Zach explains. "But I don't think it's had any effect on me."

Zach likens the women in pornography to the person behind the counter at McDonald's. "I realize the guy behind the counter has a whole life—that he's not just an object or a tool," he says. "He's got his interests, hopes, family, etc. But when I'm at McDonald's, I don't care. I just want my Big Mac." Of course, if Zach were ever to see the McDonald's guy on the street, he wouldn't treat him like a tool or an object; instead, he would say hello. "I know the girls in the pictures are real people but I just want to get off and get on with my day. I view them as tools to help me get what I want while I'm looking at porn, but if I met them on the street, I'd deal with them as real people."

The difference between real women and the women in pornography is crystal clear to him: "In porn, the women are objects and I see them that way. But if I met those women in real life I wouldn't see them like that. After all, in real life, a woman has her hobbies and interests. But you don't care about that when you're looking at porn."

When opponents of pornography talk about the ways hardcore pornography affects men, the focus is on violence and rape. But there are other, more subtle ways in which pornography operates on a man's psyche. In the Zillmann-Bryant experiments, men and women who were exposed to large amounts of pornography were significantly less likely to want daughters than those who had not. Who would want their own little girl to be treated that way? Who would want to bring a girl into such a world? It's not just hardcore porn, either. According to a large-scale 1994 report summarizing eighty-one peer-reviewed research studies, most studies (70 percent) on nonaggressive pornography find that exposure to pornography has clear negative effects.[4] Gary Brooks, a psychologist who studies pornography at Texas A&M University, explains that "softcore pornography has a very negative effect on men as well. The problem with softcore pornography is that it's voyeurism—it teaches men to view women as objects rather than to be in relationships with women as human beings." According to Brooks, pornography gives men the false impression that sex and pleasure are entirely divorced from relationships. In other words, pornography is inherently self-centered—something a man does by himself, for himself—by using other women as the means to pleasure, as yet another product to consume.

The word *objectification* smacks of 1970s feminism and outdated ideology. Yet interestingly, it tumbles unbidden out of men's mouths while discussing pornography; even porn's biggest fans readily admit that pornography treats women as objects. As an act of pure visualization, pornography legitimates, accentuates, and provokes men's emphasis on the visual—whether they have a biological predilection toward such behavior or not. Because pornography involves looking at women but not interacting with them, it elevates the physical while ignoring or trivializing all other aspects of the woman. A woman is literally reduced to her body parts and sexual behavior. Not surprisingly, half of Americans say pornography is demeaning toward women, according to the 2004 *Pornified*/Harris poll conducted for this book. Women are far more likely to believe this—58 percent compared with 37 percent of men. Only 20 percent of women—and 34 percent of men—think pornography *is not* demeaning.

With increased viewing, pornography becomes acceptable and what once disturbed fails to upset with habituation. While 60 percent of adults age fifty-nine and older believe pornography is demeaning toward women, only 35 percent of Gen-Xers—the most tolerant and often heaviest users—agree. For example, after years of heavy viewing, Harrison noticed a shift in his perspective. At first it was subtle. "It's kind of silly," Harrison says, "but my standards changed." The women he used to find attractive no longer seem quite as attractive. "Women who were otherwise good-looking but weren't as overtly sexy as the women in porn don't appeal to me as much anymore. I find that I look more for women who have the attributes I see in porn. I want bigger breasts, blonder hair, curvier bodies in general. Just better-looking overall." It's not, Harrison explains carefully, as if before he got into Internet pornography he would have dated certain women and now he turns them away because they're not porn-star material. It's not that simple. But he's noticed a change in his appraisal: "I find that when I'm out at a party or a bar, I catch myself sizing up women." The feeling troubled him. "I would say to myself, 'Wait a second. This isn't a supermarket. You shouldn't treat her like she's some piece of meat. Don't pass her up just because her boobs aren't that big.' "

You've got to keep these two worlds separate, Harrison told himself. Women in pornography are different: "There's that age-old claim that porno objectifies women and I agree with it. Women in porn become viewed as sex objects or sex tools. But it's worth noting that the same applies to men in porno. Everyone involved in porno is just an object." As a result, he says, pornography inherently cheapens sex. "These images, while they are titillating, are also devaluing our perception of what sex means between two people."

As Harrison points out, women are not the only ones who suffer. In the porn world, men tend to find themselves placed in the role of playboy or gigolo, the superficial stud whose status is attained according to the quantity and quality of women he beds. Most men would not elect to be judged in this way, particularly not those men who look at pornography because they aren't attracting women in the real world. Nor would men who fear their penises aren't large enough or who can't stay erect on demand for hours on end want to be judged. Most men do not, in the real world, measure up to the image pornography requires. In a 2004 *Elle*-MSNBC.com poll of 15,246 Americans, 13 percent of men confessed that viewing sex online caused them to worry that they might not satisfy their partner's needs. One in ten said they need to do more to keep their partners sexually interested, and 8 percent admitted that after viewing online porn, they felt bad about their own bodies.

Despite its premise of relieving tension, pornography often creates tension for men, leaving them increasingly insecure, with the need for continual validation through ongoing conquests. Pornography, with its mutual objectification and teenage mentality, can bring back the worst of adolescent fears about manhood (with its requirements for youthful vigor and a boundless constitution). This mounting tension then leads to the search for temporary relief—and a more intense drive toward more porn.

You've Seen 1,000 Women, You've Seen Them All

> It's not easy to turn me on anymore. And that's not a good thing. . . . I thought about why it is that I don't often look twice when a nearly nude 20-something walks by me in a restaurant. Or sometimes at night, when, on that rare occasion I have a woman in bed next to me waiting for me to make a move, I fall asleep.
>
> Could I have erectile dysfunction? Have I been really tired for the last year? . . . No, those weren't it. What had my turtle in his shell?
>
> Pornography.
>
> I first saw porn in my middle-teen years. It started with the late-night . . . programming. Then came the Internet e-mails. . . . It's more than five years later, and I am immune to all of it. . . . I have seen everything—things I did not know the human body could do or wanted to do. . . . When all is said and done, I have built such a high immunity to sex that the whole idea of it is demystified. There are no secrets. There are no subtleties—the subtleties that can tease a person to arousal. Nope. Not here.[5]

So many women and all so easy; a man tends to gorge. And once he's seen a thousand bare bottoms—no matter the variety of form and function—they start to look the same. Men pummel through woman after woman, plunging into an inevitable cycle of diminishing returns. In one study by James L. Howard, Myron B. Reifler, and Clifford B. Liptzin, cited in the 1970 federal report on pornography, men who were shown pornographic films for ninety minutes a day, five days a week experienced less sexual arousal and interest in similar materials with the passage of time.[6] What initially thrills eventually titillates, what excites eventually pleases, what pleases eventually satisfies. And satisfaction sooner or later yields to boredom.

Even porn stars get boring after a while. That's the way it's worked out for William, the thirty-five-year-old legal clerk from Missouri. Sometimes he'll find something "weird" or "different," but, increasingly, it feels like more of the same. After looking at pornography for more than twenty years . . . well, it's lost its novelty. "It used to be more fun looking for the right thing," he says. He enjoyed the challenge of finding just the woman to pique his interest. "But I've been on the Net since 1983, and these days, I can find what I want with just a few clicks." As a consequence, William still likes to look, but the searches are shorter and the end result not quite as sweet.

Gabe, the Houstonian who works in the oil and gas industry, noticed a similar effect when he started scoping out pornography for money. At first, the job was enormously time-consuming; he would spend most of his day at work gathering material. With time, he learned the best places to look and the task became streamlined. He searches, finds what he needs, forwards it to the sites, and he's done. Performing his online duties has taken its toll on Gabe's appreciation. "Often, I feel bored," he says. "I used to get really excited when I looked at porn. But nowadays, it's just the same poses, the same type of girls. The only time I get excited is when I see something I've never seen before or someone who's particularly attractive, but that's rare."

How can something so exhilarating turn into such a bore? It starts off with a bang. There's the preamble: stimulated by something—a woman in the office, an advertisement, a thought that crosses a man's mind, the recollection of previously viewed porn—and full of pent-up sexual frustration and desire, he decides to check out some porn. With the first glimpse, there's that strange combination of titillation and aggravation. The image is good, but not quite right. He barrels on with impatience, flipping through the pages of the magazine or scrolling from one hyperlink to the next, aroused by not yet enough, no, no, no, until *there.* That's it. The excitement reaches its limit; he masturbates and is relieved. Then he comes down. The effect wears off. He is sated, a little tired. Rather than feel nostalgia or warmth or attachment to the image, he is done with it. And it was just like the last time. And likely will be largely similar to the next time, too.

Kevin, a thirty-two-year-old photographer in Colorado, has gone through periods of porn use and disuse. While Internet pornography was exploding at the turn of the millennium, Kevin was living with his fiancée. He missed out on the early hullabaloo. But after breaking off the relationship in 2003, he fell into heavy consumption. For the first time, he looked at online porn, about five or six hours a week. The more time alone, the more free time, the more porn. "I had just bought this new computer, and started to look every other day. I was way into the discovery of what was out there." Oh, had he missed out. "In the beginning, online porn was super-awesome, this world of discovery," Kevin says. For months, he consumed on a near-daily basis. His Internet sessions would start with a casual dip into nature photography—for work purposes. In search of inspiration and ideas, Kevin would explore the great outdoors online. But it was always a progression, further and deeper into natural bodies, nudity, women. "I would want more and more," he explains. "It wasn't enough to just see bare breasts, it had to be bottoms and then it had to be couples, anal and group sex, multiple men and multiple women, bisexual porn."

"It was such a time-killer," he says now. But Kevin's excitement waned, then died altogether. Maybe he was getting too old. Maybe it had just been too much. "Ultimately it was just boredom. I was merely going through the motions." At first he felt great after his pornography fests, but he began to feel "gross" afterward. His worldview started to skew and—deadly for a photographer—his sense of the sublime faded. "It was just fucking with my head too much," he says of Internet pornography. "More than anything else, it was making me jaded. I wasn't finding pleasure in the little things, either with women or with life in general. Things that used to be erotic bored me."

Despite the physiological tumult stirred up by an encounter with porn, certain vital emotions are bypassed altogether. Pornography contains little in the way of kissing, hugging, caressing, or holding—all the supposedly "feminine" aspects of sex that, stereotypes aside, can be key experiences for men as well. No one is ever vulnerable or insecure in pornography; there are no reassurances or exchanged intimacies.

Pornography is a sure thing because the women involved don't exactly demur; it also means the implicit reward of being able to get the coveted woman is absent. She knows nothing about him—his quirks or his traits, his romantic history or plans for the future. But she doesn't like him despite all of this; she "likes" him in the absence of all this. Something about the achievement of pornography leaves men feeling somehow slighted, as if they were hoodwinked into believing something they know to be false, as if they cheated on a test and got away with it. There's an emptiness to the accomplishment. While the absence of a real woman in pornography may be welcome, it also eliminates the presence of a real man.

The inevitability of pornography can ultimately quash desire. It's not just the sameness of the poses, acts, and attitudes on display, but the risk-free ease of their acquisition. There are rarely hiccups along the way; never the awkwardness of the ill-fitting condom, the bedsheet that escapes the mattress corner, the woman's failure to achieve orgasm, the man's premature ejaculation. Nothing remotely veers from the automated path to pleasure, not even momentarily. Ultimately, there is the same ending, with no suspense whatever along the way. For this reason, many men say pornography simply can't compete with the real thing. It's intrinsically one-sided: empty-calorie sex—no risk, no effort, no reciprocity, minimal and ephemeral reward. Every once in a while, perhaps not so bad. Every day? Try eating at McDonald's on a daily basis.

Upgrade, Downgrade, More, More

It's the human condition, it's the American weakness—the desire for more, bigger, better—damn the consequences. More stuff, cheaper, easier, more exciting. In order to make that momentary gain last longer, in order to get back that sexual zing, in order to go even deeper, men go back for more pornography. Better porn. Edgier porn. Just a click away. Pornography researcher Robert Jensen has observed, "Pornography, without emotional variation, will become repetitive and uninteresting, even to men watching primarily to facilitate masturbation. So pornography needs an edge." First, Jensen explains, in the 1970s and 1980s the edge was created through anal sex; when that no longer did the trick, so-called gonzo porn became the edgier genre—with double penetration and multiple oral sex performances the main features.[7]

Since adolescence, Tyler, now twenty-one, has spent about half an hour daily with Internet pornography. His viewing patterns have been consistent. His tastes, however, have changed. "At first, I was happy just to see a naked woman. I was like 'Wow!' each time I saw a really hot girl. But as time has gone on, I've grown more accustomed to things," he explains. "I look for more and more extreme stuff." He began to search out hardcore material; close-up penetration shots became de rigueur. He developed specific interests. For example, he has "a thing" for dominant-submissive porn. "I like it when the girl is really submissive, I'm embarrassed to say.

"It's become more severe as time has gone on," he continues. "Which is weird because it doesn't correspond to how I am with an actual woman. I'm gentle, very concerned about how the woman is doing. But for some reason, with porn, in order for me to get excited, I need to notch it up one level. It's got to be more extreme. Seeing women demeaned is somehow a turn-on." Not all pornography, he points out, is demeaning to women. After all, sometimes the woman is dominating the man. "But I think most men like the portrayal of women as submissive." And not every kind of submissive pornography is a turn-on. "The women in bukkake aren't actually enjoying it—they're crying while the men come on their faces," he explains. "If the woman is crying then it seems like it's not her personal choice to be treated that way, she's not genuinely wanting it as much as she should be. It seems like it's not consensual, like it's a rape or forced sex." The difference in the woman's attitude is key. "I like it when the woman is being dominated but she appears to be enjoying herself. She's got to *really want* to be treated that way. Then it's a huge turn-on." With the endless spectrum of Internet porn, Tyler has begun enjoying types of pornography he never thought he would. "Recently—I've got to be in the mood for it—I've found that I like to see a guy pissing on a girl. I didn't think I would like it," he says. "But I can get into it."

Advocates aren't shy about extolling pornography's enticing effects. The first step is usually an increase in viewing—more times logging online or clicking the remote control, prolonged visits to certain Web sites, a tendency to fall into a routine. In a 2004 *Elle*-MSNBC.com poll, nearly one in four men admitted they were afraid they were "overstimulating" themselves with online sex. In fact, that routine is an essential ingredient in the financial success of high-tech porn. Wendy Seltzer, an advocate for online civil liberties, argues that pornographers should not be concerned over piracy of their free material. According to Seltzer, "People always want this stuff. Seeing some of it just whets their appetite for more. Once they get through what's available for free, they'll move into the paid services."[8] And once they've indulged in more quantity, they want more quality—meaning more action, more intensity, more extreme situations. As porn director Jerome Tanner explained to *Adult Video News,* "People just want it harder, harder, and harder because . . . what are you gonna do next?"[9] The impetus to find hardercore fare affects the entire industry. Says Sharon Mitchell, a former porn star, "It's multiple penetrations, it's fisting, it's all about unprotected anal sex. A few people still do vanilla regular sex, but for the most part, it's as kinky as they can get and as much as they can push it as possible. That's the majority of the porn that's out there."[10] In the same *Elle*-MSNBC.com survey, 37 percent of men admitted that Internet pornography pushed the boundaries of what they find erotic.

Particularly on the Internet, men find themselves veering off into pornographic arenas they never thought they could find appealing. Those who start with softcore develop a taste for harder-core pornography. Curiosity beckons the user to click deeper within a site, perhaps paying for something, even if only to know what the paid portions of the site offer—like picking up a copy of *Hustler* just to see what the fuss is about, back in the pre-Internet eighties. The illicitness, the total un-P.C.-ness of it all, the very idea that debasing and degrading images of women and sex are easily available can be quite enticing. So a man figures, why not, what could be the harm, and takes a look. He never knows what he might find. It might be a turn-on, after all.

Desensitization and Dissatisfaction

Sometimes the fantasy world of pornographic women provides a negative image rather than a positive one. Thomas, a tech-support staffer from Seattle, dislikes much of what pornography depicts. "There's a lot of strange stuff out there. Bestiality, child porn, rape. Men shitting in women's mouths. Things that approach snuff porn. I never seek that stuff out but occasionally they appear." When he sees it, he feels nauseated and finds it hard to shake the imagery from his consciousness. Once, Thomas saw an image—"a horrific picture"—that seared itself into his brain. It showed an extremely obese woman wearing a bikini with a caption that said, "Find a fold and fuck it." "I think I started losing hair that day," Thomas says. He has no idea who looks for this kind of thing, but notes, "They say the scary people look just like everyone else, so it could be anyone. As The Shadow says, 'Who knows what evil lurks in the heart of men?' "

Men who view a lot of pornography talk about their disgust the first time they chanced upon an unpleasant image or unsolicited child porn. But with experience, it doesn't bother them as much—shock wears thin quickly, especially given the frequent image assault on the Internet. They learn to ignore or navigate around unwanted imagery, and the third time they see an unpleasant image, it's merely an annoyance and a delay.

Rajiv was surprised to discover how, with online pornography, the rest of the world went much further than he ever imagined. He saw things that not only turned him off, they outright disgusted him. "There's a lot of weird shit online," he says. "Much of it seems focused on degradation and humiliation and that really turns me off. For me, it's not a fantasy to watch a guy pissing on a girl." On the Internet, Rajiv saw gangbangs. Violence. Scatological porn. He got upset by what he came across accidentally online. Things were different when he had his first exposure to pornography. It was "so tame"—all about women on a beach rolling around naked or touching themselves in the rain. It was sensual and erotic. But online pornography was often the opposite of what he came to think of as sexy through the pornography of his youth. "If I were a kid today, I'm sure I would have started looking online immediately upon hitting puberty," he says. "But I wouldn't want my son to get his first exposure online. There's so much fucked-up shit on there that I think it could be damaging. Women who are forced to drink a glass filled with semen or who get pissed on or who are deceived by men. My fear is that he would connect those kinds of images with getting aroused and would feel the need to treat women in his own life that way. Or that he would infer that such behaviors are normal. After all, this sort of thing does seem normal online. There's nobody on these Web sites saying, 'Guys, you shouldn't treat women like that,' so there's no accompanying voice of reason."

For years, experts and communities debated whether or not viewing rape as depicted in pornography can cause men to rape women. The research data on this question have been notoriously unreliable. However, how men perceive men who rape is demonstrably affected by their consumption of pornography. In the final session of the Zillmann-Bryant experiments with college students, participants were asked to read a newspaper report about the recent rape of a hitchhiker. The crime was described in the report, but the criminal sentence was not revealed. Students were then asked to recommend a sentence for the convicted rapist. Men who had viewed massive amounts of pornography recommended significantly shorter sentences for the man who committed the crime. Men in the "massive exposure" group recommended an average of 50 months' imprisonment for the rapist, while men who had not viewed the films recommended 95 months. (By comparison, women who had been in the massive exposure group suggested 77 months' imprisonment, compared with an average of 143 months recommended by those who had not been shown pornography.) Men who viewed massive amounts of pornography were also less likely to support women's causes in general and were about three times less likely to favor the expansion of women's rights. Overall, men's compassion toward women seemed to diminish under the influence of pornography. Repeated viewings of women debased in the vacuum of pornography apparently hits home. And the pornography they viewed was tame by today's Internet standards.

Pornography leaves men desensitized to both outrage and to excitement, leading to an overall diminishment of feeling and eventually to dissatisfaction with the emotional tugs of everyday life. Men find themselves upgrading to the most intense forms of pornography, glutting themselves on extreme imagery and outrageous orgasms. Eventually they are left with a confusing mix of supersized expectations about sex and numbed emotions about women. Zillmann describes this "satisfaction dilemma of pornography":

> What has been labeled "pornotopia" tells [men] what joys they might, could and should experience. As pornography features beautiful bodies in youthful, at times acrobatic, sexual interactions during which nothing short of ecstasy is continually expressed, consumers of such entertainment are readily left with the impression that "others get more" and that whatever they themselves have in their intimate relationship is less than what it should be. *This comparison, of which pornography consumers may or may not be fully aware, is bound to foster sexual dissatisfaction or greatly enhance already existing dissatisfaction.*[11]

Interestingly, because negative effects of pornography were demonstrated so definitively in Zillmann and Bryant's study, researchers have had a difficult time getting new studies past academic boards monitoring the use of human subjects. If a study's effects are known to be detrimental—and there is no proof the damage can be permanently reversed—ethics boards will refuse to allow a similar study to go forward. How could a university allow itself to so clearly harm students and other subjects under the auspices of social science research? Thus subsequent researchers were unable to get new projects approved. Luckily, the data provided by the Zillmann and Bryant study are thorough and solid; the only thing outdated about the study's conclusions is the pornography itself and the amount consumed. Today, men who use Internet pornography typically reach the usage levels of the massive exposure group of this experiment, and the material they look at tends to be more hardcore.

"Porn has a tendency to numb people's sensibilities toward sex," Harrison, the graphic designer, explains. "Like violence, it feeds off basic human impulses. It's so primal, there's a reason people get drawn in." And just as countless studies have shown that violent films and videos affect individuals' attitudes toward violence, pornography can make men accustomed to the heightened attractiveness and carnality of all-out porn sex, turning plain old real sex into a distant second. "Those experiences you watch in porn are just not consistent with Average Joe who meets Average Woman," Harrison says. "And I think a guy's expectations of his partner might be affected by the images he sees in porn. People's expectations of their partner's sexual performance or of what their partners might be willing to do might be unrealistic."

The more Harrison looked, especially in the online free-for-all, the less satisfied he became with his real-life sexual ventures. He wanted his partners to do more—to try positions he picked up from pornography, to be open to new things sexually, to have sex a lot more frequently. If his partner wasn't in the mood, Harrison would get annoyed. He couldn't help but be irritated if she said she was tired or didn't have time for sex.

When a man gets bored with pornography, both his fantasy and real worlds become imbued with indifference. The real world often gets *really* boring—after all, compared with the fireworks of cyber-speed porn, assuming the missionary position with an overworked wife who has cellulite isn't exactly a thrill. Porn women howl with delight at the mere sight of a man's genitals and moan with pleasure no matter what he does with them. Next to such euphoria, real women can seem staid, indifferent, or even frigid. The 2004 *Elle*-MSNBC.com poll found that as a result of viewing online pornography, one in ten men said that he or his partner was bored with their sex routine; 17 percent said that viewing pornography made sex less arousing. One in ten admitted he had become more critical of his partner's body. Without the "voice of reason" accompanying pornographic viewing, some men, particularly younger men who grew up with Internet pornography, make assumptions about what can be expected from real women, based on their experiences with porn. Just as they upgrade their pornography, they attempt to upgrade their women in real life.

Couldn't You Be More Like a Porn Star?

Pornography not only informs the male sexual appetite, it can whet it for a specific form of fulfillment, ideally achieved through real women. Though men may become accustomed to the porn star's bodily arts of adornment and performance, they still turn to their real-life partners for sex. And with 51 percent of Americans believing that pornography raises men's expectations of how women should look and 48 percent saying it changes men's expectations of how women should behave, according to the *Pornified*/Harris poll, pornography ends up having a real impact on real women.

The degree to which pornography raises standards and alters men's expectations of women likely depends on how much porn is consumed. In 2002, a professor at Texas Christian University conducted a study of online pornography consumers (heterosexual men who used pornography via Internet newsgroups). On average, respondents looked at five hours and twenty-two minutes of pornography per week. Respondents were divided into three groups: high consumption (more than six hours per week), average (two to six hours per week), and low (two hours a week or less). The study found that the more pornography men use, the more likely they are to describe women in sexualized and stereotypically feminine terms. They were also more likely to approve of women in traditionally female occupations and to value women who are more submissive and subordinate to men.[12]

Thirty-four-year-old Luis, a pornography enthusiast since the age of ten, has exacting standards for the women in his life. When he was growing up in Los Angeles, his father left porn videotapes lying around. Luis's mother, a highly religious woman from Mexico, knew about the videos, but Luis never saw her get upset about them. For all he knew, she was watching the videos with his father. After he lost his virginity at thirteen, Luis had no trouble attracting women. First married at age twenty-one for less than a year, he has subsequently remarried and divorced, remarried and divorced. As a thrice-divorced man, Luis definitely feels stigmatized on the dating scene ("Women think I'm some kind of player"), but he's hopeful about meeting the right woman. Part of being "right" for Luis is acting the part. His expectations, he says, have been raised very high by pornography: "I live sex the way it's shown in porno."

Luis encouraged all his ex-wives and girlfriends to watch pornos with him so they could see what turned him on. "If I were with a woman and I weren't getting the kind of pleasure I see people enjoying in porn films, then I wouldn't be with that woman," he says. "I've broken up with women who wouldn't perform certain things I've seen in adult films." For example, if a woman isn't into oral sex the way porn stars are—enjoying the act, the swallowing, the cum shots on her body—then Luis isn't into her. The women he dates need to be open to experimentation, he explains. "If they don't know what that means, I would suggest they watch some porn."

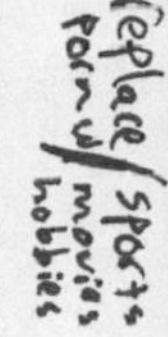

Another problem is women who take too long. "In porn, the women have orgasms so easily," Luis says. "But it usually takes longer in real life for women to have an orgasm. I get pretty impatient." One woman Luis was dating had a difficult time reaching orgasm. "It was definitely one of the factors in us breaking up," he says. Luis's demands aren't limited to his partners; he strives to maintain a high standard for himself. "I've always wanted to have a huge penis," he says. To that end, he has bought pumps and creams to make himself larger. It's worked somewhat, according to his own estimation.

At the Catholic school Luis attended as a child, there was no sex education. Nor did his parents ever sit him down for "the talk." He looked to pornography for his lessons. "I think I started looking when I was too young," he reflects. His own son, if he ever has one, won't start looking at pornography until the age of sixteen or seventeen, not if he has any say in it. "I think porn had a bad effect on me, especially on my relationships," Luis says. "I learned to live my life by pornography; it gave me my first impression of what sex is. For me, sex was all about fucking."

Compared with porn stars, real women may not have shaved their legs that morning, their stretch marks may be visible. They may not want to wear a thong that day and perform a striptease that night. They may not want to be peed on or have their boyfriends ejaculate in their faces. And when real women fail to live up to porn women, it's frustrating, annoying, and occasionally baffling to men, who ask, Why won't she do what I want her to do?

Younger men, particularly eighteen- to twenty-four-year-olds, are more likely to think pornography affects their expectations of women's looks and behavior than are older men. Tyler, at twenty-one still a virgin ("I've done absolutely everything but—it's kind of embarrassing"*), thinks men are into pornography because for them sex is more physical than emotional. His porn-infused fantasy has specific physical parameters. "I prefer a woman with a C- or D-cup—full-figured, but definitely not overweight," he says. "I don't want some small spindly girl either." Porn star Brianna Banks ("The most sensational porn star big-breasted blue-eyed-blonde beauty.") is the ultimate. "She's not only blond; she's got the right chest size." He also likes the female pubic area to be groomed. "I'm a big fan of full shaved," he explains.

Unfortunately, most of Tyler's girlfriends haven't been shaved. He regularly asks them to shave for him and some do. His last girlfriend, Betty, had not shaved her pubic hair and would not do so for him; she told him it gave her ingrown hairs. Tyler didn't get it. "Porn women don't seem to have any problem shaving their hair," he points out. "But at least Betty was blond and had very fine hair," he says. "So it wasn't that big a deal." In other areas, Betty and his previous girlfriends have been more accommodating. That's important, Tyler says, because pornography taught him that women are incredibly sexual beings. When he sees women enjoying sex in porn, it seems like the most natural thing in the world. The women tend to be slutty, Tyler says. "Both schoolgirl slutty and all-out slutty. They want it and they need it. And it's up to men to give it to them."

A year earlier, when Tyler saw pornography depicting a man fingering a woman in the ass, he didn't think that was something he would enjoy in real life ("anal had kind of been a taboo for me"). But later he tried it out with a girlfriend and realized he was wrong. Likewise, having

* Tyler defines "sex" strictly as vaginal intercourse.

cultivated a fondness for images of cum shots on the face, Tyler decided to bring the scene to life. So far, all his girlfriends have agreed to try it at some point. With one girl, he came on her breasts and she told him it wasn't nearly as bad as she thought it was going to be. "We didn't get around to the face thing, though, because we broke up."

Porn Sex vs. Real Sex

When men turn from porn stars to girlfriends, pornography doesn't always disappear. Men who look at pornography habitually can become attracted to an artificially re-created zoom-pop version of female sexuality. "When they're with their partner, they lose the ability to be aroused by her positive features," explains psychologist Gary Brooks. "Many of them then try to re-create the images from porn in their brain while they're with another person in order to maintain their arousal." Yet by doing so, men are no longer mentally with their partner, nor are they able to lose themselves in the moment.

Men are apt to say pornography has nothing to do with real women or with their sex lives, but in the same breath will extol its benefits to their sex lives and describe how they tailor their sex lives to pornography. But the fantasy of pornography seldom meshes well with the reality of sex. Since pornography is supposed to be about what you can't get from sex, or what you do when you can't get sex—not what you do when you can—the intrusion of pornography into a man's sex life can be disturbing. While some men say they try to keep pornography and real sex separate in their heads, it's not so easy; pornography seeps in, sometimes in unexpected ways. The incursion can even lead to sexual problems, such as impotence or delayed ejaculation.

Soon after he discovered Internet pornography, Rajiv would go online nearly every day, masturbating for forty-five minutes to an hour: "After I was done, I would think to myself, 'You know, that time could have been better spent some other way.' I should have been writing or working or I could have caught up on sleep." At first, pornography just filled in a hole in Rajiv's sex life. He was coming off the end of a long dry spell, and wasn't dating anyone. But after several celibate months, he started dating someone new in January 2004. The first time they had sex, Rajiv had trouble reaching orgasm. As he had always done, he conjured images from pornography in his head to maintain and enhance his excitement. But the old tricks didn't help. Perhaps it's just nerves, he told himself.

This was a strange twist in events, because Rajiv had always credited pornography with improving his sex life. Women told him he was an amazing lover, mostly, he thought, because of his staying power. He connected his ability to hold out for a long time during sex with masturbating to pornography. Whereas most guys took fifteen seconds, or so he imagined, it took him about forty-five minutes to even come close to achieving an orgasm. Rajiv figured his excellent stamina was due to the fact that he had "practiced" ejaculation control while masturbating to pornography. He thought he could come at will—that he could have a quickie or last a long time, mood depending.

Now he was just plain having trouble reaching an orgasm, no matter what he thought about. On several occasions, his new girlfriend asked plaintively, "Baby, I'm beginning to get sore, are you almost done?" Sometimes, Rajiv would just tell her, "I don't think I'm going to come." They would disengage and Rajiv would masturbate or ask her to masturbate him, in order to bring the relief of ejaculation. (In pornography films, the man routinely ejaculates outside of the woman's body.) "My heart would race less," he says. "Sex just seemed so ordinary; it was no longer thrilling or magical the way it had been before i-porn."

When he repeatedly had trouble achieving orgasm with a second girlfriend, Rajiv decided to stop looking at Internet porn altogether. "I actually had to make a conscious decision to quit," he says. "I was worried that I was becoming compulsive and even dependent on it. The fact that porn was altering my sex life scared me." Rajiv thinks he got used to seeing explicit images while becoming aroused, making him dependent on visual imagery for sexual fulfillment. "When I don't have those images in front of me, I just can't get that aroused," he says. "Sex is no longer as physiologically exciting." Rajiv hasn't had a new girlfriend yet, but when he does, perhaps things will go back to the way they once were. "I'm hoping this dependence can be reversed over time," he says with a sigh.

When push comes to shove, nearly all men say real sex is far preferable to pornographic sex. Participation trumps spectatorship. Some men say even masturbation is better *without* pornography—the creativity of open fantasy provides more inspiration than the prefab play-by-plays of porn. Freewheeling masturbation allows for a nostalgic foray into one's sexual past, where one conjures up old girlfriends or particularly erotic episodes with a current partner. Yet many men who use pornography report that they no longer masturbate without it, especially once they discover the Internet. Some confess to becoming dependent on pornographic images, whether live or conjured in their minds. Farewell to that faded memory of sex in the beachfront cabana, circa 1987.

Harrison, the graphic designer, had porn on the brain. Women he had salivated over in porn, acts he had eagerly watched, sexual styles he had admired came floating into his consciousness—while he was with his girlfriend. He would be having sex and suddenly he'd think about a threesome he'd seen in a clip downloaded from the Internet. "But during sex, that image becomes bothersome because I don't want to be in a threesome with my partner," he explains. "What may be a turn-on in a porn fantasy is actually bothersome when it comes up during real sex."

Because he always considered pornography to be a fantasy, its echo into his reality wasn't only inappropriate, it was repulsive. Of course, when Harrison sees images of beautiful women in porn, he wants to have sex with women as beautiful as they are. But the desire for porn's translation into real life ends there. "There's a reason men are into porn that involves cheerleaders and nurses," Harrison says. "They're fantasies. Of course, some men may want to act out those fantasies, but for most men, it's not something they would ever want to act out. We don't always *want* our real lives to play out like porn."

Harrison was having a hard time focusing on the woman in his bed. And because such unwanted pornographic images are a turnoff when rescreened in real time, Harrison's body got turned off as well. His difficulty achieving orgasms during sex got worse. The women he slept with found it strange that Harrison had trouble having an orgasm—usually it was the woman who would have a harder time. And there was a new problem. Harrison found it harder to maintain his erections during sex; he wasn't getting as hard as he once did. "It gets back to the expectations raised by porno," he explains. "I think my erections have been affected because I'm not as hyperstimulated by sex as I am by porno. I've gotten used to a certain heightened level of stimulation, and when compared with porn, real sex just isn't that exciting."

What scared Harrison was that even after he decided to cut back on the pornography, his dissatisfaction continued. "Had I ruined my sex life permanently?" He was worried.

Omission and Deception

Most women have no idea how often their boyfriends and husbands look at pornography. Usually, the deception is deliberate, though many men also deny the frequency to themselves. Most don't think about quantifying the amount they view. Others would rather not know. It's better to hide it, many men figure. Women won't understand. Zach's last girlfriend, Jeanne, asked if he looked at pornography and the twenty-three-year-old Web site developer admitted to her that he did. She was jealous he was looking at other girls, but he made sure she knew that porn was no competition. "You don't get attached to it," he told her. Zach doesn't understand why women take it personally, but in his experience, they do. "If a girlfriend or wife asked me not to look at porn, I'd probably look at it less and hide it, but I don't think I would stop. Because I don't understand why it would make her feel bad. Besides, it's a habit. I've been masturbating to porn online since I was fourteen. Ten years is a hard habit to break."

So despite Jeanne's worried queries and occasional entreaties, Zach continued to use pornography. He knew it would bother her, but as far as he was concerned, she didn't have to know. They didn't live together, so he could still check it out online without her ever finding out. "I don't think porn and sex are the same thing, so one doesn't affect the other," he says. "Jerking off doesn't have anything to do with sex at all. It's more like blowing your nose than having sex. A quick physical sensation, bam, you get off; you've got nothing else to worry about.

Whereas with sex, there's another person there and you have to worry about them. It takes a lot longer, and there's an emotional component. You've got a living human being who actually wants you and you want them. There's a level of trust."

But while men consider trust crucial for a healthy relationship, they seem willing to flout that trust when it comes to pornography—deceiving their significant others into thinking they're either not looking at it at all or looking at it less frequently. Fitting pornography into one's life isn't always easy. Betty, for example, made it tough for Tyler, the computer science major. She didn't approve of pornography and didn't understand why he used it while dating her. But Betty was only sixteen and came from a fairly conservative background, so Tyler made an effort to be understanding. He tried to get her into pornography, to open her mind. When she warned him that it was either her or pornography, he asked her to watch porn movies with him. "I didn't think it had to be a choice," he explains. "And I don't want anyone telling me what to do. I said to her, 'Even when I'm looking at porn, I'm thinking about you,' but she was never satisfied." Betty continued to take his pornography personally. She told Tyler that she felt she wasn't attractive or sexy enough; she couldn't live up to the women in pornography. But it was crazy, Tyler says. "She was five-nine with long blond hair. She was a dancer so she was really toned. It's true she was only a B-cup. But I told her over and over again she had amazing breasts. Betty still felt insecure." Tyler didn't get it. "Real life is entirely separate from pornography. She was so concerned that I would fall in love with the porn instead of her."

Finally, Tyler figured that what she didn't know couldn't hurt her. He told Betty he wouldn't look at pornography anymore, but looked anyway. He didn't feel particularly guilty. "I think it's okay if a guy just looks at it on his own," he explains. "Besides, even if she didn't believe me, I knew that I was always thinking about her when I looked at the porn."

Still, he worried that Betty would find out. For a month, he kept it secret, but then decided to take a stand. He told her that she needed to realize pornography wasn't a risk or threat to her. He told her that she had to let him do what he wanted to do. After seventeen months together, the two finally broke up. Moving forward, Tyler doesn't expect to have this kind of problem with a girlfriend again. Pornography is something Tyler wants in his life; ideally, he wants a girlfriend to be into it, too. "I'm old enough and mature enough to know what I want from a woman," he says. "If a girl is going to give me an ultimatum like that, then we're just not going to be in a relationship. I plan to bring up pornography very early in my next relationship. That way, if it's an issue, we just won't go anywhere."

For many men, there's the troublesome intrusion of dealing with another person's feelings or values—women who question their use of pornography or who might disapprove of it if they knew. When Jacob, the journalist who subscribed to the Playboy Channel, first moved from Washington, D.C., to New York, he started dating Carina. Carina not only didn't like pornography, she was actively opposed to it on personal and ideological grounds. Jacob, who brought some of his videos with him when he moved, was flabbergasted by her attitude. Though he found some of her arguments compelling, he had trouble with how she arrived at her conclusions. She told him that pornography was harmful and he found himself agreeing, but conditionally. He would find himself arguing, "Yes, I realize it's harmful. But how harmful *is* it in the grand scheme of things?" Where was the proof? He had trouble believing, for example, that all women who posed in pornography had been sexually abused, as Carina claimed. There had to be exceptions, he figured. Carina's sweeping statements were hard to swallow.

"It was a challenge," he recalls. "I took her ideas seriously, but it was hard to think of something that had seemed so natural as wrong." Pornography had been part of his sex life since his teen years. Giving up on it wasn't something he felt ready to do or wanted to do. So he continued to use pornography behind Carina's back. He never told her and she never asked. Jacob was happy with their sex life and they stayed together for a year and a half. But throughout their relationship, Jacob felt as though he was lying to Carina. He knew she believed he had stopped using pornography. He knew how upset she would have been to find out the truth, and he felt guilty the entire time.

Of course, for some, the taboo of pornography is the lure. For religious, moral, or personal reasons, they feel they shouldn't look at pornography—and that's part of the fun. But the bad-boy titillation can wear thin and even backfire. Men, no matter their backgrounds, can find themselves struggling with guilt and shame over pornography. It could be associated with a strict religious upbringing or it could be a product of growing up during the "Free to Be You and Me" seventies, when boys imbibed some of that decade's feminist messages. Even for men who protest to the contrary, pornography doesn't always sit well with their larger beliefs about women.

Why is pornography so complicated, Harrison found himself wondering. On the one hand, pornography is a great idea, and he certainly enjoys it. Pornography helps people explore their tastes and their fantasies. In cases where someone is repressed, pornography may help him tune in to his own sexuality, to accept feelings once thought of as naughty. "Porn helps them open up psychologically or sexually," Harrison says.

On the other hand, pornography carries a lot of negatives. For one thing, there's the guilt. Raised Catholic and practicing intermittently, Harrison doesn't have any religious convictions against porn, but he admits to having "moral questions." As a child, he was taught that pornography and promiscuity were wrong because they devalued sex. Those ideas took root early in his mind and are not easy to get rid of. But today he calls his feelings against pornography "humanistic." "I'm not an absolutist about it," he explains. "There's a reason pornography has been around for as long as it has and is so popular. But there are a lot more negatives to porn than there are positives. I can't deny having moral convictions against it. I've seen porn do a lot of harm."

Kevin, the thirty-two-year-old Colorado photographer, saw those negative influences develop in his own life. Back in college, Kevin used pornography as a "stimulant," but it had a downside: "Porn absolutely encouraged the casual hookup," he recalls. "I would never have pushed women to have sex the way I did back then had it not been for the amount of sex I could look right in the eye through porn. I became this asshole I didn't want to be because I didn't care about women."

But in his early thirties, he found he was back to pornography and back to problems. There was the question of time, first off. The average user looks at computer pornography for more than an hour a week and Kevin was no exception. Indeed, online pornography had eaten up several hours a week for the past year and a half. He hadn't had a relationship since his fiancée broke off their engagement. He hadn't been getting out as much as he wanted. And he began to feel bad about himself. "I don't think there are any taboos in my sex life," he says. "Nor do I feel like there are any taboos in porn or stripping. Yet somehow, I began to feel guilty about all the porn I was looking at." At first, this semi-practicing Episcopalian thought it was religious guilt, but he realized that wasn't the real problem: "I just felt like I was doing something I shouldn't be doing. Like porn was a secret I wasn't comfortable keeping. It felt like I was telling or living a lie." The feelings of discomfort were in part related to his family. After his brother suffered an emotional breakdown in high school, Kevin's family fell apart as well, and then was slowly rebuilt. The experience changed the way Kevin approached many things in his life. From then on, Kevin decided, no more secrets. If he experimented with drugs, his parents would know about it. If something was wrong in his life, Kevin would tell his family. Successes, failures, fears, problems—everything needed to be on the table. His family flourished under the new system. "My filter for knowing the way I want to lead my life became, if I don't feel comfortable talking about something at the family dinnertable, then it's questionable," Kevin says. And pornography . . . it was questionable.

The Blur

Harrison increasingly worried that he was spending too much time with porn. "I would be looking at it for hours before I realized how much time had gone by," he recalls. "I was spending way more time than I wanted to." A pattern developed. Often he would go online late at night. It somehow seemed appropriate. He would log on, see something he liked, find a link. Curious, he'd click on it, linking and leaping, pausing and bounding, site after site after site. "I was so turned on, so enjoying the act of tracking it down that I would sort of lose myself."

Once he realized how much time had passed, he felt awful. So much time wasted. What was he thinking? Porn was interrupting his daily schedule. He would be late to appointments. He wasn't going out as much as he wanted. Shouldn't he be spending this time looking for more work? Or a girlfriend? Harrison was conflicted. On the one hand, looking at pornography was enormously gratifying. After masturbating, he felt relaxed, sated. But he felt guilty as well. "When you realize you've spent so much more time than you intended, you feel like you're losing control," he explains. "You're not paying attention to what you're doing. Then I started noticing that porn began affecting my thoughts with regard to my day-to-day life. That's when it started to bother me. That's when I realized it wasn't healthy necessarily."

After Harrison shut down the computer and tried to go to sleep, pornography would slip into his mind. He would lie in bed as images scrolled through his head. "You begin to feel like you're losing control of your thoughts." Waking up from a night of pornographic dreams, he felt disoriented. It wasn't so much that he was afraid of what was happening, but that he *just wanted to get away from it.* Somehow, the boundaries between his fantasy life and his waking life—even his sleeping life—had blurred.

This went on for months. He wasn't accomplishing enough during the day and he wasn't getting good sleep at night. Harrison decided to get the situation under control. "I've got to curb this," he said to himself. At first he thought he would never look at online pornography again. But he soon realized that was unrealistic. What he needed was a change in attitude. "I decided to stop obsessing over it and stop letting it take control over me," he says. "It sounds kind of weird to say that, but that's how I looked at it." At times, he worried he had become addicted to pornography; it didn't seem outside the realm of possibility. "The feeling of losing control set off red flags in my head."

So he cut back. These days, he tries to limit his online sessions to a couple of times each week. He has also become more purposeful about pornography: he masturbates every single time, whereas before he would occasionally just look for kicks. When he finds himself spending too much time online, he's awash in guilt, which he hopes strengthens his resolve to cut back. There has been some improvement. He has a new girlfriend, and thinks his sexual performance may be recovering. He's getting better at maintaining an erection. If he concentrates hard, he can keep porn from popping into his head while he's in bed with her. Still, on occasion, he finds himself slipping. Harrison hasn't discussed any of this with his girlfriend. "I'm afraid to tell her because I don't think she would approve of my looking at pornography at all."

Losing control happens, men say, when pornography not only conflicts with their personal and social obligations, but when it affects their sense of self. Realizing that pornography wasn't something he wanted to share with his family was a revelation to Kevin. Everyone knows that everyone looks at porn, he figured, so what was the problem? Why did he feel as if he had to hide the fact that *he* looked at it too? He didn't know the answer. But he knew his use felt "shady" and he wasn't comfortable letting his family know about it. When he was in a relationship, looking at pornography didn't trouble him as much, but something about his solitary habit was worse. "I associated the way I was using porn with some creepy guy home alone on a Saturday night, jerking off." Sometimes, logging off from Internet porn, he felt like "a sicko."

He also felt that his attitude toward women was colored by pornography. After a year of recovering from his broken engagement, Kevin finally started dating again. "It's not that I had some kind of attitude like, this pizza girl is going to ring the doorbell and we're going to have sex, or anything," he says. "But I just didn't feel like I was coming into a new experience with a very open or positive attitude. I didn't feel comfortable going out on a date." In Kevin's mind, masturbating to computer pornography was equivalent to "going to bars randomly to have sex with whomever." He didn't feel as though he could have a relationship while maintaining his habit. "It feels like cheating," he says. "It *is* cheating. Intimacy is a big part of a relationship for me, but how could I be intimate with a woman if I were looking at all these other women?" And he felt as if he was falling into the bad habits of his college years: he was going on dates just so he could have sex. "What the hell are you doing?" he asked himself.

In 2003, Kevin decided to log off permanently. Looking back on his pornography binge, Kevin realizes pornography was wrapped up in a bad period in his life. His fiancée had left him and he was lonely. "I was feeling really shitty about myself and needed a substitute," he recalls. "I began to feel really gross. It would be a gorgeous sunny day outside and here I was sitting inside, looking at porn on the computer." He cut down dramatically, stopped drinking as much as he had been, and started exercising again. "I don't know if porn was an addiction for me," he says. "I don't think so. But it certainly was a depressant."

Many men find that pornography in the aggregate becomes a downer. Its aftermath, while relaxing, eventually brings melancholy. Even men who love pornography look down on men they see as loving pornography just a little too much. Pornography not only objectifies women, explains Mark Schwartz, clinical director of the Masters and Johnson Clinic in St. Louis, it eventually becomes self-objectifying. "A man starts to feel like a computer himself when he realizes that he's dependent on computer images to turn him on," Schwartz says. "You may be making love to your wife, but you're picturing someone else. That's not fair to the woman, and it's miserable for the man." The key, according to Schwartz, is for men to recognize that the more they focus on pornography, the less satisfying they'll find their partner, and the less satisfied they'll be with themselves. "The metaphor of a man masturbating to his computer is the Willy Loman of our decade. In a sociologist's terms, it's anomie—the completely lonely, isolated man having sex with an imaginary airbrushed woman on a computer screen. It's truly pathetic, even tragic."

Even men who frequent strip clubs talk about how "pathetic" the guys who hang out there seem. "Losers." "Desperate." Lonely, overweight, repeatedly divorced men, leering over a third Johnnie Walker at women they could never bed on their own; the women, in turn, concealing their distaste in an effort to wheedle more money. Men who look at pornography from a comfortable online or television distance deride the image of the "scumbag" characters who frequent adult bookstores. "Seedy," they call the places. "Full of weirdos and misfits."

To realize that, even in your own shiny, high-tech, private way, you are one of them, or not too far off, is an unpleasant awakening—one most men prefer to avoid. They tell themselves they're not like that. They would never stoop to visit an adult bookstore. They only go to strip clubs—high-class ones, the best—for kicks, with a group of men, or with their willing girlfriend or wife. They realize the women are getting paid. They're no fools. Yet the charade can wear off. In the 2004

Elle-MSNBC.com poll, 15 percent of men said their online habit made them feel sleazy. Seven percent had been caught or reprimanded for looking at online pornography or personals during work hours. They may be spending too much time escaping from reality, and not enough time in reality. It's no man's fantasy to spend more time virtually than viscerally.

4

Porn Stars, Lovers, and Wives: How Women See Pornography

Aaliyah, a twenty-five-year-old public relations manager from Houston, likes pornography and approves of it, though her appreciation wasn't instantaneous. Her earliest exposure was on homecoming night in high school. A friend's date had a porn video and, feeling kind of bored, the group decided to watch it together. "To us, it was gross," Aaliyah says of the reaction among the girls. "The camera was right in there up close and we didn't see anything but the sex act."

In college, Aaliyah discovered more appealing pornography. At the large Texas university she attended, groups of female friends would gather to watch a porn movie in their dorm. Mostly, they thought it was funny. Sometimes they would e-mail pornography back and forth for laughs, though now that they all have careers and use work computers, they abstain. These days, Aaliyah looks at pornography on her own, about once a month—online, on cable, or on DVD. She likes movies that have a story; there has to be "a point" to the film. But most are primarily geared toward guys. She considers many to be too low budget; many plots are terrible; black porn is cheesy. "I like it when it's realistic," she explains. "I don't like things like bondage or very aggressive sex or anything that I feel is demonizing women. That's just brutal. I would *never* watch anything like that."

Aaliyah usually watches when she's not dating anyone. A practicing Southern Baptist, she would like to get married and have kids some day, but lately she's had no love life at all. "There's nobody to date," she laments. Watching pornography alone may be fun, but it only increases her desire to have sex and to meet someone. "I'm very strict about the type of guy I want," she says. "The kind of guy who would make a porn movie isn't the educated kind of guy I want to be with." Not all men are into porn, in her opinion, perhaps just 70 percent. "No way did my father have porn in the house," she says. "My mom would have killed him." Aaliyah figures men still use pornography more than women do—maybe 30 percent of women watch. Her best friends all look at it. But in Houston, the churchgoing people she knows have a negative view of pornography. Some of her friends from church would probably be offended if they knew she indulged. "A lot of people think porn is a bad thing," Aaliyah says, "but I think there's nothing wrong with it."

Traditionally, women *have* seen something wrong with pornography. It was considered low class, uncouth, "dirty." Society encouraged women to frown upon porn and to berate—albeit futilely—their men for using it. Or to turn a blind eye on their boyish digressions. Women certainly weren't expected to look themselves.

Pornography used to be just for the boys. In 1953, the famed Kinsey Report on American sexuality found that users were almost exclusively male. During the 1970s, however, women moved beyond the de facto position of "Don't ask, don't complain." Feminists began to stake a claim on the issue. They regarded the women working in the industry with compassion, lamenting a system that valued women more for their boobs than for their brains. Such women were typically exploited, underpaid, and had all too frequently suffered from sexual or emotional abuse. The problem, many women concluded, was with pornography—an exploitative industry that not only harmed the women who worked in it but affected all women—and the solution was to get rid of it. Other feminists took a different route, declaring that pornography shouldn't be eradicated—it should be improved. Liberation, they claimed, meant securing labor rights and health standards for porn stars and prostitutes (whom they preferred to call "sex workers"). Pro-porn feminists battled it out with anti-porn feminists while most men observed the catfight in delight or ignored it altogether.

And then it was all over. By the following decade, the feminist debate over pornography retreated to academia and the legal arena. In the popular culture, women's magazines rarely discussed pornography. During the early 1990s, it was unusual to run across an occasional mention of erotica. Those who continued to question pornography were labeled "feminazis" and "radicals" by some groups, or "right-wingers" and "bluestockings" by others, depending on the political agenda and persuasion of the name caller. Together, the message was clear: "Stop whining." Having never properly addressed the feminist quandary over porn, women's roles in using and producing pornography were no longer subject to debate.

Instead, in recent years, women's magazines regularly discuss pornography from a new perspective: how women can introduce it into their own lives. While many women continue to have mixed or negative feelings toward pornography, they are increasingly told to be realistic, to be "open-minded." Porn, they are told, is sexy, and if you want to be a sexually attractive and forward-thinking woman, you've got to catch on.

Porn Is for Girls

Popular culture promotes the wild fun and whimsy of the girl who loves pornography. She is Carmen Electra, the MTV icon turned pop phenomenon, whose husband, Dave Navarro, glorifies pornography while she sells exercise videos based on strip club routines. She is Pamela Anderson, *Playboy* centerfold, who has her own column in the teenage bible *Jane* magazine. The porn girl is every celebrity who accompanies her boyfriend to a strip club, playing along and plying a few bills to get lap dances herself. "Strippermania!" shouts a headline in *Us* magazine. "Taking it off takes off in Hollywood! Ask these guys—and gals—about their XXX-tra naughty adventures," the article goes on, highlighting photographs of fans such as Kate Hudson and Christina Aguilera.

Back in the pre-"pornocopia" era, wearing a thong meant painful waxing and a wedgie, pole dancing meant emulating a low-class stripper, and taking a man for a lap dance meant tolerating and even endorsing the humiliation of watching your mate cheat. Today, the pornography industry has convinced women that wearing a thong is a form of emancipation, learning to pole dance means embracing your sexuality, and taking your boyfriend for a lap dance is what every sexy and supportive girlfriend should do. According to a 2004 Internet poll conducted by *Cosmopolitan* magazine, 43 percent of women have been to a strip club; a similar poll by *Elle* found that 51 percent of the magazine's online readers had been to a strip club.[1] More than half described themselves as "pro-stripping" (56 percent) and said they weren't bothered if their partner went to strip clubs (52 percent).

Welcome to romance in the new millennium. In the 2004 teen comedy flick *The Girl Next Door,* Elisha Cuthbert plays Danielle, a porn star turned girl-next-door crush for an innocent high school senior. As Kenneth Turan, the *Los Angeles Times* film critic, noted:

> One of the fascinating things about *The Girl Next Door* is the way it is mainstreaming pornography not only to guys but to a female audience by its adroit casting of Elisha Cuthbert. . . . Cuthbert has a sweet and appealing demeanor, an innocence that makes her look like your standard porn star the way Macaulay Culkin looks like a professional wrestler. Her persona allows a career in pornography to seem like nothing more than a kicky, kind of daring next step for veterans of *Girls Gone Wild*—a minimally risky way, less painful than tattooing, to make yourself a desirable date. . . . *The Girl Next Door* has the unsettling aspect of a porn industry recruitment film. . . .[2]

With the help of such pop culture messages, pornography has become the means to being both the bad girl who seduces the guy and the good girl who gets to keep him, a seductive and instructive combination to teenagers grappling with schoolgirl crushes.

For adults, the message is more straightforward. A number of companies are increasing production of pornography made by and for women, and the industry is keen to promote women's burgeoning predilection for pornography. In 2004, Playgirl TV announced its launch with programming to include an "erotic soap opera" from a woman's point of view, a 1940s-style romantic comedy with "a sexual twist," and roundtable discussions of "newsworthy women's topics." The result is a peculiar blend of go-girl-porn-feminism and male-directed me-tooism. While conducting research for programming development, Kelly Holland, one of Playgirl TV's executives, noted, "I have to take women at face value when they say they want to see more penises, but I factor in: how much of that is just because they want their MTV, so to speak—their right to media and their right to those sexual images? It's sort of an expression of their process of sexual liberation. It's like those rowdy women you see at a male strip club—it's almost like they're acting out some male construct of what sexual desire is supposed to look like."[3] Another female-targeted pornography network, Bliss TV, plans to offer pay-per-view and video-on-demand services with shows like *Thrust*, which will supposedly feature "the Jenna Jameson of men," and *Stiletto,* a series set in the fashion industry.

A growing number of pornography conglomerates have been launched by women. One pioneer, Samantha Lewis, has run Digital Playground, a California-based DVD company that offers films with titles such as *Only the A-Hole* and *Stripped,* for more than ten years. According to Lewis, 40 percent of retail sales of their pornographic films in 2004 were purchased by women, double the number of just two years earlier.[4] The company's Web site explains, "With a classy female in the owner's seat, Digital Playground shatters the porn stereotype, encouraging women and couples to join the consumer pool." Yet the company's Web site flashily showcases seven pneumatic models—with nary a man in sight. One of the company's most popular series, *Jack's Playground,* is described as "a collection of Jack's personal videos . . . showcasing his uncanny ability to persuade girls to perform sexual acts in front of his camera . . . real girls so thirsty for fame, they'd do anything." And this is meant to appeal to female audiences.

Online, too, women are increasingly in charge of selling themselves. New York–based pornography entrepreneurs Carlin Ross, a lawyer, and Christina Head, a documentary filmmaker, told the *New York Times* that, for them, pornography is "all about empowering and educating women."[5] The Los Angeles–based pornographic Web site

Suicidegirls.com boasts more than 500,000 visitors a month; members are 56 percent female. "Siren," the online name of one of the Web site's founders, says Suicidegirls is different from *Playboy* and other male-oriented pornography, because "what one person finds to be objectifying a woman might not be the same thing to someone else. It's all up to the women. They decide how they want to be seen. I don't feel objectified. I make my own decisions."[6] Others can take CAKE. A vaguely conceived Internet- and event-based group, CAKE was founded by Melinda Gallagher and brother-sister team Emily and Matt Kramer as a "feminist" variation on *Playboy*—"to make female sexuality a public, political movement."[7] They decry Hugh Hefner–style objectification, yet their logo is a nude female silhouette; women are encouraged to strip in front of male party guests and female lap dancers are hired to work their events. Still, CAKE effects a feminist sensibility on its Web site, with blasts at the Bush administration for rolling back reproductive rights.

Such contradictory messages are espoused without irony by the new feminist porn proponents. Molly, a twenty-nine-year-old New Yorker who works as an editor at an erotica magazine that features couples-oriented stories and women-friendly photographs, proudly refers to herself as a pornographer and a feminist. Much porn, she says, is degrading and unpleasant. "I like having a role in creating a form of pornography that reaches me, and being able to represent sex in a positive generous light," Molly explains. "What I create are better options for enjoyable, consensual, mutually satisfying sex. I feel like I'm performing a service." Molly shares her work with friends, suggesting what she considers female-friendly forms of pornography, in order to spread the gospel. "I think women aren't as accustomed to being introduced to porn the way men are by their friends," she says. "But once I show it to my female friends, they've gotten hooked."

Copping an Attitude

Some attribute the rise in female consumption to an increased supply in pornography for women. That may be part of the reason, but there's more at play than a simple supply-and-demand equation. Broader societal shifts in men's and women's roles in relationships and a corresponding swing in women's expectations and attitudes toward their sexuality are driving women to pornography as well.

Recent events on college campuses demonstrate the new approach. In March 2003, the University of Alabama hosted a debate between pornographer-multimedia star Ron Jeremy and anti-pornography activist Susan B. Cole. Sounds controversial. Yet students were far from outraged that a porn film star had been elevated to an expert panelist at a university-sponsored event, even on a moderately conservative southern campus. Nor were any feminist activists on campus rallying to Cole's side. Instead, Jeremy was greeted with cheers from students dressed in T-shirts boasting "I love porn," while Cole was booed and jeered at by the audience. Despite Cole's careful insistence that she was not opposed to sex and wasn't a member of the "sex police," she was mocked for arguing that pornography exploits women. During the question-and-answer session that followed the panel debate, which was mostly a forum for Jeremy to boast about the benefits of porn and "having a party," students took the opportunity to ask Cole questions like, "What's your fucking problem?"[8]

Sociologist Michael Kimmel, who studies pornography and teaches sexuality at the State University of New York at Stony Brook, says, "Twenty years ago, my female students would say, 'Ugh, that's disgusting,' when I brought up pornography in class. The men would guiltily say, 'Yeah, I've used it.' Today, men are much more open about saying they use pornography all the time and don't feel any guilt. The women now resemble the old male attitude: they'll sheepishly admit to using it themselves." Their attitudes have merged even more closely with men's.

Kimmel has mixed feelings about the change. On the positive side, he says, women's embrace of pornography seems to reflect increased sexual agency on their part—the Samantha of *Sex and the City* role writ large. Yet the new attitude of college women strikes him as disturbing. Female fantasies have changed over the years as a result of pornography and what Kimmel calls the "masculinization of sex." Compared with ten years ago, women's fantasies are more likely today to include violence, rough sex, strangers, and descriptions of male physical attributes. As a man who grappled with the feminist implications of pornography during the 1980s and early 1990s, Kimmel wonders how and when female liberation took this abrupt turn. "Personally, I think that for a woman to construct her sex life like that of a man is a rather impoverished view of liberation." Especially, he says, given the inequality prevalent in most pornography. From Kimmel's perspective, much of pornography enhances and supports men's sense of entitlement to look at and objectify women's bodies.

But that's not a particularly hip position. Many women today, particularly college students, consider the production and consumption of pornography a form of "sex-positive activism." In February 2004, Harvard University officials approved the launch of what the Harvard *Crimson* termed a "porn magazine"—*H Bomb,* a student-run publication that includes naked pictures of Harvard students and other sexual content. The female founders of the magazine took umbrage, insisting *H Bomb* was "not pornographic" but an "outlet" that put a "lighter spin on something that shouldn't be a restricted or delicate topic at Harvard."[9] Yet when asked if she objected to her magazine being labeled pornography, *H Bomb* cofounder Katherina C. Baldegg said she did not, adding, "I guess student porn is sort of an underground thing."[10]

Underground or out in the open, pornography is hardly rare on campuses in the new millennium. A Boston University student recently announced the launch of a new magazine, *Boink,* which she unabashedly declares is "pornography" and claims will be modeled after laddie magazine *Maxim.*[11] Female students at Smith College allegedly host a pornographic Web site, Smithiegirls;* Swarthmore publishes an erotic magazine, *Untouchables*; and Vassar has *Squirm: The Art of Campus Sex.* According to Sarah Zarrow, one of the magazine's student editors, *Squirm* tries to "explore the area in between not talking about sex and the *Playboy-Hustler* version of sex," which sounds reasonable, in theory.[12] Yet *Squirm,* which is also a campus organization, hosts a porn screening every month including, according to another editor, Per Henningsgaard, "less mainstream" pornography such as "hardcore lesbian porn, porn that depicts S&M, porn in which women are the

*This site was referred to in several newspaper articles in 2003, yet by 2004 it could not be located online. It may have been hidden or removed from the Internet.

powerful dominant figure." As for the print component, he explains, "To titillate people we call [*Squirm*] a porn magazine, but deep down, nobody on the staff considers it porn. We're certainly not hardcore porn, which needs to be bound in plastic and have an erect penis. . . . We're more of an artistic endeavor than most pornography is. We're interested in reconceptualizing what porn is."[13]

Attempting to "reconceptualize" or "redefine" pornography and disseminate it once it's found seems to be the new student project. At Indiana University, students who participated in a pornographic film were disciplined by the university in 2002 for disobeying the school's code of behavior against lewd, indecent, or obscene conduct. But girl power eventually prevailed. By 2004, a freshman at the school started her own pay pornography Web site, complete with photographs taken in school dormitories. "Keira," the woman who runs the site, created it at her boyfriend's suggestion in order to pay for college and family expenses.[14] Despite an initial uproar from campus authorities, she was ultimately not charged with violating school policy.

And why should she have been? What right did the school have to interfere with a girl's game decision to sell herself if she so chooses? "Keira" and her fellow "new school" feminists believe pornography represents the next stage in female liberation. As Abby Holland, director of Playgirl TV, explains, "Since time immemorial, it's been okay for men to be in tune with their sexuality. When it comes to porn, traditionally good girls don't do it. The third-generation feminists—the twenty-somethings—are fully aware that good girls do."[15] By redefining pornography in terms of equal opportunity and getting "in touch" with your sexuality, pornographers get women on their side—and perhaps, incidentally, also help ensure that no liberal academic institution would dare interfere.

With widespread peer advocacy and silent administrative acceptance, no wonder so many college women are eager to go wilding for *Girls Gone Wild*, the growing empire of videos, apparel, movies, music, and restaurants based on the premise that women just want to take their clothes off—for men, for free, for fame, for fun. Quite often, they are drunk when they do so, egged on by crowds of men in front of cajoling cameramen and producers, all in the name of spring break. Times

Square may have been washed of its seedy adult theaters, but in the spirit of wholesome participatory porn, a *Girls Gone Wild*–themed restaurant was scheduled to open there in late 2005. *Girls Gone Wild* founder Joe Francis, who has continually fought off lawsuits accusing him of everything from underage pornography to deceptive business practices, consistently pleads the First Amendment in his favor and denies all charges. After all, he boasts, "Everybody is doing everything by their own free choice." Francis doesn't consider his product to be remotely pornographic. He says his videos are "something that fifteen years ago would have been considered porn, now it's considered reality video."[16]

She's Got Porn

Statistics seem to suggest that women are catching on. The Internet measurement firm comScore tracked close to 32 million women visiting at least one adult Web site in January 2004. Seven million of them were ages thirty-five to forty-four, while women over the age of sixty-five totaled only 800,000.[17] Nielsen NetRatings has found figures to be somewhat lower, with 10 million women visiting adult-content Web sites in December 2003.[18] In a 2004 *Elle*-MSNBC.com poll, 41 percent of women said they have intentionally viewed or downloaded erotic films or photos and 13 percent watched or sexually interacted with someone on a live webcam.

Christina, a thirty-five-year-old mother of two, got started on pornography at age twelve, when she discovered her dad's *Playboy* stash. She wanted to compare other women's bodies to her own, so she sneaked copies to her room. Christina was a precocious young woman in many ways. At fourteen, she lost her virginity (all her friends at Catholic school already had, so she felt left behind). She began experimenting with [drugs and alcohol] at the same age, around the time of her parents' divorce, often getting into trouble at school. By eighteen she had moved in with a boyfriend, and at nineteen was pregnant with her first child. After her son was born, Christina and the boy's father, a nightclub bouncer, had a second child, this time a daughter, before breaking up four years later.

* P.P.'s claim that porn users don't fit a mold is probably right, but it seems that her interview subjects do. They are all troubled in areas other than porn. Causality?

Despite having two kids under her roof, Christina finally felt free. She went through a "wild" period. "I was just like a man," she recalls. "I didn't want commitment, I didn't want a relationship, I just wanted my booty call. Men loved it." She didn't get into another serious relationship until she married at thirty-two, but she divorced her husband, an intermittently employed truck driver, within three years. Now back on the singles scene, she has had an adventurous sex life, with about seventy-five sexual partners, male and female, in total.

People just seem attracted to her. Though Christina went through a gawky period in her preteens, she has since become the embodiment of what she calls "a typical California girl"—five feet nine, blond and blue-eyed, and thin with a 38C bust. "At work, men try to talk to me professionally, but they just can't stop staring at my chest," she says. "It's funny." Male attention has made Christina feel confident about her body, and she considers herself uninhibited and unconventional. Once she even took pornographic photos of herself, though she became wary after an ex-boyfriend sent them out on the Internet. "I was Paris Hilton'ed!" she complains playfully. But that doesn't stop her from looking online, after work, for about half an hour each night. Christina subscribes to an e-mail service called Cool Sex, through which members send one another links. Subscribers will challenge one another with pornographic Web hunts: Find the most unique and sexy shaves, like photos of heart-shaped pubic hair, was one recent quest. Christina has never met any of the other members, but they have all become "good friends," bonded around a common interest. People who are into pornography are generally open and interesting types, in Christina's little black book. "I just find porn really enticing," she says. "Some of it is raunchy, but in a good way. I like getting off on it when I'm alone and it's also a great foreplay tool."

Women like Christina attribute a number of benefits to pornography—it helps them explore their sexual side and broadens their ideas, giving them fodder for real-life sex, including positions, role-playing, and attitudes. In the 2004 *Elle*-MSNBC.com poll, 35 percent of women who had viewed adult content on the Internet said it helped them find "more ways to look or act sexy" and 28 percent claimed that it "pushed the boundaries of what I find erotic." One in four said viewing adult material online helped them talk about what they want sexually and made them feel more sexually positive about themselves. By using pornography, pro-porn women say they gain "ownership" of their sexuality, wresting it from the control of men and debunking traditional notions of women's passivity in bed. Pornography gives women "a voice" to discuss their own desires.

Denise, a single woman who works at a nonprofit organization, thinks pornography can be liberating and instructive. "It's a medium that should be completely legal and I don't have a problem with it," says the thirty-one-year-old. Having never looked online or watched a pornographic movie, she was intrigued by an old boyfriend's abundant pornography collection. He lent her a couple of Seymour Butts tapes, which they watched together, but when they broke up, he forgot to ask for them back. "I always say I got them in the divorce," Denise says and laughs. The first time she watched the movies, she was merely amused. But after repeated viewings she started to masturbate while watching. "I look at them when I want to be turned on," she explains. "And since my boyfriend now is long-distance, I don't always have someone here when I'm in the mood." Her boyfriend knows she watches tapes in his absence, and, she thinks, is turned on by the idea.

"I admit I haven't seen that much of it," Denise says. "But the online porn that I saw with an old boyfriend was all girl-next-door types. Their bodies were a lot less threatening to me than the super-thin models and actresses you see everywhere else. I thought it was kind of adorable that he was looking at these cute girls giving blow jobs." Sexual acts and positions that once seemed taboo became acceptable after Denise saw them in pornography. "I figured if all these movies show anal-oriented things, then clearly it's turning other people on. I didn't think that was acceptable until I saw it in porn."

With women increasingly learning their sexual lessons through the lens of pornography, how women construct their fantasies and pursue their actual sex lives is fundamentally shifting. Yet, on a biological level, women process pornography differently than men. In a 2004 study conducted at Essen University in Germany, researchers used fMRI scanning technology to observe brain activity in men and women as they viewed pornographic films. While both men's and women's brains showed activity in the temporal lobes, where memory and perception occur, only women showed activity in their frontal lobes, a part of the brain normally associated with planning and emotion. Whether women were plotting their morning's errands while watching pornography or having their emotional buttons pushed is not clear. Similarly, whether men get lost in the moment while watching, as is commonly assumed, or are less likely to experience an emotional reaction is also unknown.[19]

Evidence does indicate that men respond more to visual stimuli than women do, and numerous studies report that men are more visually sensitive when it comes to sexual arousal and fulfillment. Brain scans show that areas of the brain devoted to visuals come into use when men are sexually stimulated; in women, those areas of the brain remain quiet. In a study at Emory University, twenty-eight men and women were shown erotic photographs while an fMRI recorded images of brain activity. In men, the photographs triggered a whirl of activity, particularly in the brain's amygdala, which plays a key role in basic emotions like fear and pleasure.[20] Yet whether that difference is the result of biology or of cultural conditioning has yet to be established, or even explored. According to Stephan Hamman, professor of psychology and lead author of the study, one reason for the response in men could be cultural. Men tend to be inundated with sexual imagery and are possibly more likely to seek it out.[21]

As much as women want to claim a right to pornography, for most women—even those who partake—pornography is not the same for her as it is for him. Keisha, thirty-three, and her husband, Malik, thirty-six, sometimes look at pornography together, but Keisha thinks what they see is altogether different. "Men take porn more literally than women do," she says. "They use porn as a way to get hot. For me, it's entertaining. I'm not necessarily horny after I watch it." Black porn, she says, is usually just crappy. "It makes me laugh more than anything." Malik, a police officer, usually picks out the evening's entertainment. Down at the police station, guys will swap videos, which Malik will bring home with him after work. Recently, he acquired a highly recommended DVD in which a woman travels to the Italian countryside and sleeps with everyone she meets—a homeless guy, an old man in a retirement home. "I was like, ugh, gross!" Keisha recalls. "To think of somebody actually doing that."

Erotica vs. Pornography

Many of the women who say they are open to pornography are not open to what most men consider arousing. In fact, women are often talking about erotica, not flat-out male-dominated pornography, when they refer to adult material, and are unwilling to label themselves as "anti-porn" out of a reluctance to lose sex toys, lingerie, Nancy Friday, and Anaïs Nin.

Hannah, a thirty-two-year-old graduate student, makes no bones about her recent interest in erotica. Not having learned to masturbate until the age of twenty-seven, Hannah has found erotica a gratifying revelation. She keeps a small collection by her bed—old sex textbooks, Nancy Friday's compendiums of female fantasies, erotic stories, an illustrated book of sexual positions with "crazy Japanese illustrations," a photography collection from the Kinsey Museum. She has one video, a "woman's porn film" with dialogue and characters.

But a lot of pornography turns Hannah off. Internet pornography is unsatisfying, with the exception of a few independent erotica sites, such as Nerve and Cleansheets. The rest she finds too aggressive, even invasive. "You look for images you want, but end up getting all these images that are repulsive and even offensive to me personally," she explains. "Women who are clearly under eighteen, women with an emptiness in their eyes, and a hardened, professional sad attitude toward sex." She cites in particular the bad acting and depressing photography. Women being peed on and having their mouths stuffed with huge penises. "Porn on the Web reflects what so often disappoints me in male-oriented pornography," Hannah says. Male magazines aren't much better, but for different reasons. *Playboy,* with its airbrushing and fakeness, is "deeply boring"; the women are made to look like dolls rather than people. Magazines like *Maxim* are vulgar. "Women with abs of steel, gorgeous faces, and big round perfect breasts are presented with these lewd schoolboyish headlines," she says. "It appears that's what the majority of men in our culture want, and that bothers me. I'm nothing like those women, so it threatens me."

At the same time that pornography has become a mainstream component of popular culture, erotica has wended its way into suburban living rooms. Companies like Fantasia and Passion Parties are multimillion-dollar businesses that offer Tupperware-style parties selling sex toys and lingerie. In contrast to the pornography industry, which is still largely controlled by men and primarily serves men, the sex-toy industry is dominated by women and caters to female consumers. Passion Parties now employs 3,200 saleswomen, racking up $20 million a year.[22]

But what is the difference between pornography for him and erotica for her? According to Molly, the female pornographer, erotica is "just a way of marketing porn to women." As she sees it, erotica "tends to be flowery, more romantic," but in the end, "it's just a different take on the same sex act." Others see a more profound distinction. Gloria Steinem has said that erotica, based on the word *eros*, meaning passionate love or yearning for another person, is about "a mutually pleasurable, sexual expression between people who have enough power to be there by positive choice." Pornography, on the other hand, whose root word refers to prostitution, is about objectifying women. According to Steinem, the message of pornography is "violence, dominance, and conquest. It is sex being used to reinforce some inequality, or to create one, or to tell us that pain and humiliation are really the same as pleasure." Others define erotica by the quality of the imagery. Erotic films have better production values than low-budget pornos; they focus more on story line and plot, using credible characters and actors whose bodies and attitudes more accurately reflect the way women look and behave. The goal of erotica, by this definition, is mutual satisfaction rather than exploitation of women by men.

Viewing some films helps clarify the difference in approaches. Take a typical mainstream pornography video—nothing too kinky or fetishistic—sold off the Internet. *Two in the Seat #3,* a 2003 release from a company called Red Light District, concerns itself with the escapades of two men and a woman. Claire, the female protagonist, a twenty-year-old and, it happens, three-month veteran of the industry, is asked off-camera what will happen in her scene. "I'm here to get pounded," replies the pig-tailed star. Two men then enter, calling her a "little fucking cunt" and a "dirty nasty girl." While they doubly penetrate her, anally and vaginally, she braces herself, looking pained, against a couch. After both men spank her reddened buttocks, one asks, "Are you crying?" Claire answers, "No,

I'm enjoying it," to which the man replies, "Damn, I thought you were crying. It was turning me on when I thought you were crying." Claire asks if he would prefer her to cry and he responds, "Yes, give me a fucking tear." After one man ejaculates in her mouth, the second tells her to "spit all over my dick, bitch." She does his bidding, then wipes the excess semen from her face and eats it.[23] Presumably, given the popularity of the series, this is an exciting episode for many men; most women, though, would probably not find the scene arousing.

Take it down a notch to "couples porn," a genre in which porn-star-turned-entrepreneur Candida Royalle specializes. On her Web site, Royalle explains:

> I like to call my Femme movies "sensually explicit." . . . You'll find them to be less graphic and lacking in the traditional "money shot," a staple of most adult films. You'll also find story lines, good original music and real characters of all ages. Counselors often prefer to use my movies in their work with couples because of their "woman friendly" approach and what they call "positive sexual role modeling."

One such film, *My Surrender,* follows the story of April, a woman surrounded by the "tender passions" of couples who come to her in order to be filmed acting out their private fantasies. Yet April, fearful of pain and disappointment, has been unable to find "real intimacy" in her own life. Not until Robert enters her world, determined to break through April's inhibitions and weaken her resistance, will her "erotic flower" bloom. Viewers are invited to watch to see if Robert will truly make April surrender herself in the way the other couples she films have done. Can April become truly uninhibited like a porn star? The Web site provides a hint, cooing, "Ah, sweet surrender. So delicious. So pure."

Or, as a male reviewer on the Web site notes of the female-styled fare, "I am not sure it would be that great to sit down to alone. I might want something a little less 'lovable,' but for my wife and I it was great to spark up the night." Other "couples-oriented" pornography seems more geared toward men. The Web site Adam & Eve boasts *Group Sex: Pure*

Ecstasy: "The gang's all here! It's a 4½-hour showcase of 9-person orgies, group groping, all-girl box-banging, deep-throat action and anal invasions—plus every juicy variation on the 3-way! See gorgeous groups of fresh-faced babes get it on with some of the horniest cocksmen in XXX. Along the way you'll witness Nikita Denise . . . showing off her rear-entry talents . . . and Brianna 'No Gag Reflex' Banks going down on everyone in sight!"

Despite the efforts of female erotica and pornography producers, and the women who enjoy their work, most men do not find truly female-targeted erotica appealing, and the men who do watch them with their partners say they do so only for their girlfriends' or wives' sake. For their own arousal, they watch male-oriented pornography on their own. Meanwhile, erotic material for women is more likely and effectively found in mainstream Hollywood films. As pornography scholar Diana Russell notes, the mainstream media have readily adopted much that she would categorize as erotica—sex scenes in R-rated movies, for example. "There's nothing wrong with arousal," she emphasizes. "The issue isn't about being against arousal, it's arousal to degrading material that is so destructive." Take *Unfaithful,* an exploration of a married suburbanite's affair with a hunky downtown New York book collector played by international sex symbol Olivier Martinez. Throughout the film, the protagonist, played by Diane Lane, is both in control of the situation and emotionally conflicted. There are steamy nude sex scenes, but the focus remains on the woman and the emotional and practical effect her affair wreaks on her marriage.

True male-oriented pornography still offends the vast majority of women. Yet popular culture and the media today conflate the two, referring to them interchangeably. A recent feature by a female journalist in the *Chicago Sun-Times* entitled "The Language of Love" is a good example: "Feminists often decry pornography as evil and based on the objectification of women," the article begins darkly. The author then goes on to say that "pornography and erotica can play a useful role," and briefly attempts to differentiate between the two; pornography is "thought of as more hardcore" while erotica "is considered to be softer sexual imagery that appeals to our sensual side." By the fourth paragraph, the article eliminates the discussion of "pornography" proper, referring only to erotica, and urging women to try out female-friendly fare: "How do you find erotic videos that are female-friendly?" the article asks. "You can always visit your local erotica shop, but any online erotica shop has a variety of options. . . . There's nothing shameful about curiosity or exploring your erotic side."[24] The result is that not only have the two ideas—erotica and pornography—become blurred in the public's mind, but that pornography has become further defined into acceptability. Now that mainstream media, from R-rated movies to HBO television shows, regularly depict erotica that used to be considered pornography, those seeking to adopt porn are pushed further to the limits of what they may have once considered acceptable.

Women Who Don't Like Pornography

Lauren wants to believe that pornography is okay. The thirty-two-year-old mother of two majored in women's studies in college, and works as an educational consultant advocating progressive education. She and her husband are raising their children as equal partners. "The radical feminist in me wants to like it," Lauren explains. "And there are parts I do like—that women acknowledge that sex is for sale all over America and they're getting in on the game. That there is theoretically room for them to be active personal agents." She pauses and sighs. "But the way that porn plays out is usually pretty repulsive. For the vast majority of women in porn, it's not a real choice. And as a mother of two girls, married to a guy with a stack of *Playboys* in the closet, I can't abide by it. We're moving next month and those *Playboys* will *not* make the move."

As much as women are touted as the new pornography consumer, they still lag far behind men. The spitfire headlines do little to reflect the reality of most women's experiences, and statistics belie the assertions of the pro-porn movement and the go-go girl mentality espoused by female pornography purveyors. While some polls show that up to half of all women go online for sexual reasons, the percentage of women who say they do are likely exaggerated by the inclusion of erotica, dating, and informational sites in the definition of "adult" Internet content, areas to which women are disproportionately drawn compared with men. Many women who are tracked through filtering sites are linked to pornography by accident, visit out of curiosity, or are tracking down a male partner's usage. Others feel that admitting they don't look at pornography at all is akin to affixing a "frigid" sticker to their chastity belts: better not to come off as uptight.

Women who don't log on to Internet pornography express a number of reasons for abstaining. In the *Elle*-MSNBC.com poll, six in ten said they just were not interested in Internet sex sites or didn't like them, 35 percent said they had no desire or need to look because they already had a fulfilling sex life, 29 percent said it would make them feel sleazy, and 24 percent said they don't want the pop-up ads and cookies that come with the package. Not everyone wants to be a porn star, particularly women with a greater range of options. In a 2004 survey of 107 female students at California State University, 96 percent claimed they would not participate in a *Girls Gone Wild* video. And in certain corners, porn star fatigue is setting in. In her February 2004 editor's letter, *Elle* magazine editor Roberta Myers championed the new modesty in women's fashion as a backlash against the ubiquity of pornographic imagery in mainstream culture. Myers noted that such styles will likely be embraced by women "who were just never quite able to find their inner porn star, despite a cultural atmosphere suggesting that not to was to be somehow a sexual failure, a prude, a woman out of touch with her own goddess."[25] Later that fall, fashions for teenagers were noted for reflecting a new preppy modesty.

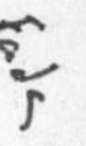

Other signs of female protest percolate. At the University of North Carolina at Chapel Hill in 2004, ten female students decided to protest against *Playboy*'s "Girls of the ACC" photo spread by signing up to pose themselves. They then canceled their appointments via a letter to the magazine. The women carefully framed their protest in impersonal terms: "This is not about porn being offensive; that is, hurting our feelings or sensibilities," they wrote. "It's about the pornographic videos and magazines, like *Playboy*, that reinforce women's sexual objectification."[26] On campus, fifteen female students gathered to protest the pictorial. (But while the activists took their stand, fifty other female students showed up, decked out for their *Playboy* appointments.)

Among women in their teens and twenties, pornography is now openly used, advocated, and celebrated, without the desire for privacy that continues to characterize older generations. Like many college students and recent graduates, Ashley, a twenty-four-year-old who works in advertising in Baltimore, feels alone in her dislike of, and disdain for, pornography. At the Catholic university Ashley attended, men were open about their love of pornography, with videos and DVDs strewn around their rooms and *Playboy*s scattered among their textbooks. Ashley can't remember a guy's bathroom that didn't have a pile of *Maxim*s or *FHM*s shelved high atop the toilet. Before *Maxim,* she says, you had to be eighteen to buy *Playboy,* and doing so was considered embarrassing; today it's perfectly acceptable to buy magazines with explicit photographs of women on the covers. The Internet especially has made pornography omnipresent among her peers. Male friends gleefully beckon one another to their computers to behold porn of particular interest. Trips to strip clubs are a regular outing. "All the men I know feel like there's nothing wrong with pornography," she says. "They don't even try to hide it." Instead, guys try to pass it off as something funny. "It's all very ironic to them," Ashley explains. "Which I think is a lie. They say they look at it because it's hysterical and that it's a hoot to get lap dances. They never admit to using porn for what I think they're using it for." All of her female friends act as if they're okay with it, too, though Ashley doesn't buy it. But it's better for women not to complain. "Guys think it's really uncool for a woman to get pissed off about it."

For Ashley, who is a Republican, pornography is not about politics. She believes in free speech and dislikes the mixture of religion and politics that often grips denunciations of pornography. Nor is it about God. She isn't strongly religious and never goes to church. And she considers herself far from a prude. She lost her virginity when she was sixteen and has had sex with ten other men since, five of them serious boyfriends. Instead, pornography is "personally offensive" to Ashley. Seeing her male friends and boyfriends use it is upsetting. Moreover, as a feminist ("I know that word has negative connotations these days"), Ashley believes pornography is inherently demeaning and objectifying, "impeding the progress of women." As for feminists who believe pornography should be an equal opportunity enterprise, Ashley considers it wishful thinking. "I don't think we're far enough along as equals in men's minds to get away with the pro-porn stance," she says. "I think that until men view us as equals, it's not smart for women to encourage men to objectify us."

Playing Along

Many women learn to objectify themselves. Just as some men observe a shift in their sexual behavior stemming from pornography, women sometimes experience an effect on their own sexual behavior. Valerie, thirty-two, first saw pornography when she was twelve. She would steal her parents' magazines and sneak glimpses on cable TV. "I have that imprinted in my brain," she says.

Valerie, who is single, admits to having an active sex life with more partners than average, though she can't come up with an exact number. She goes for younger men, artistic types, men with whom her relationship is overtly sexual. "When I'm with a guy and he starts pulling moves from porn movies, it's familiar to me and that's exciting," she admits. "My sense of eroticism has definitely been influenced by similar pornographic forces that men experience, and so I respond to those same attitudes and positions and types. I've been brainwashed, too." But while the sex that results is often physically satisfying, there's a negative side. "At the same time, it's icky," she says, trying to explain. "I don't just want to become Body A. I want men to feel like they're with *me,* Valerie, a particular woman with a particular body and my own unique personality. I want them to be in the moment, as opposed to going through some form of learned behavior. I want it to be our own experience as opposed to an imitation of porn."

Because she's so aware of pornography from her own early exposure, whenever Valerie becomes sexually involved with a man she can easily tell if he's into porn. Her first such experience was with Bill, a hotshot lawyer. She was twenty-five at the time and infatuated with Bill's good looks, charming demeanor, and professional ambition. "He was an educated, really smart guy," she says. "But he was obsessed with porn. He had it all over his apartment, cutouts of women pasted on his walls—and mind you, he's a lawyer." Intimidated, Valerie didn't feel she had a right to complain. But the porn showed up in their sex. "He was really into fucking," she says. "You know, bright lights on, staring at my body parts, going through the motions." After a few months, she and Bill went on a trip together and had sex in the airplane bathroom. Afterward, Bill told her that she got "a lot of points" for doing it, but Valerie felt inadequate. "I didn't feel like I was a sexual enough person for him. And it felt strange that he was giving me 'points' for doing this. To me, you get points if you give money to a homeless person or do something meaningful."

She tried to get into Bill's porn-sex style, but the lack of sensuality and romance got to her. It seemed as though he was trying to push her away subconsciously, to keep her at an emotional distance. "I'm sure he thought I was lame and I thought he was scary," she says. In retrospect, it was strange that Bill, at twenty-six, had clippings of women pasted on his walls. "I mean, girls do that when they're twelve or thirteen, put up pictures of models and pretty actresses," she says. "He was acting like a twelve-year-old, very into the beauty of various body parts." The two remained friends, however, and Valerie wasn't surprised to hear when, years later, Bill turned to various self-help groups in an effort to get over his "womanizing" ways. "He is finally struggling with his whole commitment issue," she says. "He has this ideal of what a woman should be, but once a woman becomes available, he doesn't want her anymore." Pornography, she hypothesizes, seemed wrapped up in a number of related relationship problems for Bill.

After dating Bill, Valerie went for a few years in which pornography didn't seem to influence her male partners as much, though it continued to play out in her own head. Then the familiar struck. At twenty-nine, she started to date Miguel, a musician. The first night they slept together it was the same old thing: lights glaring, gaping at her body parts, manipulating her into positions popular in pornography so he could admire her. He was aggressive, he was confident, he was following a formula. It was cold. "I almost felt like he was in the sex industry," she says. "As if we were performing on the porn screen." Afterward, she turned to him and said, "Do you watch a lot of porn?" He thought she was asking because she liked pornography, too; it was clear he was impressed.

"Yeah," he replied. "What are you into?" Instead of answering, Valerie told him, "I could tell by the way you had sex with me." Miguel was taken aback. He had no idea a woman could trace his moves back to pornography; he didn't even realize that was what he was doing. "He just thought it was hot, that he was a stud," Valerie says. It felt bold for her to mention her reaction after the first time they had sex, but Valerie was compelled to do so. "I felt cheapened," she says. "It wasn't as if because he diminished me, I had to diminish him back. I just had to get it out there. I felt so empty after the experience."

For other women, the raw sexuality they observe in pornography is something they appreciate in real life. Christina, the thirty-five-year-old who subscribes to Cool Sex, says pornography has broadened her sexual horizons. She graduated from "standard women and men sex" to pornography showing group sex and edgier fare. Open to anything except "really raunchy" stuff—scatological sex, for instance—Christina likes imitating the women in pornography. She collects sex toys and accessories that she's noticed in pornography, and keeps them by her bed, making sure to lock the door when she's not home so that her fourteen-year-old son and twelve-year-old daughter won't find them. She often thinks about porn while having sex. "It lights a match to your senses," she says. "And gives you crazy ideas of stuff to try." For a while, she and her now ex-husband attended sex clubs together. That ended when he eventually became too obsessive and jealous to watch her having sex with other men, and was physically abusive.

Most men, Christina finds, are into the fact that she likes pornography, and that helps her relationships. She and her boyfriend of seven months went to a hotel recently and ordered a huge array of pornos. He said, "Man, this is so great. My friends aren't gonna believe that we're watching this together and that you enjoy it even more than I do." His reaction was typical: "Men think women who are a little freaky will have no inhibitions and be super adventurous in bed," she explains.

As Christina sees it, her greatest attribute and chief downfall is that she's a people pleaser. "Especially with dating, I never want to say no. Rather than hurt someone's feelings, I end up doing what they want." Her daughter takes after her in this regard, and Christina fears she'll become promiscuous in order to please men. For Christina, trying to please has meant putting up with things she thinks she maybe should not have accepted. One ex threw food at her and spit in her face; her blue eyes were often black and swollen from abuse. Her ex-husband raped her, forcing her to get a restraining order.

Pornography can be a tool for women who aim to please. The message to women is clear: Want to be sexy? Want to win that man? Want to make him stay? Look like a porn star, or, at least, enjoy looking at women who look like porn stars. And needless to say, don't be uptight if your man wants to look. In a 2004 issue of *Glamour* magazine, in an article entitled, "31 Essential Sex & Love Experiences," readers are told that watching porn is one of the "ultimate milestones on any relationship résumé." The article advises, "Consider this your happy love life to-do list."[27] A 2004 article in *Self,* "Jump Start Your Sex Life," included porn on its "Lust List" of things to do. "It's true that hardcore porn can be offensive," the article acknowledges. "But when you select carefully, some of these flicks can also be exciting." It goes on to suggest spending a few days viewing pornography and then laying off for several months to make the activity "fresh again."[28]

For Keisha, the stay-at-home mom married to a police officer, looking at pornography with her husband is a way to stay hip, to "keep your freak card."* Keisha explains, "Especially after you have kids, a lot of women become prudish. There's less time for sex and men get disappointed. They think they married a freak but end up with a prude. If porn is something he likes, he'll be happy you're willing to share it."†

Other women make an effort to accommodate or incorporate a man's pornography into their relationship. After their rather dispiriting first encounter and continually unfulfilling sex, Valerie and Miguel tried to improve matters. Miguel, who grew up in a wealthy Puerto Rican family, had a "typically Latin" approach to sex and relationships, according to Valerie. He thought he knew how to please a woman. "He really hated the idea that I felt such an unspecialness when we had sex,"

*"Freak" is commonly used to denote a person who enjoys pornography and/or adventurous sex.

†Several months after our interview, Keisha and her husband got divorced.

Valerie explains. "I tried to go with it. After all, I had been raised on porn from a young age, too. I couldn't help but find that kind of carnal sex exciting, and I tried to accept that this was something deep inside me." They would cuddle afterward and kiss, but it wasn't the same as connecting during the moment.

They attempted various solutions. One night, they rented a porn film together. Valerie tried to get into it, continuing to watch while Miguel started making his moves. "It was a total disaster," she says. "He got mad because I was looking at the movie while we were having sex." Valerie protested that she thought that's what he wanted, which escalated into a blowout. "Every time I thought I was being cool, I somehow upset him," she says.

"Don't Pornify Me"

Most of the time, when it comes to porn, what turns him on turns her way off. One woman's erotica is the next man's snoozefest. Lauren, the mother of two from Virginia, says that though she "wants" to be able to approve of pornography as a radical statement of women's liberation, she has doubts about the way her husband views his *Playboy* collection. "They irritated me on one level because I'm not sure he necessarily had them for revolutionary purposes," she explains. "My husband is clearly not using them for that—he's using them in the totally generic guy way. It's not necessarily problematic, but it's not my favorite thing. Certainly, I would prefer he contribute to the National Organization for Women than look at *Playboy*." In fact, her husband has toted his *Playboy* collection along in two family moves. "He insists they're going to be valuable someday," Lauren says, laughing. "I guess there's part of him that doesn't want to acknowledge that contradiction with his otherwise liberal, feminist outlook."

Lauren believes men's and women's sexuality aren't that different biologically, they're just socialized differently. Theoretically, men who are psychologically sound and in good relationships, who like and respect women, could still look at *Playboy* or a nonviolent form of pornography privately. "Who am I to judge?" she says. After all, her own husband holds views that are supportive of women. "I don't think that having porn in your life means you're unable to engage in normal healthy relationships with women." In fact, she has no idea whether he even still looks at his *Playboys*. "I've never walked in on him," she says. "Quite honestly, with two kids under the age of two in the house, I don't know where he would find the time. If he *does* have time, he ought to be doing the dishes."

For many wives and girlfriends, it becomes immediately clear that the kind of pornography their men are into is all about the men—about their needs and about what they want, not about their women, their relationships, or their families. Men aren't completely in denial, either; they often recognize that their kind of pornography doesn't exactly reflect well on themselves or on their partners. It's usually not surprising to either party when a woman ends up feeling second-rate.

Eventually, Valerie went "to war on the porn thing." She had her ammunition. When she and Miguel started dating, he had just broken off a five-year relationship with a live-in girlfriend. Yet when Valerie stayed over in the apartment they had shared, she found a faded girlie photograph pasted inside Miguel's medicine cabinet. Valerie was fascinated that Miguel's ex-girlfriend put up with it. She asked Miguel if Edie had minded. "She was totally cool," he insisted. From then on, every time Valerie objected to Miguel's pornography, Miguel held Edie up as the exemplary girlfriend. Why should Valerie mind if Edie hadn't? Couldn't Valerie be cool, too? Finally, during one heated argument, Miguel told Valerie she should talk to Edie herself.

So Valerie called Edie, who told her that she and Miguel hadn't had sex for the last two years of their relationship because Edie felt so bad about herself while she was with him. For a while, she had tried to accept Miguel's behavior. She even threw him a birthday party at a strip club. But inside she felt terrible. She hated her body, she felt degraded, the sex was no good. After her talk with Edie, Valerie confronted Miguel again. "He needed to understand why Edie stopped sleeping with him, and how his pornography affected women." When Valerie told Miguel the truth, he lost all color in his face. He had had no idea. Valerie took it upon herself to teach him how his "porn lifestyle" hurt people. It became her mission.

She was quickly thwarted. One day, Miguel was sick and Valerie took the day off from work to care for him. She ran around buying groceries to make him lunch, but when she came back to the apartment, she saw that far from lying sick in bed, he had been on his computer while she was gone, masturbating away. "I freaked out," she says. "I felt completely betrayed." After two years of trying to make things work, Valerie and Miguel broke up. Now she's trying to change her approach. "I never want to be in the kind of relationship where it's just physical. I want my lovemaking back." Part of the problem has nothing to do with the men she dates. "I think I'm creating that carnality myself," she says. "It's like a habit I have and a pattern I inadvertently promote. Men respond to my acting so wild and that just encourages them."

Nowadays, Valerie would prefer to be with a man who isn't into pornography. "I don't know any man who is into porn who has been able to be truly intimate," she says. If she could be a "fascist dictator," she'd make 95 percent of male-oriented pornography illegal to move both sexes toward using erotica. "It sounds so girlie," she says. "But I think that when there are stories and characters involved, it humanizes it."

When men view pornography, they absorb messages about what it means for a woman to be sexy. Not only does pornography dictate how women are supposed to look, but it skews their expectations of how they should act. Men absorb those ideals, but women internalize them as well. According to the *Pornified*/Harris poll, most women (six out of ten) believe pornography affects how men expect them to look and behave. In fact, only 15 percent of women believe pornography *does not* raise men's expectations of women.

Even Molly, the feminist pornographer, finds a disconcerting link between her job selling fantasy and the reality of her love life. On the dating scene, she encounters men who practically salivate when she tells them about her profession. "It's a huge thing with guys in a lascivious way," she explains. "Once I tell a man what I do, it weeds out the idiots. The skeevy guys are almost undressing me immediately." Because she is voluptuous and doesn't dress "conservatively," she says, their misperceptions grow "out of proportion."

Men on Women and Porn

And what do men make of women's feelings toward pornography—pro or con? Thomas, the single, thirty-four-year-old tech support worker from Seattle, says that in his experience, about half of women like pornography and the other half are offended. "There's nothing like a girl who goes through your pornographic video collection and pops one in," he says dreamily. "It means they're sex positive. It shows they're interested in sex in general and there's a higher percent chance they'll have sex with you." As opposed to women who don't like pornography. Affixed to the walls in Thomas's house are posters of women, mostly models. One girlfriend greeted a poster of *Sports Illustrated* model Kathy Smith on his wall with a look of revulsion. "I can't understand that attitude," he says, exasperated. "I mean, this was a fitness model, and she was in a one-piece swimsuit. But this woman just did not like the 'idea' of me having that poster." A woman who would be offended by a poster like that wasn't a good match for him, he decided. "She would be too controlling and demanding, and that's not sexy."

As far as Thomas can tell, a woman who doesn't like pornography is either prudish or judgmental. Or she thinks of sex in a very limited arena—only within a relationship or a marriage. "I can't imagine why a woman wouldn't like pornography, but I guess that's because I'm not a woman," he notes. If he were ever in love with someone who was opposed to pornography—not that he thinks that would happen—he would have to discuss it before getting too committed to the relationship. "I would tell her that it sounds like she has some jealousy issues," he says. "I would want to get to the bottom of why she hates porn so much and why she would feel hurt if I looked at it." He laughs. "Who knows? She might convince me to give it up. I've done stupider things."

In an ideal world, the right woman—the woman he would marry—would make pornography unnecessary. "I've had the feeling before," he says. "She was all I thought about night and day." With that relationship, he went so far as to throw out all his pornography—not at her request, but because he wanted to. (Ultimately, the woman left Thomas for someone else.) That was the only time Thomas gave up pornography altogether, though when he is in a good relationship his use drops dramatically—from a couple of times a day to a couple of times a month. Not that pornography has been an issue every time he's dated a woman; he doesn't exactly bring it up: "I always want to make a good impression, so I'm not going to say something that makes me sound like an ass or a pervert. It's hard to know how a woman will react, so you have to be careful."

Men tend to be of two polarized schools when it comes to women and pornography. They either like their women to be interested in pornography or they don't want their women to have any part of it. Many try to draw a distinct boundary between the women in pornography and the women in real life. A Manhattan woman writes to the advice columnist of *New York* magazine: "I'm a straight woman in my twenties and ever since the first few intense weeks, my boyfriend of eight months has been more distant than I would like during sex (he closes his eyes or watches porn, for instance, and doesn't initiate things as much as I do). When questioned, he said that I'm 'so beautiful and smart' that he has trouble seeing me 'like that.' It wouldn't bother him at all that our sex life had faded if it weren't for my complaining. . . . I can't help feeling lousy and rejected."[29]

Most men tell women their consumption of pornography is natural and normal. The implication is that if a woman doesn't like it, she is controlling, insecure, uptight, petty, or a combination thereof. The woman is demanding. She is unreasonable. He has to give up something he's cherished since boyhood. She's not supportive. She blows everything out of proportion. "Men look at porn," wrote an angry male to Dear Abby successor Ask Amy, in response to her suggestion that a woman confront her fiancé about his propensity to e-mail nude photos of women to his friends:

> They always have and they always will. For women to demand that their husbands or boyfriends give it up is unreasonable and unrealistic. . . . [This woman's] fiancé looks at nudie pictures with his buddies. He's most likely done this since one of his junior high friends sneaked a copy of his dad's *Playboy* into the locker room in 7th grade. . . . If she lets a small thing like this

> ruin what sounds like an otherwise loving relationship, then she doesn't deserve him anyway. And I think it stinks that you agreed with her insecurities.[30]

While many men hope their partner approves or remains agnostic about their own use, they can be outright intimidated by or disapproving of women who use pornography themselves. The 2004 *Elle*-MSNBC.com poll found that six in ten men were concerned about their partners' use of pornography Web sites. One in four said they found such material demeaning to women and online sexual content sleazy. A man usually doesn't want his porn star to be his wife nor his wife to be a pornography devotee; if she's going to look, she should only do so in his presence, when they share it as a couple. No matter what women think, most men still see pornography as "a guy thing." One woman, twenty-two, tells a story to "Cosmo Confessions" about her boyfriend's discomfort with her intrusion into his porn world. "Once a month, my boyfriend has a guy's night out with his buddies. Normally, they shoot pool or go to a ball game. But last month, I overheard him making plans to go to a strip club. It really upset me that he didn't bother asking how I felt about his sticking dollar bills in other women's G-strings. Instead of confronting him, I did some investigating and found out that the night he was planning to go to the club happened to be amateur night, which meant that any girl could get on stage and dance. So I called a few girlfriends, and we headed to the club. After a few drinks, I surprised my guy as one of the novice strippers. He was so shocked that he just froze—until I started undressing. Then he jumped up on the stage and begged me to come down, promising me he'd never go to a nudie bar again."[31]

Denise, the owner of the two Seymour Butts films courtesy of her ex-boyfriend, was surprised by a recent incident with her current beau. Two years ago, she had gone to a strip club with a group of friends and loved it. "The women were gorgeous," she says. "The whole idea was titillating—seeing these men get so turned on. It was very voyeuristic." Eager to return, she asked her current boyfriend to join her. "Why would I want to go watch these women who are all fake when I can have the real thing?" he asked. Denise was taken aback. On the one hand, she was embarrassed that she had been so gung ho to take him to a strip joint. On the other hand, she was pleasantly surprised. "I guess I had this assumption that all guys want to go to strip clubs and having their girlfriends take them there would be a turn-on," she explains. "But it was nice that he just wanted to be with me, and look at me rather than look at other women. That made me feel good."

Individualized.

5

You and Me and Pornography: How Porn Affects Relationships

It wasn't until four years into their relationship, after Kara, a thirty-year-old physician, and her writer boyfriend Rob moved in together, that she realized Rob went online every day for pornography. She knew he liked porn and seemed preoccupied by it, making frequent jokes on the subject, but she had no idea of the extent of his viewing. Still, she didn't think it was a major issue. "I'm very open-minded," she says. "I've done a lot of experimenting. I think I've been with more men than he's been with women." She wants to be clear: "I'm definitely not a prude."

So Kara suggested they watch together. She and Rob rented a video one night, but it didn't turn Kara on at all. "Of course, the men weren't attractive. And the women were all fake, made-up, overly accessorized," she recalls. "There was no intimacy, nothing sensual about it." The tenor of the flick, in fact, resembled their sex life. "Even when he and I were intimate, the sex wasn't intimate. We were two people just sort of taking care of ourselves with each other." Moreover, Rob didn't seem to have much interest in her. "He never told me I was sexy and beautiful," she says. "I don't look anything like a porn star. I'm athletic and slight, not voluptuous in the least."

Rob was picky about the way women looked. He would tell Kara she wasn't getting waxed often enough, and asked her to get the full-on Brazilian wax with centerfold-style "landing strip." "God forbid I ever had a hair on my nipple," she recalls with a laugh. Rob didn't think Kara dressed sexily enough, either. "But if I did put on something sexy, he'd make fun of me. He would say, 'Ooh, those are sexy pants. I don't know if you can get away with those!'" While Rob seemed to like ultrafeminity from afar, if it were staring him in the face in reality, he would run the other way. She thought perhaps he was afraid of the fact that she had more sexual experience than he did, and was generally more comfortable with her sexuality.

Their relationship began to founder for a number of reasons, and they entered couples therapy. Kara thought Rob used pornography as a way to get himself off without having to deal with a woman's vulnerabilities or confront his own insecurities and fears. He wanted no strings attached, no responsibility, no risk. "I think he was intimidated by real-life sexuality and porn was a safe fantasy for him," Kara says. "In retrospect, I don't think he really liked women." At one point, she recalls, they had a huge fight over whether getting a lap dance was cheating. "I said it's cheating because the woman is touching you," Kara explains, "but Rob didn't think so."

Last year, Kara and Rob broke up. "Now if I found out a guy I was dating looked at pornography, honestly, it would set off alarm bells," she says. "That makes me sound so Dr. Laura, but it's true!" Luckily, her new boyfriend, a musician, doesn't look at pornography. Kara asked him outright and he was open with her. "He thinks porn is silly, a waste of time, not a turn-on. It was a huge relief." Moreover, he considers a lap dance cheating, no question. "And it's not like he's Mr. Conservative or anything," Kara says. "He's probably been with more women than I want to know. Maybe it's just that he's more confident and doesn't have something to prove."

Me and Your Fantasy

Monogamy isn't always easy, and each individual brings his or her own desires and fantasies to their sex life as a couple. Indeed, those fantasies can help maintain and enhance a relationship. Nor is it an acceptable alternative to eradicate such fantasies. Is it not his right—and hers as well—to have private fantasies? One partner cannot control what goes on in the other's mind; at some point, one person ends and the other begins.

So what's wrong with fantasizing, assuming one can keep fantasy separate from reality? Eliot, a twenty-eight-year-old musician from New York, would say, "Not a thing." Eliot doesn't look at pornography. Sure, he's seen it, and he can't deny that a lot of it is arousing, but he prefers to let his fantasies fly free-form. "For the most part, I connect best with people I've had some kind of contact with," he explains. "Whether it's a girlfriend or a woman I just met at a party." Eliot has been dating Sophia for six years, and living with her for five. Sophia, who like Eliot considers herself a feminist, is strongly opposed to pornography. Having grown up with a father who not only consumed pornography, but was unfaithful and left her family when she was young, Sophia may have been predisposed to dislike it. Plus, according to Eliot, Sophia isn't a very sexual person; she's too cerebral to completely let loose. They don't have sex as much as he would like; it's a frequent topic of discussion. But he has no intention of breaking up with her; he wants to do what it takes to make it work. For him, fantasy fills that empty space.

Eliot has always masturbated about once a day, whether he has a girlfriend or not. "As a man, you just get this urge to get it out of you several times a day," he explains. "I don't think you can be sated by being in a relationship." He fantasizes about Sophia only a fragment of the time he's masturbating; plenty of other women flit in and out of his mind. "I'm sure if she knew that, she could intellectualize it," Eliot explains. "But I think that she would still find it emotionally disturbing and scary. I bet she would wonder if I would be willing to go off and act out those fantasies anytime." Eliot sees no cause for worry. His father confided to him that after nearly forty years of marriage, he's never been unfaithful, yet to this day, he fantasizes about other women of all ages, whether it's an actress or one of his friends' wives. "Fantasizing about other people helps with fidelity," Eliot says. "I think so-called impure thoughts are actually important. It helps to engage in fantasy so as not to do these things in real life."

In its myriad forms, fantasy is often a component of matrimony. Mark Schwartz, director of the Masters and Johnson Clinic, notes that married couples are contemplating sex with the same person for forty or fifty years. "Naturally people think, 'Why not add a little salt and pepper?' " he says. "I don't think fantasy is necessarily dangerous. There's nothing wrong if it enhances a man's relationship with his wife. But with pornography, what happens too often is that the man starts making love to a picture rather than to his partner." There's a distinction between free-flow fantasy and porn-induced fantasy. While both often involve "other" women, fantasy is an individual's prerogative; pornography is an industry prescriptive. Fantasy is all in the mind; pornography is in print, on video, and online. Fantasy inspires a man to seek out and understand his desires; pornography lets others decide for him. Fantasy is open-ended; pornography designates a beginning, middle, and end. Fantasy is private; pornography is mediated. Fantasy is natural; pornography is artificial and commercialized. Pornography also comes across differently to women than it does to men. "Tell me your fantasies" typically reads as appropriate pillow talk, whereas "Hey baby, check out my favorite porn site" does not.

Many men argue that the women in pornography aren't "real" to them, but that may not comfort a wife whose husband regularly masturbates to schoolgirl images or enjoys watching women receive double penetration coupled by slaps on the rear. Women are significantly more likely than men to say pornography harms relationships (47 percent versus 33 percent).[1] Fewer than one-fourth of women see no harm to relationships resulting from porn, according to the *Pornified*/Harris poll. For a man to say, "Don't worry, you're different from the girls in porn; you're my wife," is hardly reassuring.

Most porn-centric fantasies are far from matrimony-oriented. In the study conducted by Zillmann and Bryant, where a group of adults were exposed to heavy sessions of pornography viewing for a six-week period, 60 percent of those who viewed no pornography during the experiment endorsed marriage as "an important institution"; only 39 percent of those who viewed "massive" amounts of pornography agreed. This shouldn't be a surprise: loving wives and faithful husbands rarely feature in a porno. Pornography is the fantasy of permanent and unfettered bachelorhood; married characters who do appear are pursuing sexual adventures on the side. In pornography, partnered life hampers sexual pleasure.

Yet, despite appearances, pornography isn't precisely a solo activity either. As interviews with men and women attest, porn plays into how people approach and function in relationships. Whether a couple watches together, or one or both partners uses it alone, pornography has a significant role not only in sex but in a couple's sense of trust, security, and fidelity. As Mark Schwartz says, "Pornography is having a dramatic effect on relationships at many different levels and in many different ways—and nobody outside the sexual behavior field and the psychiatric community is talking about it."

Porn Together

When people do discuss the role of pornography in relationships, they assume it's a plus, particularly given the dominant media messages affirming men's involvement with pornography, encouraging women to try pornography themselves, and urging couples to use it together. A March 2004 *Today Show* segment shows just how acceptable pornography has grown:

> Katie Couric: We're back with more of our special *Today's Woman* series and answers to your e-mail questions. . . . Let's go to JW. "My husband likes to look at pornography and it makes me feel inadequate later when we're in bed. How can I compete with this?"
>
> Dr. Gail Saltz: This is also a very common scenario. . . . [Y]ou need to talk to your husband and tell him how it makes you feel. Now, it could be that he would curb it somewhat, but hopefully, what he would do is actually say to you, "But this is what I love about your body." . . . [I]f he really likes that kind of more in-your-face sort of sexuality and you're comfortable with it, you too can put on sexy underwear, you know, do a little striptease.
>
> Katie Couric: But, but, I mean, I—I'm not really into pornography, I just, but, but a lot of, I guess a lot of couples are and why not say—
>
> Dr. Gail Saltz: Just do it together.
>
> Katie Couric: I mean, isn't that what some people do?

Dr. Gail Saltz: [M]en tend to like sort of harder-core stuff than women. Women like sort of softer, romantic, sexy films. So you might say to him, "Let's get something that we'll both enjoy," which is probably going to be a little different than what he's looked at.

Katie Couric: All right. Let's move on, shall we?[2]

Still, discrepancies between what's urged by pornography advocates and sex therapists and what the average American wants in her sex life persist, as reflected in Couric's ambivalence. This is also demonstrated by conflicting poll results. In the Kinsey Institute online poll, which recorded the opinions of a self-selecting group of respondents, 55 percent of Americans professed to believe that pornography can improve relationships. But such polls, despite the attention they generate, likely exaggerate the truth. In contrast, the nationally representative *Pornified*/Harris poll found that only 22 percent of Americans believe pornography improves the sex life of those who look at it. Indeed, only one-third of respondents to this book's nationwide poll believe looking at pornography won't *harm* a couple's relationship.

Nevertheless, many consider pornography to be fine in a committed relationship as long as a couple uses it together. People in their thirties—members of the so-called Generation X—are most likely to believe pornography improves one's sex life, even more so than people in their twenties.[3] Nina, thirty-two, and Sam, thirty-five, both lawyers, are happy to talk about how pornography works for them. Married for a little over a year after a yearlong courtship, the two occasionally watch films together to "spice things up." Usually, they save their pornography for travel. "It's always available in hotel rooms," Nina says. "That makes it something special—part of being away as opposed to just having sex at home. Or we'll watch if we've been working a lot or haven't had as much sex as we'd like. It's almost an aphrodisiac; it gets you going a little faster." Sam agrees: "It's a jump start. In fact, we usually only watch for about five or ten minutes. It's like drinking a martini instead of three glasses of wine."

Sam thinks pornography is just a part of life. "As a guy, you're used to this kind of stuff," he says. Poll data back Sam up. Nearly three in ten men think pornography improves their sex lives, compared with only 17 percent of women. "Guys always look at nudie magazines or whatever it might be. You're likely to hang out at a guy's house and have a beer and pass porn around, or surf the Internet for porn. We like to show each other the good Web sites, that kind of thing."

"You *do*?" Nina interjects, with a startled laugh. She apparently didn't know that Sam looks at Internet pornography on his own, but quickly adds, "I'm not threatened by it or anything. There's something that's so removed from reality about pornography. With women like Jenna Jameson, everything is so perfect, it's beyond the everyday." Nor is the comparison necessarily negative. "On the other extreme, there's porn out there where I feel like I look better than those women," she says. "If I had a lower self-image or if I were much heavier than I am, I might be more sensitive."

Nina believes pornography has improved their sex life. "If we watched it all the time, we'd probably end up stopping," she says. "I don't think we'd get the same benefit if it were just an everyday thing. And I'm sure if I told Sam it bothered me, he would stop." She doesn't completely disagree with those who oppose pornography, which includes many of her friends. "There are a lot of things in our society that could be improved, particularly in the realm of people being objectified. It's probably not a great industry. That being said, I think it's possible for consenting adults to use it in a positive way. We're certainly using it for a good reason. But I would give it up if it meant the industry would be cleaned up." Sam takes "a more First Amendment stance" on pornography. "I don't see anything wrong with it all," he says. Besides, "Nina and I have such a good relationship. Lots of people we know wouldn't allow pornography in their relationship. My friends and I will go out for a bachelor party to a local nude bar and certain guys won't be allowed to go in—I mean, they'll choose not to go in—because it upsets their wives. But Nina and I agree it's human nature to look at other women."

Sex therapists and couples counselors are often behind the move toward mutual acceptance of porn. Sometimes they recommend couples view "erotic" films together, suggesting that, particularly for couples with low sexual desire, such images can generate new ideas, increase tolerance for each other's predilections, and enhance arousal. If a woman is upset or confused by her male partner's interest in pornography, therapists often suggest that perhaps she'll better understand her husband's desires or needs if she explores them as well. Perhaps she'll learn how to better please him or will share in his extracurricular pleasures. And if she finds she enjoys pornography herself, the two of them will have found a bonding mutual interest. In this view, pornography is not an obstacle to the relationship unless a woman allows it to be, and for a woman to judge pornography as anything but positive is considered a condemnation of her man or, at the very least, his sexual life. Discomfort with pornography also becomes a woman's discomfort with her own sexuality.

Some therapists, however, insist certain guidelines be followed. Lexington, Massachusetts–based psychologist and sex therapist Aline Zoldbrod says a close emotional foundation must be in place before they introduce pornography into their sex life as a couple's activity. In the best cases, both people are equally interested. When one person isn't turned on by a particular kind of pornography the other agrees to turn it off, and it's always consumed together. Moreover, Zoldbrod recommends erotica over pornography, though, she admits, some "perfectly normal" couples enjoy raunchier fare. "But you get on a real slippery slope," she cautions. "The majority of porn out there is degrading to women and it's only gotten worse. The women are plasticized; there's no longer as much diversity or naturalism as there was two decades ago." Many people find themselves humoring their significant others through movies specifically selected with their partner's enjoyment in mind. Women will rent slightly more hardcore films in order to win over their men; men suffer through flowery erotica or softer videos to appease their women. What appeals to him rarely appeals to her and vice versa. Nearly all the men interviewed for this book scoffed at the idea of erotica, which they see alternately as "boring," "stupid," "pointless," or a figment of women's imagination. Moreover, given the plethora of edgier choices online, many men prefer looking at Internet pornography to watching movies, but sidling up beside each other at a computer screen hardly sounds like a sexy evening together to most women. And anyway, most men prefer to keep their computer pornography private. Watching pornography as a couple almost becomes a diversionary tactic: If she thinks they're using porn together she's less likely to imagine that he looks at it alone. If she thinks what they watch together is what he likes, she's less likely to be curious about his *real* porn preferences.

What starts off as sexy sometimes ends up disruptive or alienating. Thirty-three-year-old Nathalie, recently married, recalls a turbulent four-year relationship during her twenties in which sexual exploration played a major role. Her then-boyfriend, a musician, was interested in openly watching pornography and re-creating sexual adventures. She was curious and wanted to be a part of his life, so the two watched retro porn from the 1970s together, mutually excited by some of the scenes as well as intrigued by the scenarios in vogue during the early days of home video. One Christmas, the boyfriend bought Nathalie a dildo, which they played with together.

But Nathalie was also curious about her boyfriend's private sex life. When he left her alone in his apartment, she would spy on his computer to see what he looked at when she wasn't around. Porn sites clogged his browser history. As time went on, her boyfriend's private practices seemed to overtake their mutual enjoyment. Toward the end of their relationship, he was looking at what she calls "ridiculously bad porn movies with Robin Hood plotlines." Nathalie felt estranged from the women she saw in these new videos—girls with long nails and cheap hair. "When he started watching these things alone while I was at his place, that spelled the end of our relationship," she recalls. "At about the same time, he bought me a vibrator. It was as if he were saying, 'Here's your toy. You don't need me anymore.' I felt like it cheapened everything."

Women often assume that when they use pornography with their partner, they're satisfying all his sexual needs. That's rarely the case. Judith Coché, a therapist in Philadelphia, tells the story of one couple's spiraling experience. Leigh was an extremely attractive woman—free-spirited, sensual, a provocative dresser. She enjoyed watching erotic movies with her second husband, Max. Leigh thought she and Max had a great sex life—exploratory and a bit risqué. But one evening, checking her e-mail on Max's computer, she found hundreds of porn sites bookmarked on his browser. At first she was taken aback. She told him what she had seen, but rather than get upset or angry, she said she would be happy to make his pornography part of their relationship. "Let's look at it together," she suggested. So they would sit by the computer side by side, exploring at his favorite sites.

Only Max didn't seem into it. Then Leigh caught him looking at the same Web sites secretly. When she confronted Max this time, she was upset. After all, hadn't she been open, hadn't she been willing? Leigh asked Max to go into therapy with her and he agreed. They saw a sex therapist and things seemed to improve. Except for one thing: Max refused to stop looking at pornography on his own. Leigh couldn't understand why. Ultimately, pornography created a wedge in their relationship, and the couple parted.

Leigh is not alone. A woman from Colorado writes to the advice columnist of a women's magazine:

> My boyfriend and I live together. Three months ago, I found him on the Internet looking at porn. I was shocked! We discussed it and decided that if either of us was going to view porn, it would be together and it would be a movie. I felt this arrangement was perfect. He gets his porn and his own porn star—me. Last month, I found him viewing Internet porn AGAIN! We talked about it, he said he was sorry, but I was so upset I couldn't even bring myself to sleep in the same bed with him. He promised all porn would stop. . . . Then I came home last week, and guess what? He's viewing porn on the Internet. . . . I told him it makes me feel that I'm not good enough in bed for him. . . . I love him, he's fine in all other areas, but isn't it time to move on?[4]

Despite the apparent shift among women toward accepting pornography as part of men's sexual nature, the vast majority of women do not like when men look at it. In the 2004 *Elle*-MSNBC.com poll, nearly six in ten women believed their partner was using the Web for sex. Taking part in pornography themselves doesn't seem to alleviate their concerns. Of women who consumed online porn, 37 percent admitted that as a result they worried they might not be able to sexually satisfy their partner. More than one in five felt they needed to do more to maintain their partner's interest, 15 percent felt pressured to reenact scenes their partner had viewed on Web sites, and 12 percent blamed the Internet for the fact that they were having less sex.

Porn Apart

No matter how willing a woman is to participate alongside her man or how much she's willing to compromise, many men do not like using pornography with women, and the vast majority do not want pornography to be an exclusively mutual activity. Some therapists suggest that under the right circumstances a man's use of pornography on his own can still work. Provided, that is, the woman doesn't object to pornography, the man uses pornography in moderation, and he is always emotionally and physically available for his wife. Rarely do all these factors line up. "Pornography is like an escape for men," explains one thirty-one-year-old woman from Ohio. "The man just turns to that instead of his partner as a way of not having to deal with things or go through things with his partner. It prevents people from having intimate, vulnerable relationships." Before she married, one of her boyfriends was an avid user and it showed. "He was obsessive about sexual things—pornography seemed to infiltrate his whole approach to sex." If she were ever to discover her own husband using pornography she would feel hurt more than anything. "I would worry we would no longer be close."

There are reasons men prefer to keep their pornography to themselves; porn is their private realm in which they can do as they please. One of the major attractions of pornography is that it is dissociated from real-life pressures, emotional entanglements, and commitment. For many men, any conscious intertwining or overlap can feel unpleasant and even threatening. To consume pornography in the presence of a flesh-and-blood female, for whom one has feelings and with whom one has developed a relationship, seems disconcerting at best, upsetting at worst. Jonah, a twenty-nine-year-old religion teacher at a Jewish school in Chicago, tries to share some of his pornography with his live-in fiancée of four years, Stephanie, in the hope of improving their sex life. For the past three years, Jonah has had intermittent trouble during intercourse. For a few months, everything will function as it should, but this is followed by months of difficulties in which he is unable to maintain an erection or reach orgasm. Masturbation is an entirely different matter. When Jonah looks at pornography online, he ejaculates with ease. Though Stephanie usually understands, she gets frustrated and feels hurt or annoyed by Jonah's difficulty with her and his pleasure without her.

Sharing Jonah's pornography with her might help, they figured, but Jonah doesn't feel comfortable. "I expect that somehow she's judging me," he says. "Even though we've talked about it and she says she's not. Deep down I feel like she thinks I'm this lecherous or bad person." Watching pornography in a woman's company strikes Jonah as cheesy or ridiculous in a way that makes him want to laugh rather than get turned on. "I guess I generally feel inhibited sexually, and that's part of the problem with having sex," he explains. "I'm afraid of being in the moment because I'm scared of being judged." With pornography, of course, there's no performance anxiety; naturally, he looks forward to it on his own, about five days a week. "Porn is a way for me to celebrate my privacy. I have this space and time to find ways to make myself feel good."

Some women resign themselves to their partners using pornography without them. Boys are raised on it, they figure, and should be expected to indulge. Even if a woman objects, there's not much that can be done, especially if her partner seems unwilling to share the experience or the woman decides she doesn't want to participate. Lily, a part-time secretary and student in Boston, expects her husband to look at pornography; he watches adult pay-per-view a couple of times a week by himself. "Men are visually stimulated and that's what does it for them," she says. "It's like Harlequin romances—women masturbate to the same thing, just a more romanticized version."

Growing up, Lily was exposed to the vagaries of male sexuality. "I lived with a dirty old man," Lily says of her adoptive father. Married later in life, he and her adoptive mother never had a particularly sexual relationship; they were more like roommates than lovers. They even slept in separate beds. Lily suspects her mother may have been raped or molested at some point; she didn't seem interested in sex. Meanwhile, her father would frequently go to strip clubs; he would get so drunk, the club's proprietor would have to call Lily's mom, and the two would roll into the car late at night to pick him up. "I think my dad's porn habit could have definitely contributed to their lack of sex life," she says. "I know my own husband tends to watch more porn and masturbate more frequently when we haven't had sex for a while."

Lily explains, "I'm more tolerant of men's sexual behavior as a result of my upbringing." Some of her friends have criticized her for tolerating her husband's forays to strip clubs. They get upset when their own husbands express their desire to take part, and the men retaliate with, "But Lily doesn't mind when her husband goes!" Lily doesn't think she's being unreasonable. "It's not like I would excuse *everything* under 'boys will be boys,' " she says. "But I've come to expect certain things." For her, lap dances are okay, and a drunken kiss with another woman could be permissible, depending on the context. The only thing she asks is that if her husband plans to cheat, he will divorce her first. Lily isn't as particular as most women are toward the extent of her husband's dalliances.

The Selfish Sex

Still, more often than not, women profess to tolerate men's porn. Jessica says she's okay with it. "I think it's unnatural to expect someone to never look at someone else or fantasize about being with another person," she says. "And doing it with an inanimate object like a porn star as opposed to doing it with a real human being alleviates the risk of becoming attached emotionally." Jessica has had to get used to it. "My boyfriend has a lot of pornography. It's like falling out of his closet and under the bed." She doesn't want to sound uptight. "I mean, most people look at pornography—I even look at it sometimes." Like many women, she is eager to sound game.

But lately Jessica, a twenty-eight-year-old product manager in New York, and her boyfriend, Joe, have been having "a debate" about his habit. "I don't have a problem with his pornography, but to be honest, I feel like our sex life isn't as good as with previous boyfriends." Joe seems sexually selfish and doesn't make as much of an effort to please her. Nor is there much sexual energy in the relationship. "Pornography is about him avoiding his own insecurities. It's safe for him to 'get' his fantasy woman without having to risk his self-esteem in any way," she explains.

At a certain point, Jessica said to Joe, "I think you substitute reality with pornography and, as a result, the real live person you're with isn't getting the same thing you're getting." Joe got defensive. "I use pornography to fall asleep," he said. "It's a comfortable place to be for me."

Many women remark on the lack of foreplay from men who watch a lot of pornography. Because porn is typically about male gratification, it rarely takes the time to plow through any preamble. As Aaliyah, the Southern Baptist from Houston, explains. "I've been with guys who watch a lot of porn and that affected how they view sex." Such men pushed for oral sex all the time, even if she wasn't interested, and they expected her to be over-the-top enthusiastic about it. The problem, she says, is that in pornography, women are always servicing men. "If some guy is watching porn a lot, they're not necessarily going to please women in real life because porn never shows that. There's no foreplay; there's no romanticizing sex. It's just, let's do it." The first man Aaliyah ever slept with insisted on watching pornography while they had sex. They were both twenty years old. "He'd be watching TV while we were in bed. It definitely distracted him." Aaliyah also found herself watching rather than focusing on her partner. "It felt like we weren't even having sex. I was just lying there for him and watching sex on a TV screen." Meanwhile, the sex itself was far from satisfying. He would just "ram into" her. "That's the way he knew how to do it."

Aline Zoldbrod believes many young men today are terrible lovers because they've been raised in a pornified culture. "In real life, sexually speaking, women are Crock-Pots and men are microwaves," the sex therapist explains. "But in pornography, all a man does is touch a woman and she's howling in delight in two minutes. If men think this is how real women respond, they're going to be horrible lovers. Today, pornography is so widely used by young men, they learn these falsehoods. That becomes what it takes to arouse them. There's good evidence that the more men watch porn, the less satisfied they are with their partner's looks and sexual performance." And the more skewed their expectations. According to studies conducted on men during the 1970s and 1980s, men who were continually exposed to pornography were more inclined to agree with statements such as "A man should find them, fool them, fuck them, and forget them," "A woman does not mean 'no' unless she slaps you," and "If they are old enough to bleed, they are old enough to butcher," demonstrating an increase in what researchers term "sexual callousness" among men who consume porn.[5] Habitual male consumers of mainstream pornography—that is, nonviolent but nonetheless objectifying images—appear to be at greater risk of becoming sexually callous toward female sexuality and concerns.[6]

Women can tell. In a 2003 story in *New York* magazine, Naomi Wolf wrote, "Young men and women are indeed being taught what sex is, how it looks, what its etiquette and expectations are, by pornographic training—and this is having a huge effect on how they interact." Wolf cites her interviews with college women, who complain about the effects on their sex lives—the "deadening male libido in relation to real women," the inability of women to be "porn-worthy" in the eyes of young men, the hopelessness of competing on the basis of pornography, and the loneliness induced by porn-infused sex.

Not knowing who to turn to when their boyfriends turn away from them and toward pornography, many women write in to magazine advice columnists for help or ask for support in online forums. Female-oriented Internet communities (chat rooms, bulletin boards, online forums, etc.) teem with discussions on the subject. Every week, an advice columnist across the country addresses the issue; presumably many similar letters go unanswered in print. A woman from Atlanta writes in to "Playboy Advisor," of all places: "My boyfriend is 28, reads *Playboy,* goes to the mall during lunch to check out chicks with his 20-year-old friends, spends around $100 a month on Internet porn, not to mention all the free photos and movies he downloads, and has at least 1,600 images in 'secret' places on his computer. . . . He constantly asks me to dress like I'm a 15-year-old slut and doesn't think twice about starting a fight because I won't wear sluttier clothes. . . . Do you honestly think he doesn't have a problem with porn obsession?"[7] Another woman writes to a local newspaper, "We've been together five years, lived together half that time. . . . Recently, I discovered via the computer that he's fascinated by hardcore pornography, lots of it. When confronted, he said I have no right to be upset, though he's aware it offends me; he insisted I let it go. He's still spending hours looking at this and I'm disgusted. . . . I feel I'm not going to be able to satisfy his urges because I'm unwilling to do what really turns him on. I've tried to discuss how degrading and controlling this seems to me but he's not willing to give it up. I know many people think it's harmless, but it's making me question whether I'm willing to continue a relationship with someone who can disregard my feelings so easily."[8]

Time for Porn

A man has only so much sexual energy. Especially once he's past his sexual peak and easing into his thirties, it's not easy to reach orgasm two or three times a day. Many men are drawn to pornography because it's an emotionally and physically easier route to sexual satisfaction than dealing with another human being, even a willing partner, wooing and pleasing her. Yet pornography further drains men of sexual and emotional energy. In the 2004 *Elle*-MSNBC.com poll, 45 percent of men who used Internet pornography for five or more hours per week said they were masturbating too much, and one in five confessed they were having sex less often with their partners. Which isn't surprising, given that 35 percent said real sex with a woman had become less arousing and 20 percent admitted real sex just couldn't compare to cybersex anymore. "What bothers me is, he claims he's too tired to make love with me, yet he's not too tired to go to these sites and pleasure himself," writes a woman named Madison on the Web site iVillage, under the heading "Husband Porn Watching Hurts My Feelings." "As far as me not being able to reach orgasm, this is going to sound a wee bit gross, but I *am* able to reach orgasm . . . just not with him anymore. . . . He's turned me down so many times claiming he's tired that I often take care of it myself." Dear Dr. Shoshannah, writes another woman on iVillage, to the resident advice columnist, "My husband won't stop looking at porn. He knows that I don't approve and how much it hurts me, but he still does it. . . . The worst part is that I know he does it while I'm at work, and he's home with our 10 month old son. How can I make him stop?"[9]

Many men nonetheless feel the right to reserve a place and time for their pornography. Jonah, the religious-school teacher, cherishes his time alone with porn, a time when he can pursue interests that exclude his fiancée. He likes to view hardcore S&M, going through different phases and fetishes: women in prison, genital torture, rape enactments, water bondage. It excites him to see a woman restrained and helpless, with the man firmly in control. "I like to hear women crying out in pain," he says. "I have these impulses and dark desires, and porn is a way to vent them in a healthy way."

What Jonah likes in pornography is not necessarily how he lives out sex in real life. Though he admits to harboring a lot of anger, he considers himself gentle and considerate, not violent in the least. His sex life with Stephanie, his fiancée and girlfriend of six years, sticks to the tame side. He would like to try light bondage with her—just tying her up, no violence—and she has agreed, but Jonah fears being out of control with her; it's safer to confine those desires to porn. And that means he's getting sexual satisfaction from someone else. "I've had moments where I felt like, I shouldn't be doing this, I should be having sex with Stephanie instead," he admits. "If I would rather masturbate to other women in porn, then it was like I was stepping out on Stephanie. That I wasn't devoting that time to improving our sex life or to our relationship meant something was very wrong with us."

Never mind what a man looks at—where does he get the time? Take your average husband and father. A full-time job often means he's up at six and out of the house by 7:30. Sometimes he goes to the gym after work, but usually he comes straight home for dinner. He would like an hour with the kids at night, to spend more time with his wife, to get in some reading. But there's always something that needs to get done—the dog to be walked, bills to be paid, a bit of housework perhaps. On weekends, he's running between the kids' soccer game, Home Depot, and the occasional round of golf. An extra two or three hours for pornography every week necessarily takes away from something. Of course, it's conceivable that he's all caught up with everything and has time to spare that couldn't be better spent with friends, his wife, his kids, his parents, or himself—reading, improving his tennis game, catching up on paperwork. But for many men, pornography takes away from time and energy that could be better spent on marriage and family.

Tina Tessina, a psychotherapist in Long Beach, California, notes that in her practice problems related to pornography are the impetus for one-fourth of the couples who seek counseling. "It keeps men from dealing with problems that exist in their marriages," she says. "And they need to talk about that, rather than substitute those emotional and sexual needs with porn. It's avoidance." Couples, particularly dual-career couples, already complain about how little time there is for their spouses and families. Imagine the toll that devoting five or so hours a week to pornography takes on family life. Meals that could have been prepared and eaten together, homework that could have been pored over, family movies that could have been watched in each other's company. Imagine the anxiety and tension caused to a mother who knows her husband is online looking at pornography while his son is desperate for Daddy's company.

Pornography isn't just about how the wife and kids feel. Not surprisingly, researchers have found that prolonged exposure to pornography fosters male sentiments *against* having a family at all. For those who already have a family, the urge is to withdraw. In 2000, psychiatrist Jennifer P. Schneider conducted a study of ninety-one women and three men whose spouses or partners had become involved in cybersex. Among couples with children, 37 percent reported that children lost parental time and attention due to a parent's online sexual activities.[10] In the 2004 *Elle*-MSNBC.com poll, men confessed that online pornography was eating up hours formerly devoted to other things. One in five said pornography took away from time they used to spend working, and another fifth said it took time away from hours they used to devote to their partner or their children. Heavier users (five hours or more online per week) were more likely to experience the crunch: 37 percent said time had been eked away from work and 37 percent admitted it took time previously devoted to family.

Furthermore, that so many men consider pornography a private matter, one hidden or downplayed, necessarily creates distance with girlfriends and wives. According to Schwartz, no matter how you look at it, pornography is always a sign of disconnection; those who seek it out often do so because of boredom or dissatisfaction elsewhere in their lives, particularly in their relationships. In his research he's seen a "whole new epidemic," largely related to the Internet, of people using pornography to disconnect from their wives. "If porn is increasing involvement with your partner—you're getting turned on and then running to be with your wife, that's one thing," he says. "But we're seeing more men and women with an intimacy disorder, having trouble connecting with their spouse."

Jealousy

Bridget, a thirty-eight-year-old accountant from Kentucky, had been married for seven years when she witnessed something curious. One evening, she walked into the family's home office and could have sworn she saw a pornographic image flicker across the computer screen in front of which her husband, Marc, sat staring raptly. In a second, it was gone, but Bridget's suspicions were aroused. A few days later, Bridget was using the computer when she saw a strange file listed among the downloads. She opened it to an unmistakably pornographic photo. "I got butterflies in my stomach," she recalls. "I didn't know what to do or say or how to handle it." Bridget decided to confront Marc outright. He said it wasn't his—but who else was there? Of her two sons, the elder, thirteen at the time, lived with his father, her first husband. Her younger son was only eight. "I knew Marc was lying," she says. "And I felt awful." But the couple was on their way to a dinner party and Bridget let it go.

She couldn't stop thinking about it all night. Was this the man she married? Marc had been an exemplary stepfather. A respected man in their hometown. He sang in the church gospel choir. He worked for the state government. Most of his friends were people he had met through church and he was greatly admired by his peers. "When we married, everybody told me what a great guy he was," Bridget recalls. Bridget broached the subject again when they got home. After asking him about it repeatedly, Marc confessed everything. He had been using pornography on a regular basis throughout their marriage—with careful precautions. Pornographic magazines had been delivered to their home in plain wrappers. He religiously deleted the pornography he looked at online (except for that fateful oversight). When looking wasn't feasible at home, he went to adult bookstores and spent money on XXX movies there instead.

Bridget couldn't get over the rejection. "He chose to dwell on these images of other women when he could have been with me at any time," she says. She thought back over their life together. In recent years, Marc hadn't seemed as sexually interested in her; Bridget felt dissatisfied by the frequency with which they had sex. "When I found out he was looking at all this porn, I felt like I had just been thrown away."

According to Lonnie Barbach, a sex therapist in Long Beach, California, when a wife finds out her husband has been using pornography, she feels as if she's not good enough: "Otherwise, why would he be seeking this?" Evan, a twenty-one-year-old college junior majoring in computer science, admits there's truth to women's fears. One of his ex-girlfriends was bothered by his pornography. "She took it as a personal insult," he recalls. "She felt like she wasn't good enough." If his girlfriend saw him reading *Maxim* or *Playboy* or watching a DVD, she would say, "Why do you want to look at that? Aren't I good enough?" The truth, Evan admits, is she wasn't. No woman can possibly be as attractive or sexy as the women in pornography—that's why Evan likes them so much. Moreover, his girlfriend had some self-esteem issues. No matter how many times he told her she was just as good as the women in porn, she wanted him to stop looking. Evan felt as though she was fishing for compliments.

No matter what men tell women, many women feel "less than" the porn girls to whom their boyfriends seem so sexually drawn. As Mark Schwartz of the Masters and Johnson clinic explains, "Imagine if you're a man who has gained some weight and your wife began to subscribe to a magazine where every month she looks at six-pack abs and says, 'Wow, check out those muscles.' Think about how the man would feel. Each time a man looks at a picture of a woman who's eighteen and airbrushed, it's an insult to the woman he's with. He's basically saying, 'This is what really turns me on—not the woman besides me.' "

When Mia and Jesse started dating, she noticed he had stolen cable. As a lark, the two of them began watching porn movies together. At first, Mia, a thirty-four-year-old New Yorker, was into it. There was the novelty factor and a bit of the risqué. "I wanted to be the cool girlfriend," Mia says. "Like, I'll be cool and watch porn and fuck you. I didn't want to come across as Pollyanna-ish." But before long, Mia realized Jesse wasn't watching pornography quite so cavalierly; he insisted they turn on the TV before fooling around and gazed intently at porn movies while they had sex. He seemed more turned on by the television than he was by her. "I'm tired," he would announce during sex and would lose his erection.

"There was something about him needing the objectification of another woman to turn him on," Mia says. "Then he could transfer that excitement to my body." She didn't feel they were truly connecting. "I've had one-night stands that were more intimate," she says. Finally, one night in bed, Mia asked Jesse to turn off the porn. Jesse demurred: "I really like it. It makes me feel more turned on." Mia began wondering if something was wrong with her. Her sexual needs weren't being satisfied; perhaps she was oversexed. Her self-esteem plummeted. "I began feeling very insecure about my body image and I had never been self-conscious before in my life," she says. "I started feeling like I was fat. Like I wasn't sexy enough."

In *Glamour* magazine (interestingly, the same issue that encouraged women to give porn a chance), an article on body image included "the explosion of porn" on a list of reasons why women struggle with their appearance. The article cited a woman who works in a treatment center for eating disorders describing her female patients bemoaning the effect that the pornified culture has on their body image: "They think the guys who look at it are creeps, but they also wonder how they can live up to the surgically enhanced breasts on unnaturally thin women. And they say it's hard to find a guy whose standards haven't been distorted by porn or the media."[11]

For Ashley, the twenty-four-year-old woman from Baltimore who faces her peers' open usage of pornography, the result is major insecurity. Her ex-boyfriend of a year and a half visited a strip club for lap dances every couple of months. "I tried to explain why I thought it was offensive by saying, 'If I walked into your apartment and saw a naked woman straddling you, I would walk right out and never talk to you again.' Just because the same thing happens in a club that sanctions that behavior doesn't make it okay with me." She felt constantly insecure in the relationship, knowing that for her boyfriend, she alone would never be enough. "My body image suffers tremendously," she says. Ashley shared her lack of self-confidence with her ex-boyfriend to no avail. "He reassured me that my body was 'perfect.' A statement that was blatantly contradicted by the porn magazines lying on the floor just a few feet away."

Ashley, an attractive, slender five-foot-five blonde, is otherwise comfortable with her looks. But a "small B," her breasts are not what she sees most men fantasizing about. In bed, she says, men seem to give her breasts cursory attention. "I assume they just aren't turned on by them and so they move on to other parts," she says. Her current boyfriend, whom she's been dating for two months, has done nothing to boost her confidence. He has difficulty maintaining an erection, which she can't help but take personally. An open fan of pornography, he constantly talks about women's breasts. "That's his thing," she says. One time, she swallowed her shyness and mentioned her insecurity with her own endowment. "Yeah," he agreed, "it's such a shame because I'm a real boob man." She almost didn't talk to him again. But, she says, what can she do? "As a heterosexual woman, I can't help but want to attract and please the opposite sex."

Competition

Many women who discover their mate's pornography preferences feel pressured to pony up. If he's not getting it from me, she'll reason, he'll get it from pornography. She's got to compete. Jessica, the twenty-eight-year-old whose boyfriend, Joe, openly consumes porn, is making the effort. "Most of the porn stars he looks at have had a lot of surgery. I don't think most men have a realistic idea anymore of what a normal body looks like," she complains. A small-framed woman, Jessica says she'd never felt uncomfortable or insecure with previous boyfriends. In fact, she loved to undress and prance around naked in front of them. Not with Joe. Once she realized the extent of Joe's pornography habit, Jessica didn't "really like to get undressed in front of him anymore." Instead, "I'll kind of go to the bathroom or wait until the lights are off. I mean, compared with the women he likes to look at, I feel like a little girl." After all, she explains, when you're constantly exposed to women with large breasts and that's what your boyfriend gets off on, you can't help but feel, Well, I'm just not attractive. "Honestly," she says, "I think if I had a C- or D-cup, I'd be a lot more comfortable and I'd probably ask him to throw all his pornography away. But as it is, I can't blame him for what he likes and for making up for the fact that he's not getting it from me. I'm sure he wishes on some level that I were more like Jenna Jameson, so I guess I can't get mad at him."

Jessica is trying to please him instead. At Joe's suggestion ("A lot of my friends' girlfriends have done it"), Jessica consulted a plastic surgeon and she's planning to get implants. "Joe said to me, 'Imagine what an awesome body you'd have if you had big breasts.' Unfortunately, the doctor told me that given my small frame, I shouldn't go bigger than a B. Joe doesn't think that's big enough, but he wants me to do it anyway. I may try to find another doctor."

In recent years, women in the United States and the United Kingdom have gone so far as to get plastic surgery on their genitals. One form of surgery, vaginal tightening, involves cutting a piece of the vagina to make it smaller. Another is more aesthetics-oriented: in a labial reduction, fatty tissue is removed from around the vagina, giving the area a neater, more childlike appearance.[12] But pleasing a man raised on pornography goes beyond improving upon or changing one's appearance. Not only have one in ten women told the 2004 *Elle*-MSNBC.com poll her partner seems more critical of her body since he started looking at Internet porn, one in five said that as a consequence, they felt compelled to do more to keep their partners sexually interested.

Women may be on to something. "The worst is how they say that [porn] makes women feel that they're not good enough, assuming that all women are NECESSARILY good enough, without even wondering if they make enough efforts to be better than porn for their man," complained one man recently in an online "support group" discussion about pornography.[13] According to Diana Russell, a sociologist who has researched pornography for decades, men who look at pornography repeatedly "come to think that unusual sex acts are much more frequently performed in sexual relationships all over the country, because of course that's what they're seeing in porn." They begin to believe that anal sex and S&M are common practices, part of every happy-go-lucky couple's repertoire. And if they're not doing it, something's wrong with them. They're not adventurous enough. They're missing out. And what to do about it? Bring it home to your wife. Introduce it to your girlfriend.

Because all her male friends and every man she has dated is fixated on porn, Ashley can't help compare what they view in pornography with what they expect from real sex. "Their view of sex is really skewed. It's gotten dirtier, raunchier. They want you to do a lot of degrading things." Many men don't even realize that what they're asking for is degrading or unpleasant to women. The pornographic videos and online clips they watch show women smiling in anticipation of "facials" (the term for men ejaculating on a woman's face), lapping up the semen on their faces and breasts, wiping it all over their bodies, savoring its effects, cooing with delight, and thanking their sexual partner for his generosity. What transpires rarely in real life is especially appealing as a fantasy, so pornography glorifies the practices that women are least likely to accommodate. No wonder male expectations shift. Every guy, Ashley says, asks for anal sex—"It's huge now." The most popular thing these days is to "do it from behind." All the men she's been with since college—and her friends remark on this, too—want to ejaculate on their faces (and their bodies, to a lesser degree). The big thing is "neck and above." Ashley refuses to give in unless she's in a serious relationship. The last two guys both asked her to do so. "I think they were testing the waters," she says. "And I think if I had done it, they would have seen that as the norm. Whereas for me, that's definitely *not* the norm." With her ex-boyfriend of a year and a half, she eventually let him ejaculate on her. "I didn't mind so much because we were very close."

Trust

Surprisingly, many women have no idea their husbands or boyfriends would even consider looking at pornography while in a monogamous relationship. Couples therapists tell stories of wives shocked to find their husbands glued to their computers at night blearily masturbating away. They find pornography downloaded onto the family's computer hard drive and are scared to ask whether it belongs to their husbands or their teenage sons. A girlfriend discovers an online cache of sites on her boyfriend's computer that baffles as much as it repels: prepubescent girls, hairy women, two-men-on-one-woman action, group sex in Thailand. Is *this* what he likes? "Men I counsel generally keep pornography a secret from their partners," says Marlene Spielman, a New York psychotherapist. "They know they shouldn't be doing it because they're in a relationship because—let's face it—when you masturbate with pornography, you really are with someone else, one way or another."

That's not how most men see it. Boys often look at their first pornography together and sign a wordless pact: This is our secret. And those boys grow up to be men who don't tell their wives what they're looking at. Scott Halzman, a practicing psychiatrist who specializes in counseling married men, says that if a client came to him and said he was enjoying a "healthy use of pornography" and not telling his wife, Halzman would urge him not to confide. "If you want to call that secrecy, fine," Halzman says. "But like most fantasies it's more exciting if it's kept personal. It loses its mystery if your wife knows." Halzman has struggled with how to handle the issue in his practice. "Yes, it creates a fundamental deception in a relationship," he acknowledges. "But I'm torn. The hallmark of my work is to teach men how important it is to respect their wives' opinions and to find ways to meet their wives' needs, and if you're off masturbating to pornography it would seem you're somehow robbing your wife of something that belongs to her. But I have to believe that it's not necessarily the case if the man isn't addicted to porn but is just using it." As Halzman sees it, if a man uses pornography, he either doesn't tell his wife or he does and risks her wrath and disappointment. "Some of the men who are most successful in marriage are not open with their wives all the time," Halzman allows. "The reality is most women feel a shudder of discomfort about pornography. I think women say intellectually that it's okay for a guy to look at pornography, but psychologically, it makes them feel bad. It's difficult to justify to them."

Once women discover their spouses' pornography use, most are shocked that their husbands would blatantly disregard their feelings on this matter, but women are very naive about the way men operate, says psychotherapist Tina Tessina. "Every woman seems to think her man is some kind of saint. But most don't realize just how susceptible men are to sexual activities." Women in her practice get very upset about it. "They're usually shocked when they find out their husbands are looking at porn." Bridget, the mother of two in Kentucky, says finding her husband's secret stash "pretty much wiped out the trust in our relationship." Once she knew about Marc's years-long subterfuge, "I would find myself worrying all the time. If I were going to take a trip for my job, I'd wonder about what he might be looking at while I was gone." She tried to keep her eyes peeled, maintaining a tight rein on the family finances and monitoring Marc's computer use. She couldn't trust his promise not to use pornography anymore. There's an inevitable side effect of men's secrecy around porn: if men are hiding it, women figure, there's got to be a reason. If they're hiding it, they don't want their wives and girlfriends to know. If they're hiding it, there's got to be cause for worry. If they're hiding it, it's got to be wrong.

Cheating

A man spends more time away from his wife. And the time is spent with other women. He's getting sexual release from these women. He's getting a certain kind of "emotional" satisfaction, be it excitement, relaxation, an ego boost, a sense of power. Sure, in an affair, there's another human being involved, whereas in pornography there isn't, or, at least, not quite. But there is still one human being involved: the husband. According to Jennifer Schneider's study, about one-third of those married to a cybersex user consider their partner's online sexual activities akin to adultery.[14] In the 2004 *Elle*-MSNBC.com poll, one-third of women said they considered their partner's online activities to be cheating, and one in three felt "betrayed." The nationally representative *Pornified*/Harris poll found that overall, 34 percent of women see men using pornography as cheating in absolutely all cases. Ashley, the Baltimore twenty-something whose boyfriends are open about their porn, says she knows "rationally" that pornography isn't cheating, but emotionally, it feels as though it is. "Because you're getting off to other people, not the person you're with," she explains. "How is that supposed to make me feel?"

Yet only 13 percent of men in the *Elle*-MSNBC.com poll considered online sexual activity to be cheating; in the *Pornified*/Harris poll, only slightly more—17 percent—of men equated pornography with cheating. Indeed, most men tend to see pornography as *not* cheating: a man has his needs and he's fulfilling them in a way that prevents him from cheating on his wife with a real woman. According to the *Pornified*/Harris poll, 41 percent of men say pornography should never be considered cheating (only 18 percent of women felt the same way). Trey, a married film editor, explains, "There's a big difference between porn and having sex. Porn is just an extension of fantasizing and if porn is cheating, then everybody cheats all the time." No, Trey would never cheat on his wife, Eliza. Whereas in previous relationships he felt he had to keep his porn secret (his other girlfriends all disapproved of pornography), with Eliza he can be more open. At the same time, were Eliza to insist he stop, he would probably continue to use it privately. "What she doesn't know doesn't hurt her," he explains.

This is how men deal with monogamy, Trey says. Part of him wishes he had slept with ten other women before marrying—in addition to the fourteen women he did sleep with—but it didn't work out that way. Pornography helps him cope with that reality. "This probably contradicts what I said about cheating," he hedges. "But there's very little that's different about fantasizing and having sex." For men, he continues, having sex with a woman for the first time is always the best, and with pornography, Trey can have that "first time" *all* the time, with as many women as he likes. "You get to be with her once—see what she looks like naked and have sex with her—then never see her again. It's so much less complicated than having an affair in real life."

The opposite sex doesn't always see it that way. "Dear Harlan," writes one woman to the syndicated male advice columnist, "I have been dating a wonderful man for a little more than a year. . . . Last night, I walked in on him masturbating while looking at porn on the Internet. . . . I couldn't help but feel betrayed, as if I was cheated on. It makes me think he will cheat on me someday. It also turns me off from him, because now I worry that he's thinking about someone else when we're together. . . . Am I overreacting? Should this be a major issue that I should debate breaking up over, or is it something that guys just do and I have just been naïve about before this?"[15]

Not all men are unaware of how pornography can signify betrayal. After a year of complaining about her boyfriend's lap dances, Ashley felt as if she finally broke through. "We had this big talk toward the end of our relationship," she says. "For most of the time we were together, he thought I was being ridiculous when I got upset about pornography. But eventually he told me he had no idea it seriously hurt me." Ashley believed him. After all, nobody had told him that what he was doing was wrong. His parents knew about his strip club partying. "They just laughed," she says. "Their attitude was, 'Boys will be boys.'" The last time his friends planned a strip club jaunt, her boyfriend stayed behind for her sake. That was a big step in Ashley's mind. "But he lied to the guys so they wouldn't know the real reason he wasn't going."

The lies of pornography. "No matter what you do, you cannot hide your porn from friends and family," says a married father of one. "Despite the fact that my wife doesn't care that much, it is still awkward and embarrassing when you leave porn in the VCR and her sister finds it, or the video store sends out a notice about a porn video being late, or she walks in on you whacking off." Pornography, he explains, leads to "lots of small lies." Some of his friends who have been caught with pornography have claimed to their girlfriends that it was his (even when it wasn't) in an effort to avoid repercussions. The pain of uncovering pornography is clearly not an isolated or easily resolved problem.

Rupture

Once she's discovered his pornography, what next? Psychotherapist Marlene Spielman says when a woman finds out about a man's pornography habit, the result is usually a back-and-forth of strong emotions. The woman typically feels hurt, angry, and betrayed. Confronted husbands often begin with denial before confessing the truth, followed by a big fight, blaming, and accusations. He may accuse her of driving him to it; she might point to his avoidance of problems in the relationship. After Bridget reproached her husband, Marc, about his pornography, Marc promised to change. Bridget asked him to talk to their pastor, and Marc reluctantly agreed—after she threatened to tell the pastor herself. The pastor, she says, was merciful with Marc, perhaps too merciful. Bridget felt as if their church's attitude was, "You gave in to a natural weakness. It's understandable." So while Marc continued to see the pastor, Bridget took additional measures. She bought a new computer and programmed it with children's settings, creating special e-mail accounts for all members of the family. Only her elder son, then nineteen, was allowed full access. Problem solved.

Three months later, her nineteen-year-old approached her privately.

Someone had been using his e-mail account. His search history revealed Web sites he hadn't visited; his account was loaded down with porn. Bridget was devastated. "I felt so betrayed and hurt," she says. "It was like being stabbed in the back. The person you're supposed to trust and depend on being honest with you . . . and then you discover they've been lying to you about their secret life." The episode set Bridget "way back emotionally." It had been four years since her initial confrontation with Marc, and she thought "all that" was behind them. Too angry to cry at that point, Bridget demanded that Marc apologize to her son.

Around this time, Bridget also learned that her younger son, now thirteen, was looking at pornography as well. He had installed another Internet provider service on the family computer and was spending hours online. Bridget found a hardcore lesbian movie downloaded on the computer. At first she wasn't sure who was at fault—Marc had supposedly stopped again. When she realized it was her younger son, she broached the subject with him and, after several denials, he confessed. "My reaction was much worse than it had been with my husband," she recalls. She told him that though what he was looking at might seem innocent now, he didn't know where it might lead and how it might affect his life. But Bridget feels she has only so much control. Her son lives primarily at the house of his father, who doesn't think pornography is a big deal. The boy's father shrugged off Bridget's concerns, which didn't surprise Bridget since she knew from her first marriage that he liked pornography himself.

More women are installing programs like NetNanny on their computers to limit home computer Internet access to PG-rated Web sites. According to one filtering company, WiseChoice.net, more than half the company's 3,000 customers are adults who use the software not to block their kids' access but to keep themselves and other adults from looking.[16] Others see the need for a stronger dose of intervention. In the *Elle*-MSNBC.com poll, one in four women said they were concerned their partner had an "out-of-control habit" with online pornography, and one in four divorced respondents said Internet pornography and chat had contributed to their split. At the 2003 meeting of the American Academy of Matrimonial Lawyers, a gathering of the nation's divorce lawyers, attendees documented a startling trend. Nearly two-thirds of the attorneys present had witnessed a sudden rise in divorces related to the Internet; 58 percent of those were the result of a spouse looking at excessive amounts of pornography online. According to the association's president, Richard Barry, "Eight years ago, pornography played almost no role in divorces in this country. Today, there are a significant number of cases where it plays a definite part in marriages breaking up." In an online forum on the Web site Women Online Worldwide, a woman who identifies herself as "anti-pornography" explains:

> A couple of years ago I discovered that the man who had lived with me for ten years, had supported my activism in every way—ideologically, practically, and emotionally—was in fact using Internet pornography himself. . . . What did I do? Banished him from my life. . . . No personal relationship is worth more to me than the lives of the women who are hurt and abused in the making or consumption of pornography. . . . They say pornography is "free speech." Um . . . who, exactly, is speaking here? Pornography is men telling lies about women. Pornography kills love and any sense of humanity so that some big fatcat somewhere can make megabucks through hate speech against women.[17]

Matrimonial lawyers across the country attest to the growing docket of cases. "Pornography wrecks marriages," says Marcia Maddox, a Vienna, Virginia–based attorney. Among the five attorneys in her office, there's always a case involving pornography under way. In one case, a wife found out her husband was involved in Internet pornography while she and their daughter were working on a school project. The two were seated at the family computer together when suddenly a large window popped up depicting a giant penis ejaculating. Horrified, the mother quickly shut down the computer. She then hired a computer technician, who discovered a trove of hardcore pornography on the hard drive. The couple divorced and the mother was awarded sole custody. In another case that also ended in divorce, the husband was regularly using porn on the computer until two o'clock in the morning. According to Maddox, most cases settle rather than go to court because it's embarrassing for the man's pornography to come out in public, particularly when children are involved. "I'm sixty-two," Maddox says. "I didn't grow up with computers and these cases blow my mind." The fact is, "using pornography is like adultery. It's not *legally* adultery, which requires penetration. But there are many ways of cheating. It's often effectively desertion—men abandoning their family to spend time with porn." Often the judges find that even if children aren't directly exposed to a father's pornography, they are indirectly impacted because their fathers ignore them in favor of porn. Visitation in such cases may be limited.

Mary Jo McCurley, an attorney who has practiced family law in Dallas since 1979, agrees. In the past five years, more and more cases are brought forth in which a husband's pornography is a factor. "We see cases in which the husband becomes so immersed in online porn it destroys the marriage," she explains. "Not only is it unsettling for the wife that he's using other women to get off, but it takes away from the time they could spend together as a couple." In divorce cases these days, enormous amounts of time and money are spent recovering pornography off computers. "You can hire experts who specialize in digging through hard drives," McCurley says. "There are people who have made a profession out of it. It's become quite common in Texas divorce."

Still, many women equivocate over how to handle their husband's use, questioning themselves and their feelings. "Dear Abby," writes one woman from Kentucky, "My husband has run up telephone bills amounting to $15,000. . . . When I leave the house, he immediately puts our daughters in their rooms and goes online to porn sites or to talk to women. He is taking much-needed money from me and our children to get his kicks. I have begged him to stop, but the problem is getting worse. Should I stick to my word and leave him if he doesn't quit?"[18]

Denial and Rationalization

Sadly and perhaps not surprisingly, women tend to blame themselves when their partners stray into pornography. "Dear Dr. Ruth," writes a woman, "I've been married for two years now (second husband). My husband seems to be very interested in sex, i.e., Internet pics, magazines, watching Playboy, tele-companions; however, I'm not getting any! . . . We've talked some about it, but I feel that at this point I'm begging. . . . I love my husband with all my heart. We are raising two teenagers. Sometimes it seems like we're a great team at being parents, but not at being a couple. What should I do? I am seriously concerned with this problem and need some help."[19]

But rather than be consoled for their distress, women are reinforced in this self-blame—not only by their partners, but also often by advice columnists, sex therapists, and other members of the therapeutic community. Such experts would sooner urge a woman to ignore the problem, stop complaining, or learn to better "understand" her man than to tell the woman she's normal for feeling the way she does. The days are long past when using pornography was considered denigrating to one's partner and to women overall. Such ideas have been shuffled aside like a dreadfully un-revivable 1970s fashion trend. Instead, women are told to get with it. One woman, writing to an online sex coach about the trauma of discovering pornographic pictures on her partner's computer after seven years together, is summarily dismissed and reprimanded: "There is a wise old saying. 'One man's trash is another man's treasure.' What appears disgusting and dirty to you may be your partner's path to sexual pleasure. . . . I know that for you and many women who trip over sexy pix of women on their loved one's computer (or elsewhere), this can be a shock. . . . It may even trigger reactions such as, 'Am I not enough for him? . . . Does he want to be with them instead of me?' Let me assure you that throughout time, men have been and will be peeking at pictures of pretty women, clothed and naked. Even cave-dwelling dudes probably did this. And typically, it has nothing to do with their feelings for the women in their lives. In fact, perhaps YOU violated HIM by peering into his stash of images, which he may have reserved for his most private moments away from the real woman he likes or loves. . . . I say let him have his toys. And stay out of his files. . . . You're going to have some explaining to do about that deleted file, especially if your relationship matures into a long-term trusting bond."[20]

Thus women are told that their man's consumption is not only okay, but they're wrong to get upset by it. And it's not just men delivering the bitter medicine. "Here's the hideous truth," *Elle* magazine columnist

E. Jean Carroll advises a reader distressed over her boyfriend's habit. "Almost every guy you know is looking at this odious tripe. And the reason? Your man is simply following the plan Mother Nature devised. To ensure the propagation of the species, Ma created a rabid desire in the male beast to gaze at (and poke the blazes out of) naked women. . . . So if your man watches too much porn (more than an hour a week, in my opinion) . . . What to do? I love your anti-bourgeois 'Baby, let's look at dirty movies together' idea."

Jonah, the S&M fan from Chicago, used to feel terrible about his habit, but now, with the help of therapy, he's changed his attitude. His therapist, a woman he's been seeing for several years, tells him there's no reason to feel guilty; there's nothing wrong with pursuing his fantasies through pornography. "She's really encouraging," he says. "It's helped me get over the guilt." Nowadays, Jonah is trying to convince himself that pornography is a harmless outlet for perfectly human desires. As he sees it, men are wired to want to have sex with everyone, but social and psychological reality dictate that they can't. Still, that's not *his* fault. He used to feel bad when he walked down the street lusting after every attractive woman he saw; he worried intensely that pornography was affecting the way he viewed women, that it gave him a low opinion of women and corrupted his idea of what an attractive woman could be. His therapist disagreed. She told him pornography had no impact on how he viewed or treated women.

Jonah used to think pornography got in the way of his sex life; now he views it as an enhancement. He has trained himself to think about pornography while having sex with his fiancée, Stephanie, in order to keep himself excited and involved, and told her what he was doing. At first, it affected her sense of self, as she revealed during couples therapy. But after three years of intermittent impotence, Stephanie is willing to let Jonah do whatever he can to maintain his erection while they're together. She's desperate to be sexually satisfied in her relationship, and Jonah thinks pornography helps. What once felt like cheating to Jonah now feels like a boon to his sexuality.

Meanwhile, women beat themselves up over "driving" their partners to porn. Perhaps it was her own fault: she wasn't a good enough wife or sexy enough lover. Women married to pornography users echo each other's pain. A thirty-eight-year-old mother of two from a Chicago suburb says her husband's pornography made her feel inadequate. Her husband seemed to demand perfection and she felt like a constant disappointment. She didn't wear the right clothes. She didn't look right when she wore them. She never performed in bed the way he wanted her to. "I began to feel physically like I was not a sexual being," she recalls. "I knew I could never measure up, so I couldn't compete." She tried watching pornography with her husband. "If you can't beat them, join them," she figured. "But I also had this sense I was reaching new lows. I was compromising my own feelings and beliefs." A teacher from Dallas says that when she found out her husband was using pornography behind her back, she felt sick and angry. "Those women are so unreal," she says helplessly. "They're so different from the normal average person. I didn't measure up at all." She wondered if it was because she was a bit overweight. "Maybe that's what drove him to this," she worried. But then again, even if she were her perfect weight, she would never look like them. She figured she may as well just give up.

Women tend to reach the same sad conclusion: Porn is inevitable and there's nothing they can do. Part of the reason men and women come to believe that pornography is so excusable, so natural, so unavoidable stems from what they learned growing up—the lessons their parents taught them, the shrugs and excuses from other adults, the advice and encouragement from friends and peers, and the messages from the media surrounding them during their formative years. Boys who are told that "boys will be boys" become men who are boys. Dads who hand down pornography teach boys a lifelong lesson: Pornography is a natural male imperative. Mothers who pretend not to notice set standards for the wives who follow. Today, a pornified culture reinforces and expands on those messages. And then the next generation comes along.

Could they all be right?

6

Born into Porn: Kids in a Pornified Culture

How does a boy become a childhood user of pornography, grow up to be an adult user of child pornography, and eventually become the father of children who use pornography? Looking back over his lifelong involvement with porn, Charlie feels as if he can spot the signs. His life seemed overly sexualized from a very early age. Growing up, he heard his father make constant references to sex, either overtly or through innuendo. Yet his dad had a poor image of the opposite sex, treating his mother and other women in ways Charlie deems "sexist." He maintained an authoritarian home with strict rules and discipline. On the outside, Charlie obeyed his father. He became a "stoic and disciplined person." Inside, Charlie developed into an introverted young man, socially inept and ill at ease.

Charlie first saw a softcore magazine when he was eight years old, in 1973, at a friend's house. He turned to hardcore magazines, again with friends, at age eleven. The boys would fool around while gazing at the magazines together, mostly group masturbation. Around this time, Charlie says, he became aware of his father's video collection. He didn't actually see his father watching them or view them himself, but he knew they were around.

Even as a child, Charlie felt that looking at pornography was wrong. His family regularly attended a Presbyterian church. His religious upbringing made him feel guilty about pornography and he fell into a cycle of compulsive behavior and remorse. But despite his doubts, Charlie's use escalated. He became the school's purveyor of pornography, buying magazines in bulk and reselling them to guys at school at the time. He earned the nickname "Pervert," a moniker of which he was proud. Preoccupied with sex, Charlie took to peeping, sneaking glimpses into the girls' locker room at school and watching his neighbors through the bedroom window at night. At eighteen, he saw his first porn movie at an adult drive-in theater. He didn't have to wait for another porn flick to roll into town; it was 1983 and the Betamax revolution had begun. Charlie started to rent his movies. He soon learned that he and his father were frequenting the same video rental store.

My First Porno

Children come across pornography in a variety of ways. The old-fashioned way is through older peer or family introduction: a cousin, brother, or uncle gives pornographic magazines to a boy on the cusp of puberty, or the boy discovers a relative's stash on his own. Parents might pass along pornography inadvertently or carelessly. "Dear Amy," writes a seventeen-year-old girl to the *Chicago Tribune* advice columnist, "I used my father's computer and found something very alarming. In addition to an adult entertainment toolbar, I found various pornography sites . . . most of the sites were teen pornography . . . I would like to blame this on the male nature; however I can't get past the fact that my dad is looking at obscene pictures of girls my age. I approached my mom about this, but she just blamed it on the fact that he is a man and men 'do things like that.' "

Some parents, especially fathers but mothers as well, actually encourage their kids to pick up on pornography or knowingly look the other way. Christina, the divorced mother of two who subscribes to pornographic Web sites, has a fifteen-year-old son who has kept pornographic DVDs and comic books lying around since he was twelve. His father, an ex-boyfriend of Christina, supplies him with pornography, which

Christina allows him to hang on his bedroom walls. Her twelve-year-old daughter thinks the pictures are "gross," though Christina is fairly certain she has also looked at porn online, mostly out of curiosity. From what Christina has observed, her son has some "pretty far-out tastes"—bondage, girl-on-girl, bukkake, cum shot videos—admittedly far more hardcore stuff than she herself saw at his age. "It doesn't bother me," Christina says. "When I was that age, I was just as curious and would be looking through my dad's stuff." Still, Christina tries to keep her own pornography out of her children's reach. She makes sure to erase her Internet history every night after being online. Yet there are no rules, no Internet filters, no discussion.

Whether parents pass down their own pornography deliberately or inadvertently, whether they try to hide it from their kids or keep it out of the household, children today often come across pornography on their own and don't necessarily wait for hormones to kick in. They might flip to a cable channel on television, find a public access program, or order a pay-per-view movie. They might discover a video or DVD tucked away in their neighbors' or older brother's collection. According to a 1995 study of teenagers in California conducted by Gloria Cowan and Robin Campbell, 83 percent of high school boys and 48 percent of girls said they had seen explicit pornographic videos or films. Three in ten boys admitted to watching pornography at least once a month (compared with one in ten girls). On average, boys said they saw their first film at age eleven; girls at age twelve. Boys admitted to having seen a dozen pornographic films or videos, while girls saw an average of five.

Those figures are surely much higher today, with children increasingly discovering pornography on the Internet. According to a 2001 study by the Kaiser Family Foundation, seven in ten fifteen- to seventeen-year-olds admitted to "accidentally" stumbling across pornography online. Girls were more likely than boys to say they were "very upset" by the experience (35 percent versus 6 percent). While a majority of fifteen- to twenty-four-year-olds (65 percent) said they thought viewing such pornography could have a serious impact on people under eighteen, younger kids were more likely to take it in stride: 41 percent of fifteen- to seventeen-year-olds said it wasn't a big deal. Learning to like pornography online is fast becoming the new norm. According to the

Pornified/Harris poll, 71 percent of eighteen- to twenty-four-year-olds agreed with the statement "I have seen more pornography online than I have seen offline (in magazines, movie theaters, TV)"—which was twice the number of baby boomers who agreed with the statement. More than half admitted it's hard to go online *without* seeing pornography. This isn't an exclusively American phenomenon. A 2004 study by the London School of Economics found that 60 percent of kids who use the Internet regularly come into contact with pornography.[1]

It's easy for kids to come across pornography online, considering the ploys pornographers use to lure them, whether through deceptive URLs or by linking pornographic pages to more innocent content. Pornography has become seamlessly integrated into the mainstream World Wide Web. In a study of peer-to-peer file-sharing networks, the U.S. Customs Department's CyberSmuggling Center found that searching for innocuous phrases normally used by children (phrases included the name of a popular female singer, child actors, and a cartoon character) elicited a slew of pornography. More than half of the downloaded images were either adult pornography, cartoon pornography, child erotica, or child porn.[2] In another nationwide study of children ages ten to seventeen, conducted in 1999–2000, nearly three-fourths of kids' accidental exposure to online pornography occurred while they were searching or surfing, often through misspelled Web site addresses; exposure through e-mail and instant messaging also ranked high. Of the images encountered, 94 percent were of naked people, 38 percent of people having sex, and 8 percent involved sexual violence.[3] A more recent study by Congress found that of the nation's 70 million Internet pornography users, 11 million—or 16 percent—were under the age of eighteen.[4]

If kids can't get pornography at home, there's always the library. "I love the library," writes Stephen Jones, a fourteen-year old boy from Washington State, in his home newspaper. "I love to read. I love the Internet service the library provides; but we have a problem. Pornography is available through the library Internet. The library has filters, but as it stands now anyone over the age of 12 can have the filters taken off."[5] A study of the nation's public libraries in 2000 confirmed the scope of the problem. David Burt, a public librarian, discovered more than

2,000 complaints involving pornography at libraries in 1997 and 1998* (29 percent of the country's 9,767 public library systems participated in the study). Cases involved children accessing pornography on the library's computers, situations in which adults exposed kids to pornography in the library, cases in which pornography was specifically left for children, and instances when pornography was left on the printer or computer screen.[6] In his study, Burt cites one librarian in Washington who told him, "On Monday of last week a group of about eight to ten teenage boys came to the library and asked if they could get pornography on the Internet. I replied that they could. . . . Later that afternoon, one of the younger boys (elementary age) said that the big boys had shown some dirty pictures on the computer. . . . When I applied to work at the library, running a porn shop was not in the job description. . . . We are supplying pornography to minors without their parents' permission or knowledge."

Kids can also find pornography at school. At Monessan High School outside of Pittsburgh, male students learned some interesting lessons in their social studies class. The thirty-five-year-old teacher, Joseph Fischer, showed boys pornography on the Internet during "free time" that Fischer, who also served as the football coach, allowed students to take during class. Two students alleged that between December 2002 and December 2003, Fischer downloaded pornographic photographs and film clips for the kids' consumption. It was only after Fischer allegedly assaulted a fifteen-year-old student that other students came forward with their complaints.[7] At North High School in Arizona, a student reported witnessing his math teacher, Richard Hutchison, fifty-one, viewing pornography on his computer while in the classroom. Hutchison, also the school's tennis coach and a nine and a half–year veteran in the Phoenix Union High School District, was given thirty days to fight his firing. Hutchison claimed he visited the site by accident. This wasn't the first time Arizona's school system has faced the problem. Every year, five or six complaints roll in, all with the same charge: teachers

*Imagine how much higher the number of incidents by 2005—an eon in Internet time.

looking at Internet pornography while in the classroom.[8] A history and government teacher at the Tulsa High School for Science and Technology in Oklahoma resigned after three students between the ages of fourteen and sixteen spotted pornographic pictures on his computer. The teacher, Donald Eric Cherry, twenty-seven, quickly hid the pictures, but when students asked to see them again, Cherry complied. Eight of the photographs on his computer allegedly depicted child pornography. Cherry pleaded guilty to three felony counts of exhibiting obscene material and was sentenced to prison. As he explained in court, "I'm very big into escapism and leaving reality behind." In going to prison, Cherry also left behind a nineteen-month-old daughter.[9]

If their teachers don't show it to them, kids find it on their own. At Richland Middle School in Texas, students learned to bypass the school's Internet filters and look at pornography during computer class. According to one female student, age thirteen, kids congregate in the back row of the classroom after finishing their exercises in order to look at pornography. The computer teacher has never once tried to monitor their activities. "Everyone tries to tell us there are blocks on it, but half the kids are looking at this stuff on the computer," she explained. Students would create pornographic screensavers, but simply clicked them off when the teacher walked by. At the same school, another teacher was disciplined for accessing pornography from the school's computers. All this happened despite the administration's insistence that their filter system effectively stymied all attempts to access inappropriate material.[10]

Statistics show that about half—if not all—teenagers are exposed to pornography one way or another. A 2004 study by Columbia University found that 11.5 million teenagers (45 percent) have friends who regularly view Internet pornography and download it.[11] The prevalence of teens with friends who view and download Internet pornography increases with age, from nearly one-third of twelve-year-olds and nearly two-thirds of seventeen-year-olds saying they have friends who use online porn. Boys are significantly more likely than girls to have friends who view online pornography: 46 percent of sixteen- and seventeen-year-old girls say they have friends who regularly view and download

Internet pornography, compared with 65 percent of boys the same age; the comparable percentage for twelve- and thirteen-year-old girls and boys are 25 percent and 37 percent, respectively.[12]

"Who Would Ever Be Interested in *That*?"

Despite his childhood interest in pornography, Charlie's real sexual experience lagged; ironically, he was afraid of sex and still felt morally conflicted about sex outside marriage. When he married his high school sweetheart, Elise, at age twenty, Charlie was still a virgin. Elise knew of Charlie's "pervert" reputation, but only in the abstract; she had no idea he looked at so much pornography himself. She didn't learn about Charlie's habit until after the wedding. At first, they had sex about once a week, but after a year of marriage, if tapered off. Charlie was still interested in sex with his wife, but Elise's desire seemed minimal. In order to entice her, Charlie tried to get her to watch porn videos with him and encouraged her to do things he saw on film, which Elise didn't appreciate. "In truth, I found the videos more satisfying than going through the trouble of having sex with her," he admits. "But I was never unfaithful."

After twelve years of marriage, Charlie discovered the Internet. It was 1997, and Charlie was going to grad school for social work; a friend suggested he visit an adult Web site. He was immediately sucked in. Every night he would go online for hours, preoccupied, he says, "with the hunt for the one piece of porn that would give me that buzz."

His tastes changed quickly. He started out with traditional pornography and very attractive women. Then he became interested in amateur women, not even that good-looking. Next he turned to cheerleaders and younger women made up to look like young teens. Then he was all over the map—whatever struck his mood. At one point, he became interested in mature and elderly women. He was curious about bestiality; not any particular animal, just generally. It started off with pop-ups depicting women with animals. "I remember thinking, who would ever be interested in *that*?" he says. "What kind of person could get off on dogs and horses?" But the direction Charlie was going in, "any kind of sexuality with any type of thing could be a turn-on." He recalls thinking, "If

I'm into things now that I didn't think would ever turn me on, what could that possibly mean? Where could this go?"

When Charlie discovered chat rooms, he began to participate daily in chats devoted to a variety of fetishes. Online chats made him feel better about his curiosity and his predilections. "Talking openly with people in those chat rooms distorts your reality," Charlie says. "I felt like there were plenty of other people who shared my interests and therefore there couldn't possibly be anything wrong with it."

Meanwhile, Charlie's wife, Elise, didn't have a clue what Charlie was doing. Often she was sleeping when he went online. When she woke up, he would usually tell her he was studying for grad school. Sometimes he admitted he was looking at pornography; other times he would deny it. He never told her what he was looking at specifically and, afraid she would find out, was careful to clean the computer cache each time. Nevertheless, Elise felt hurt, betrayed, and demeaned. Why wasn't he available not only to herself but also to their family? What's a mother to say when the kids ask, "Where's Daddy?" He's not there to help with homework, go to the zoo, pick up the kids after softball practice. Running a household with a heavy pornography user in it takes a toll on family life. But what could she do about it?

Despite his marriage and family obligations, Charlie—whose early sexual life had been completely defined by pornography—was sliding deeper into porn sex. Charlie doesn't remember exactly when it happened, but he eventually crossed the gender line. It began in chat rooms, where he started talking to men as well, at first discussing women and couples. "My theory is that all porn is focused on ejaculation," Charlie explains. "All men talk about the 'money shot' and if you immerse yourself in porn, you eventually become obsessed with ejaculation and that can become an attraction in itself. Which then can lead to an attraction to male sexuality." Charlie purchased a Web camera and communicated and masturbated not only with women and with couples but eventually with other men who were by themselves, too. He would hole up in his home office for hours, corresponding visually with whoever interested him at the moment. If all these other people were into it, how could it be so bad?

Porn Is Cool

It's not easy to shock Judith Coché. "I've had my own therapy practice for over twenty-five years," says Coché, a clinical psychologist who runs the Coché Center in Philadelphia and teaches psychiatry at the University of Pennsylvania. "I feel like I've seen everything." She pauses, and says almost apologetically, "I'm going to say something really strong. I've been walking around my practice saying, 'We have an epidemic on our hands.' The growth of pornography and its impact on young people is really, really dangerous. And the most dangerous part is that we don't even realize what's happening.

"Frankly, I'm alarmed for today's preadolescents and teenagers," she continues. "I've been working with a number of kids who are stuck on the Internet. I've had two cases recently that blew me away. In one instance, a married couple, both professors, discovered their eleven-year-old daughter using very sexually explicit language in e-mails to her friends. She was discussing her clitoris and describing an incident in which a boy she knew grabbed her by the crotch. Her parents had thought she was completely naive—she hadn't even had sex education at school yet. They were appalled—and these were well-educated, liberal people. They just didn't expect their daughter to be aware of, let alone conversant in, these kinds of things. The other case was even more disturbing. Another girl, also eleven, was found creating her own pornographic Web site. When her parents confronted her, she said that pornography was considered 'cool' among her friends. Perhaps it wasn't a very good idea, the girl admitted, but all her friends were doing it. Her parents were horrified." More boys—often preadolescents—are being treated for pornography addiction, Coché says. "Before the Internet, I never encountered this."

According to Coché, the effects of such ever-present pornography on kids who are still developing sexually—or who haven't even reached puberty—have yet to be fully understood. Coché has talked to parents who have witnessed their sons playing computer games when pornographic pop-ups come onto the screen. "Pornography is so often tied into video game culture and insinuates itself even into nonpornographic areas of the Web. It's very hard for a twelve-year-old boy to avoid." As a result, boys are learning to sexually cue to a computer rather than to human beings. "This is where they're learning what turns them on. And what are they supposed to do about that? Whereas once boys would kiss a girl they had a crush on behind the school, we don't know how boys who become trained to cue sexually to computer-generated porn stars are going to behave, especially as they get older."

Pornography is wildly popular with teenage boys in a way that makes yesteryear's sneaked glimpses at *Penthouse* seem monastic. For teenagers, pornography is just another online activity; there is little barrier to entry and almost no sense of taboo. Instead, pornography has become a natural rite and acceptable pastime. One teenage boy in Boston explained recently to the *New York Times,* "Who needs the hassle of dating when I've got online porn?"[13] Pornography is integrated into teenage pop culture; video game culture, for example, exalts the pornographic. One 2004 video, *The Guy Game,* features women exposing their breasts when they answer questions wrong in a trivia contest; the game, available on Xbox and PlayStation 2, didn't even get an "Adults-Only" rating. (The game manufacturer is being sued because it is claimed that one woman included in the footage was only seventeen and didn't give her consent to be filmed.)[14]

With no one telling them it's wrong or inappropriate, it's no wonder kids have become audacious in their consumption of pornography. In 2004, a student at Weston High School in Connecticut tried to take a porn star to his prom after winning a date with her on Howard Stern's radio program.[15] At St. Xavier High School, a prestigious all-boys school in Springfield, Ohio, two students were charged with selling pornographic DVDs on school grounds to thirteen classmates. They were caught when the assistant principal for discipline told a student to tuck in his shirt, causing a concealed DVD to drop to the ground.[16]

By the time boys get to college, pornography is more than accepted—it's exalted. Jim Weaver, a professor of communication and psychology at Virginia Tech, has taught a course on pornography for years. "Young men in my classroom today don't even understand why we should be talking about it," he notes. "They see it as harmless entertainment. Their attitude is, 'It's a free country and I've been watching porn since middle school on the Internet and there's nothing wrong with it.' Most recently, students have become radical supporters of pornography. I didn't used to see that at all from young men. It's a huge shift in attitude." At Jacksonville University in Florida, students were reprimanded for installing a stripper's pole in an on-campus apartment and hosting a party in which drunken freshmen females were asked to compete for a $100 Victoria's Secret gift certificate by dancing on it while being photographed.[17] According to college-age men and women, and recent graduates, at colleges nationwide, guys are known to scribble on their dorm room message boards: "Leave me alone, I'm watching porn."

Boys are into porn, and girls, they claim, should be in on the game. At Scarsdale High School, a videotape of two fourteen-year-old female students in a sexual encounter was widely disseminated among the student body. In the film, an off-camera boy urged them on. "Everybody does it these days," he cajoled. Another onlooker told her to get more "hardcore." When one girl seemed reluctant to continue, pleading, "Stop," an off-camera boy called her a prude. "Please, we'll pay you," coaxed a second voice. Another assured her if she kept going, she would be "the coolest girl in the world."[18] Lots of girls go along. On Jenna Jameson's book tour promoting *How to Make Love like a Porn Star,* the pornography star was surprised by her young female fans. "It does make an impact on me that thirteen-year-old girls are coming up saying that I'm their role model," she told the *Los Angeles Times*. A gaggle of eighteen-year-old female fans were in attendance at a reading in Los Angeles. One girl explained, "I just like her because I want to be like—" "A porn star!" her friend interrupted. "No. Sexy and confident," the first girl explained. "Just, like a cool woman."[19]

Girls who aren't cool are condemned. In Orange County, California, three teenage boys videotaped themselves having sex with an apparently unconscious sixteen-year-old girl, allegedly assaulting her with a pool cue, juice bottle, juice can, and lit cigarette.[20] All the while, a hip-hop song boomed, "We like pussy. We like pussy . . . Fuck an asshole too. . . ." While the boys took turns putting their penises into her mouth and vagina, one of them held a camera, often rushing in for close-up penetration shots. They used a pool cue to penetrate the girl anally, slapping her stomach in time to the music. Afterward, when they used the cue on her vagina, the girl urinated on herself to the boy's laughter. "Fuck yeah!" one of them yelled.

When the case went to trial, the boys' lawyers tried to bring two porn stars to the stand to testify that the victim could have just been acting out a homemade porn movie.[21] Their attorney made the case that the girl had enticed "sweet," "caring," and "kind" boys into a sexual frenzy. During the trial, one of the defendant's lawyers referred to the girl variously as "a tease," "a porn star," an "out-of-control girl" and "a cheat."[22] The defendants claimed the girl said she wanted to be a porn star—and it wasn't their fault for believing her. Sharon Mitchell, a former porn star turned sexologist, briefly took the stand to explain that the actions shown in the footage were "consistent with pornography," explaining that many of the "positions" adopted on the tape are popular in porn films.[23]

Girls sometimes complain. In 2004 a thirteen-year-old girl from New Jersey told *People* magazine that the fact that boys look at Internet pornography makes her feel bad. Of her ex-boyfriend's interest in Internet pornography she said, "He told me he wanted me to look skinny like the porn girls. He told me I was fat, that I was a hippo."[24] They also sometimes play along. Also in 2004, a sixteen-year-old student was suspended from a high school in Fort Worth, Texas, after she allegedly showed a videotape of herself and other underage students engaged in sex acts with classmates. The boy in the tape was the girl's cousin; two other girls were fellow tenth graders. When initially questioned by the police, the girl said the videotape showed her getting her hair braided. She faces charges of delinquent conduct and sale, distribution, or display of harmful materials to a minor. Whether she is victim, perpetrator, or a combination thereof will surely be addressed in court.[25] In another case, a fifteen-year-old girl in Pittsburgh was arrested for taking nude photographs of herself and posting them online. She depicted herself in various states of undress, performing a variety of sex acts, and sent the photos to people she met online in chat rooms. After the police seized the computer, complete with photos of herself stored on her hard drive, the girl was charged with sexual abuse of children, possession of child pornography, and dissemination of child pornography.[26] In April 2004, a thirteen-year-old eighth grader at a prestigious private school made a porn video of herself masturbating and simulating oral sex for a classmate crush, who promptly put it online. The three-minute video immediately wended its way through the New York City private school circuit and then onto the Internet, where everyone from extended family to summer camp friends to unknown sexual predators could see it.

These are dangerous days for any attention-seeking tween with access to a digital camera or, worse, a webcam. One of the most recent trends in homemade, "amateur" pornography is entrapment porn, in which a man (usually a young man) coaxes a woman into sleeping with him and unbeknownst to her films the episode, posting it later on the Internet. Such footage is often accompanied by commentary in which the successful entrapper makes fun of his victim, mocking both her gullibility and her technique for the amusement and titillation of audiences worldwide.

It's not surprising that girls today emulate porn stars in the same way earlier generations gyrated to Madonna. *Playboy* bunny Pamela Anderson has become someone girls look up to; in addition to her column in *Jane* magazine, she also stars in a TV cartoon *Striperella,* in which she plays Erotica Jones, stripper by night, superhero by day. Christina Aguilera titled one of her albums *Stripped* and its first single "Dirty." The stripper/porn star look is popular among young women today. Delia's, the popular mail-order teenage apparel line, sells thongs to tweens emblazoned, "Feeling lucky?" In 2003, girls between the ages of thirteen and seventeen spent $152 million on thongs, from Hello Kitty designs to red-hot glitter. Teen girl mall store Hot Topic sells Playboy bunny trucker hats, pajamas, and pillows.[27] As Tom Connelly, publisher of the trade magazine *Adult Video News,* explains, "I think [Larry Flynt's name] used to be something pornographic, but now it's the ultimate in hip, trendy and cool . . . kids want to wear T-shirts with *Hustler* on it."[28] Little surprise then that the number of eighteen-year-olds who got breast implant surgery nearly tripled, from 2,872 in 2002 to 11,326 in 2003—a far greater increase than the 12 percent rise in such surgery among adults overall, according to the American Society for Aesthetic Plastic Surgery.

Like all good marketers, pornographers know it's important to reel in consumers while they're young. MTV recently announced the launch of a Stan Lee–Hugh Hefner collaboration, *Hef's Superbunnies,* an "edgy, sexy animated series" from the creator of the *Spider-Man* comic book series featuring a buxom team of specially trained Playboy bunnies.[29] Marketers have extended the porn brand to everything from sporting equipment to clothing. Two snowboarding companies, Burton Snowboards and Sims, now offer boards emblazoned with images of Playboy bunnies and Vivid porn stars. Sims boasts that their so-called Fader boards, which feature photographs of Jenna Jameson and Brianna Banks, are their bestsellers. Such boards are clearly marketed to teenagers, who form the backbone of the snowboarding market. Mainstream video games regularly feature pornographic elements. BMX XXX, for example, adds a pornographic sheen to bike stunts and racing. Another game, Leisure Suit Larry: Magna Cum Laude, features full-on nudity as gamers live out the player lifestyle, trying to score hot babes. The game's manufacturers are fighting to obtain an M rating (the equivalent of a movie's R) in order to ensure being carried at Wal-Marts across America.[30] Groove Games and ARUSH Entertainment have developed Playboy: The Mansion, a video game in which gamers adopt the role of Hugh Hefner as they "live the lifestyle" by hosting "extravagant parties" and undertaking "empire-building challenges." Given that *Playboy* readers already spend $300 million on video games annually and more than three million readers own a video game system, paying "residents" of the new mansion look to be built in.

What Kids Learn from Pornography

"Guys will ask if I've gone to first base yet, so I got to figure things out," a thirteen-year-old boy from New Jersey told *People* magazine. "If you don't know they laugh at you. Some guys look at porn out of curiosity and to figure out what they want to do with girls in the future." In his eighth-grade class, all forty-two students admit to looking at Internet pornography.[31]

Some people pose the question: What's so wrong about kids seeing a couple have sex? Is it wrong for children to see naked women? Not necessarily, but pornography isn't mere depictions of couples having consensual sex or respectful photography of naked men and women. Those who suggest otherwise clearly haven't been exposed to much pornography. Pornography, particularly online, offers a very different view of sex from *Where Did I Come From?*

Kids also absorb and process pornography very differently from the way adults do. Not only are kids like sponges, as the cliché goes, they are also quite literal. Even young teenagers are generally not sophisticated enough consumers to differentiate between fantasy and reality. What they learn from pornography are direct lessons, with no concept of exaggeration, irony, or affect. According to the 1995 Cowan-Campbell study of teenagers in California, six in ten boys said they had learned "some" or "a lot" from porn. Nearly half of girls agreed. They learn what women supposedly look like, how they should act, and what they're supposed to do. They learn what women "want" and how men can give it to them. They absorb these lessons avidly, emulating their role models. Still, many older kids at least partly recognize the negative side. When asked in a 2001 study by the Kaiser Family Foundation, 59 percent of fifteen- to twenty-four-year-olds said they thought seeing pornography online encouraged young people to have sex before they are ready, and 49 percent thought it would lead people to think unprotected sex is okay. Nearly half (49 percent) thought Internet pornography could lead to addiction and promote bad attitudes toward women. In a 2002 nationwide Gallup poll, 69 percent of teenage boys between the ages of thirteen and seventeen said that even if nobody ever knew about it, they would feel guilty about surfing pornography on the Internet. An even greater number of girls—86 percent—felt the same way.

Pornography in all its permutations affects developing sexuality; the younger the age of exposure and the more hardcore the material, the more intense the effects. Even *Playboy* has "a highly harmful effect on men's sexuality and ability to be in a serious relationship," says Gary Brooks, a professor of psychology who studies pornography's effects on men. "Boys learn to become sexual by masturbating to unreal images of women and in the process lose the emphasis on sensuality and interpersonal connection. Through masturbation, they become conditioned to arousal by these objects, and can lose touch with everything else," he explains. "Sex becomes something you do in a disconnected way—looking at a person without actually being with that person." Boys who look at pornography excessively become men who connect arousal purely with the physical, losing the ability to become attracted by the particular features of a given partner. Instead, they re-create images from pornography in their brain while they're with a real person. "It's sad that boys who are initiated in sex through these images become indoctrinated in a way that can potentially stay with them for the rest of their lives," Brooks says. "Boys learn that you have sex in spite of your feelings, not because of your feelings. Meanwhile, girls are taught that you don't have intimacy without relationships."

The effects on children can be disturbing and devastating. In the spring and summer of 2003, in Ontario, Canada, two boys, twelve and thirteen, and one thirteen-year-old girl decided to play a new game. The kids were good children from solid homes. None had been in trouble before. But what they did together that summer was engage in sexual acts that the police deemed to be "far beyond any normal sexual experimentation that might occur at that age." The thirteen-year-old boy performed sex acts on a seven-year-old girl he was babysitting. The thirteen-year-old girl also chose her victims from among her babysitting charges, touching them sexually while watching cable TV. The twelve-year-old boy convinced an eleven-year-old girl to engage in mutual sexual petting, along with three siblings, ages eight to ten. When the parents overheard the children talking about their new games, they confronted the kids. Their inspiration? They had learned it via Internet pornography, mostly pop-up ads, and from cable TV.[32]

Kids typically learn about the opposite sex through interaction. A boy tells a girl he likes her, but chooses the wrong words or says them in the wrong way and she gets annoyed and tells him to get lost. Lesson learned. A boy shyly and sweetly tells a girl she's pretty and she's touched, and even though she's not sure she likes him, she blushes and kicks the ground and smiles. Lesson learned. If instead of taking his hopes, fantasies, and ideas to the girl in math class, a boy takes all that bridled sexuality online to a porn star, what is the lesson he learns? No matter what he does, no matter what he's thinking, the porn star will do what he likes: deliver sexual pleasure. And she is certainly going to do so in a faster, more direct manner than even the most accommodating thirteen-year-old girl would consider.

Watching pornography, kids learn that women always want sex and that sex is divorced from relationships. They learn that men can have whomever they want and that women will respond the way men want them to. They learn that anal sex is the norm and instant female orgasm is to be expected. "Kids today are going to run into pornography online, *not* erotica," explains Aline Zoldbrod, the Lexington, Massachusetts–based psychologist and sex therapist. "They're getting a very bad model. Pornography doesn't show how a real couple negotiates conflict or creates intimacy." For girls especially, Zoldbrod believes pornography, particularly online, is a "brutal way to be introduced to sexuality," since much of it she deems "rape-like" in its use of violence. When asked in the *Pornified*/Harris poll what the greatest impact of pornography on children is, 30 percent of Americans said that it distorts boys' expectations and understanding of women and sex; 25 percent said that it makes kids more likely to have sex earlier than they might have; 7 percent cited the way it distorts girls' body images and ideas about sex; and 6 percent said it makes kids more likely to look at pornography as adults (men were twice as likely to believe this last as women). Only 2 percent of Americans actually believe that pornography helps kids better understand sexuality. And only 9 percent think it has no impact on children at all.

Lauren, the thirty-two-year-old mother of two from Virginia, fears her children might learn about sex in a pornographic vacuum. She hopes if she has a son he wouldn't look at pornography until he is sixteen or seventeen, and only after she has a chance to discuss sex and pornography with him. "Developmentally, young teens don't have the cognitive ability to put together what porn is and the place it holds in our society," she explains. "They might fall into traps that an adult could more easily avoid. Pornography could impact what they think about the girl next door or how they relate to girls and women they know." As for her daughters, her concerns are as great, but different. "I hope my girl has a healthy sexual identity and only sees pornography when it's age-appropriate," she says. "I hope she can experience her own sexuality in positive and real ways that are particular to her." As an educator and parent, Lauren believes it's her responsibility to talk to her children about the role of sex in society and to put pornography into context. "I don't buy the idea that you may as well just throw up your hands because you're not going to be able to change society anyway," she says of the prevalence of pornography among today's youth. "You don't *have* to have a TV in your house or give your kids access to the computer when you're not there. That lets parents off the hook. You have to be protective and mindful."

Yet many parents leave such potentially uncomfortable discussions to the classroom—where sex education is on the wane. Although students in 89 percent of American public schools took a sex education class as of 2002, one-third of those schools taught abstinence-only education. The Bush administration proposed $258 million for abstinence-only sex education programs in 2005, twice the amount in 2004, and nearly five times the $59 million spent in 1998, despite teenagers' need, and desire for, more information.[33] According to a 2004 Kaiser Family Foundation survey of American teenagers, 69 percent of teens say it's very important to have sex education as part of the school curriculum, and 21 percent say it's somewhat important. Only 9 percent believed it was unimportant or shouldn't be taught at all. As it is, sex education in America rarely touches on the subject of pornography. Although media education is increasingly taught in many curricula, kids aren't typically taught to put pornography into context.

In the absence of such education, the onus is on parents to explain sexuality and pornography to their kids. Child therapists advise parents to tell children about pornography at the age when children may become exposed so that they are prepared to handle it. Kids should understand that pornography purports to depict a fantasy and is a far cry from reality. At the same time, kids need to make a connection between fantasy and the real culture and economics of pornography production. A father can ask his son how he would feel if the woman depicted were his mother or sister, so he understands that while pornography projects a fantasy, the women who appear in pornography are real people. Zoldbrod argues that parents must remain available to their children so their kids can come to them with questions about pornography, since kids are bound to discover it with or without their parents' knowledge or approval. Better to shape children's responses than to leave them to figure it out on their own. Looking for answers, they'll likely turn to the Internet.

The Return of Child Pornography

Parents not only have to fear their child looking at pornography, they have to fear their child coming across child pornography—or their child becoming an unwitting subject for the next child pornographer. Such fears, once considered paranoiac, are increasingly realistic. For a long time, child pornography was not considered a problem in this country. In 1970, the nation's first National Commission on Obscenity and Pornography noted that "the taboo against pedophilia" had "almost remained inviolate" and that the use of prepubescent children in pornography was "almost nonexistent."[34] Once child pornography became explicitly illegal and the laws enforced, authorities believed the scourge had been largely wiped out.

This, however, was prior to the Internet. Between 1996 and 2004, the total number of child porn cases handled by the FBI's cyber-crime investigators increased twenty-three-fold.[35] By 2003, there were more than 80,000 reports of Internet-related child pornography made to CyberTipline, a service provided by the National Center for Missing and Exploited Children (NCMEC), up 750 percent in five years.[36] According to a November 2003 study by the New Hampshire Crimes Against Children Research Center, 2,577 people in the United States were arrested for Internet sex crimes against children between July 1, 2000, and June 30, 2001; 39 percent were alleged to have violated children and 25 percent were caught through law enforcement stings in which pedophiles set up rendezvous with undercover agents.[37] Child pornography is back—and a bigger problem than ever before.

It's particularly prevalent on peer-to-peer (P2P) file-sharing networks. According to a federal study of P2P networks such as Gnutella, BearShare, LimeWire, and Morpheus conducted by the Government Accountability Office, a huge quantity of child pornography is readily available through file sharing. In one search, using twelve keywords associated with child porn, the GAO identified 543 titles and file names that linked to child pornography content.[38] Kazaa, for example, yielded 149 child pornography images and 44 child erotica images (erotic images of children that do not depict sexually explicit conduct). Since the National Center for Missing and Exploited Children began tracking child pornography on P2P networks in 2001, there has been a fourfold increase in reports, from 156 in 2001 to 757 in 2002.[39] NCMEC also found that the number of reports about child pornography Web sites increased from 1,393 in 1998, to 10,629 in 2000, and to 26,759 in 2002.[40] Still, such measures do not nearly capture the full gamut of child pornography online. Most users are not so foolish as to label kiddie porn explicitly; established code words such as "Lolita" and "nymphet" guide those in the know.

Attempts to limit or patrol child pornography have been thwarted in court. The government attempted to expand federal child pornography laws with the Child Pornography Prevention Act of 1996 to include not only pornographic images created using real children, but pornography that depicts virtual or simulated images of child pornography—with cartoons, for example. However, in 2002, the Supreme Court struck down the law, arguing that limiting material that does not involve and thus harm actual children in its creation is an unconstitutional violation of free speech rights. This means that in order to prosecute on grounds of child pornography, authorities must prove that the depictions of children in child pornography are actual children. "Morphed" child porn, for example, which uses images of adults digitally altered to appear like children, doesn't fall under regular anti–child pornography laws because, it has been ruled, it would limit artistic expression.

While controls on child pornography have been hindered by American courts, other countries have taken measures to fight back. On April 22, 2004, the International Centre for Missing and Exploited Children announced the launch of a Global Campaign Against Child Pornography, with the help of a million-dollar grant from philanthropist Sheila C. Johnson and Microsoft. The campaign plans to create an international child pornography monitoring and oversight system, help law enforcement investigate and prosecute child pornography, and develop stronger laws between governments and private-sector organizations to fight against child pornography, and build public awareness of the problem. Norway recently introduced a nationwide child pornography filter on all Internet access. "If police authorities and Internet suppliers in other countries follow our example, we could succeed in destroying part of the client base of a cynical, international industry which exposes children to violence and sexual assault with the aim of making money," explained Arne Huuse, head of the Norwegian National Criminal Investigation Service.[41]

Meanwhile, in the United States, the FBI, the U.S. Department of Justice's Child Exploitation and Obscenity Section, and the U.S. Customs Department are using what means are at their disposal. The FBI launched a $10 million campaign, Innocent Images, which tracks down child predators. Since 1996, the campaign has opened 7,067 cases, obtained 1,811 indictments, performed 1,886 arrests, and secured 1,850 convictions or pretrial diversions in child pornography cases.[42] Local courts are also strengthening law enforcement's hand. In June 2004, the Supreme Court of California reversed a 1983 precedent by requiring people convicted of child pornography possession to register as sex offenders for the rest of their lives.

"I Essentially Stumbled Upon It"

It was only a matter of time before Charlie was exposed to child pornography. "I essentially stumbled upon it," he explains. "It wasn't something I sought out or even thought I would ever be interested in." His foray began innocently enough—checking out nudist Web sites, where he observed families frolicking in the buff. Then there were naked children alone. Child porn. "At first it was a real turnoff," he recalls. "But there was an aspect of curiosity as well." He kept clicking back, intrigued. What was it about those young girls that was so seductive? Why was he getting so excited? Within a month's time, Charlie was seeking out child porn regularly, with the explicit intention to masturbate. Between 1997 and 2000, Charlie became a habitual user of child pornography. "That whole period is like a blur to me," he says.

Meanwhile, his pornography habit began to spill over into real life. After hesitating and fantasizing, procrastinating and finally taking the plunge, Charlie arranged a meeting with one of the women he met through the Internet. When the appointed hour arrived, Charlie had second thoughts and couldn't go through with it. He did this repeatedly. He met a woman or couple online, interacted over the webcam and in chat rooms, proposed a meeting, then chickened out at the last minute. He didn't even bother canceling their rendezvous. It was so easy to arrange, it would be so easy to go through with it . . . but something wasn't right. The whole thing terrified him. He was spending hours online, going nights without sleep. Elise constantly complained about the time he was spending on the computer. He was always exhausted. "I realized I didn't seem normal," he says.

What really started to scare Charlie was when he began lusting after people he encountered in his everyday life. That hadn't happened since puberty. In fact, he had long ago concluded that pornography helped keep his desires in check, satisfying them virtually while maintaining his perspective in real life. Now, pornographic thoughts began intruding into everyday activities. "I was teaching Sunday School to high schoolers," he recalls. "The whole time I would be lusting after the girls in their short skirts. And, of course, I felt overwhelmed with guilt."

Who Uses Child Pornography?

In most people's minds, the child pornography user is the ultimate transgressor—perverted and dangerous, a person who has fallen beyond the boundaries of society and morality. When asked about child pornography, men who are regular users of pornography typically become incensed. "Those people should be executed," they say. *Disgusting, horrible, troubling, scary* are words they use to describe men who enjoy sexual depictions of children. "They're ruining it for the rest of us!" three men fumed separately in interviews.

Fear of child pornography is pronounced and growing more intense. Every day, at least fifty newspapers worldwide contain stories—outraged, sorrowful, fearful—about child pornography. Headlines are filled with attention grabbers like "Nuclear Physicist Arrested for Third Time on Child Porn!"[43] "Disgraced Former Judge: I Downloaded Child Porn."[44] "Kiddie-Porn Suspect Worked with Children."[45] The men seem at once suspicious and unlikely, like all other men, and yet somehow terribly different. True to terrifying stereotype, the child pornography user often works with children. Here they are, the lineup:

- Harold Shaw, fifty-nine, was a regular churchgoer, a "good guy" according to neighbors. The former gymnastic coach worked as a volunteer at a summer camp run by the Mormon Church. Fellow churchgoers affectionately called him "Brother Shaw." Since leaving the school system, he worked as an electrician, sometimes doing free repairs for neighbors and watching after people's dogs and mail while they were away. He also welcomed teenage girls from his church and young female relatives to his home. But in February 2004, Shaw was arrested on charges of child pornography. The walls of his Las Vegas home were lined with photographs of girls between the ages of eleven and fifteen, featuring close-up shots of their genitalia while performing gymnastics. The police also discovered a videotape of Shaw performing sex acts on an eleven-year-old girl, who appeared to be either drugged or drunk in the footage. "I can't imagine that he would do something like that," said a shocked neighbor. "He's never been anything but a good person. I would trust him with my kids any time."[46]
- In March 2004, Joseph Thomas Nurek, fifty-four, a school principal on Chicago's North Side, was arrested for possession of child pornography. Federal authorities found more than a hundred images on Nurek's computer, as well as CD-ROMs, videos, and DVDs, with pictures of boys as young as twelve performing sexual acts. Nurek had served as an administrator and principal for four and a half years at the Chicago International Charter School. A criminal background check prior to his hiring had come back clear.[47]
- That same month, a former navy physicist and weapons designer was convicted for using the Internet to seduce teenage

girls and for possession of child pornography. The defendant, forty-six-year-old George Paul Chambers, argued that he had just been role playing when he exchanged graphic sexual e-mails and photographs with a thirteen-year-old cheerleader in an AOL chat room called "I Love Older Men." It was all an elaborate fantasy—just for fun. When he arranged to meet the girl at a local mall in Maryland, FBI agents tracked him down and arrested him. His lawyer claimed that his client, a "socially awkward" and "sexually inexperienced" middle-aged man, had been a victim of the "thought police."[48]

- David Deyo, forty-three, was a Sunday School teacher and youth group leader in North Palm Beach, Florida. He was also a pedophile and child pornographer who had more than a hundred images stored on his computer and computer disks. According to the U.S. attorney who prosecuted his case, Deyo portrayed himself as a clown, a babysitter, "someone who could be trusted."[49]
- In February 2004, Kerry Dwayne Stevens, forty-eight, of Aberdeen, Mississippi, pleaded guilty to charges of child pornography. Stevens photographed his daughter and two of her friends' genital areas while they slept, and uploaded the images to his computer for distribution. Prior to this incident, Stevens worked as a radio show producer for a children's program on American Family Radio, a Christian radio station.[50]
- Donald Edward Godman, a twenty-seven-year-old percussion instructor and band assistant at North Carroll High School in Halethorpe, Maryland, was charged with sending child pornography over the Internet to his teenage students and soliciting teenagers to pose naked for him. One of the teenage girls Godman had allegedly sent pornography to, a fifteen-year-old color guard member, said she considered Godman a "mentor."[51]

Few studies quantify how many people use child pornography, but all indications point to a growing prevalence of child pornography with the Internet's expansion. In the United Kingdom, the Internet Watch

Foundation found that between 3,000 and 3,500 child pornography sites are added to the World Wide Web each year. When British Telecom, an Internet service provider, introduced a filtering technology to prevent child pornography Web sites from being downloaded in 2004, more than 20,000 attempts were blocked every day. British Telecom, which serves 2.9 million customers, is only one of many ISPs in the United Kingdom.[52]

Most men come across child pornography for the first time inadvertently. Among those interviewed for this book, three-fourths of pornography users said they had encountered child pornography while online, nearly always by accident. Miles, a thirty-three-year-old military man from Indiana, saw child pornography back when he was a frequent pornography user (he has since stopped looking altogether). "The Yahoo! groups and chat rooms are renowned for people slipping child porn in, so you come across it whether you're looking for it or not," he explains. "Sometimes it would horrify me, but after a while, it would occasionally excite me." A father of two, Miles says he "compartmentalized" his enjoyment. He would be online for a couple of hours, euphoric with the buzz of porn and masturbation, and find child pornography staring him in the face. At some point, he would tell himself, "I can't look at that." He would see his own children and think, "If something like that ever happened to them, I would be sick." He would force himself to pull away from the computer. Forty-four-year-old Ray felt a similar push and pull. While online for pornography, he would inevitably come across child pornography. He looked at it a little bit, though it was never a major draw. "It was more curiosity," he explains. "I just wanted to see what it was." After a while, he would become "shocked and disgusted" by what he was getting into. Especially as a high school teacher. Especially as his own five children had reached the age at which kids are featured in pornographic Web sites. "The idea that my son could be dating a girl I think is really hot is kind of scary," he says.

Men who use adult pornography think of themselves as fundamentally different from the perverts and "sickos" they believe venture into child pornography. Yet the distinctions aren't quite so clear, and for many men it's a slippery slope. Randy Brown, a former basketball coach for the Iowa State Cyclones who was arrested in 2004 for child pornography use, slipped into child porn in the typical manner. After using adult Internet pornography for months on and off, he began veering younger. "In my mind I was envisioning the fifteen-year-old who looks twenty," he said, emphasizing that he had never been interested in prepubescent children. "I know that sounds horrible. Let's face it—the whole thing is awful. What was it about being on the computer that made it worth compromising everything in my life that I love?" Brown hated himself every night, but "it just seemed so harmless at the time. You engage yourself in fantasy, then it's over and you're out of there." Child pornography wasn't even a particular interest of Brown's; when his computer was ultimately confiscated, only 26 of the 2,600 pornographic images on the computer were judged "problematic." He was ultimately arrested for trying to pick up a fifteen-year-old girl—who was actually a grown man posing as a young girl for his own enjoyment in an online chat room. Alarmed by how far Brown took the fantasy (sending the supposed fifteen-year-old a series of photos of nude minors, asking her to meet him), the man/girl turned Brown in to the authorities.[53]

But is it a surprise that men who never thought they would do so end up using child pornography? "Teen porn" Web sites, videos, and magazines abound, showcasing "barely legal" young women, fully shaved of pubic hair, cavorting in schoolgirl outfits and pigtails. Many of the sites and films are voyeuristic, featuring peepholes into girls' locker rooms and showers, slumber parties and schoolhouse toilet stalls. In sex scenes, these "girls" are typically depicted having sex with much older men. And that's assuming the "teens" are actually eighteen or nineteen years old. Though a woman must be eighteen years old before legally posing for pornography, underage women slip through, especially in the world of amateur porn and on the World Wide Web, where standards and laws in Southeast Asia and eastern Europe, for example, may differ from American practices. The supply exists to serve the demand. There's an illicit, voyeuristic pleasure to the enterprise. There is also a tinge of revenge. Men in their teens, twenties, thirties, and even fifties regularly seek out the youngest women online or look for women who emulate their schoolboy crushes, bedecked in cheerleading costumes and Catholic school uniforms with their short skirts. Men feel an emotional tug toward these figures, hoping to "get" the girl who once rejected them and fulfill their long-delayed fantasies. The gazer longs for what he could not have long ago and what he certainly cannot have—at least, legally—today. These girls may not actually be underage, and therefore no "harm" was done to an actual child in creating the pornographic image. But the desire for a child and the desire for a childlike woman blur and overlap.

The Effects of Porn on Kids

Adults aren't the only ones looking at child pornography. One teenage boy in Granville, Ohio, was said to be "mentally and emotionally troubled," according to local press reports. "At the time I did it, I wasn't me," he told Judge Robert Hoover in the Licking County Juvenile Court. "I wasn't in the right state of mind because I don't remember doing it." What he did was download more than one hundred child pornography images from a file-sharing service. When arrested in 2003, he denied having done so and initially cooperated with authorities, though he later tried to escape from the sheriff's car and at one point threatened to infect the juvenile court system with a computer virus. A troubled child, the boy had been diagnosed as schizophrenic and depressed, put on medication, and sent to counseling. Sitting in court beside him, his mother cried periodically.[54] Ultimately, her son was found delinquent on two counts of pandering sexually oriented matter involving a minor and eight counts of felony pandering. He faces three years in detention and will likely be required to register as a juvenile sex offender, a label liable to stick for the rest of his life.

No matter what kind of pornography they look at, spending one's prepubescence and puberty on porn can have lifelong implications. Masters and Johnson clinical director Mark Schwartz has seen fourteen- and fifteen-year-old boys who are addicted to pornography. "It's awful to see the effect it has on them," he says. "At such a young age, to have that kind of sexual problem." Schwartz isn't surprised about the growing number of young addicts in the Internet age. "Your brain is much more susceptible," he explains. "Many of these boys are very smart and academically successful; a lot of computer geeks are the ones who get drawn in. It affects how they develop sexually. Think about a twelve-year-old boy looking at *Playboy* magazine. When you're talking about Internet pornography, you can multiply that effect by the relative size of the Internet itself."

Research trickling in has begun to document the effects of pornography on kids, a difficult area to study given obvious ethical challenges. Certainly, no parent would consent to have their children view pornography in order to further research on the damage done nor would respectable institutions fund or support such experiments. Still, some evidence has been gathered. A recent study of 101 sexually abusive children in Australia documented increased aggressiveness in boys who use pornography. Almost all had Internet access and 90 percent admitted to seeing online porn. One-fourth said an older sibling or friend had shown them how to access pornography online, sometimes against their will; another fourth said that pornography was their primary reason for going online. When questioned separately, nearly all of their parents said they doubted their child would access any pornography via the Internet.[55] In Ireland, scientists are reportedly developing a program, in conjunction with the National Society for the Prevention of Cruelty to Children, designed specifically for teenagers who have become addicted to pornography.[56]

Interestingly, when asked about the effect of pornography in the *Pornified*/Harris poll, young people between the ages of eighteen and twenty-four were often most likely to report negative consequences. Four in ten eighteen- to twenty-four-year-olds believe pornography harms relationships between men and women, compared with only three in ten twenty-five- to forty-year-olds. The Internet generation is also more likely to believe that pornography changes men's expectations of women's looks and behavior.

"I Spent a Lot of Time Lusting After My Niece"

Scared by the force and frequency of his desires for the women and children around him, Charlie discovered a local 12-step program for sex addicts online. The program's Web site included a questionnaire to ascertain whether a person was sexually compulsive or not. Charlie answered all but two questions in the affirmative. Shaking, he e-mailed the group's leader but was told he would have to go to a group in person. That ticked Charlie off, though his anger was mostly a cover for embarrassment. He was too nervous to go to a meeting, so several months went by before he contacted a different group, this time an hour away. By this point, his wife knew he had a problem and, though she resented that he needed to take even more time away from her and their family, she knew he needed help.

Over the next few years, while his three kids were exiting childhood and entering preadolescence, Charlie attended regular meetings with his sex addiction group, though he suffered through several relapses. In addition to the 12-step program, he saw a traditional psychotherapist. He went on Prozac, then went off. Nothing seemed to help. He couldn't stop thinking about pornography and slipping back into old habits. Charlie decided just to wallow in his own degradation and returned to pornography full force. Then, in the spring of 2003, during one of his relapses, Charlie's therapist asked if it would be okay to give Charlie's phone number to another patient who might need a 12-step group. Charlie agreed. The guy who called Charlie for help was being sent to jail for molesting his stepdaughter. He begged Charlie to start a new sexual addiction group with him. Charlie didn't want to. What was the point?

But the man seemed desperate, so Charlie agreed to meet him; soon the two men were meeting regularly. After a few weeks, his friend started talking to Charlie about religion. Why, if Charlie called himself a Christian, was he still suffering from so much denial? At the time, Charlie had stopped going to church altogether. "At the church I attended you couldn't dare admit that you had a problem with sex," Charlie says. What could such a church do for him if it wasn't even willing to acknowledge his problems? But through his conversations with the child molester, Charlie began to question those assumptions. Over the course of several months, Charlie joined another congregation. "At my new church they have pamphlets for people overcoming all kinds of addictions and they included pornography," Charlie explains. "I was shocked to know that they even used that word in their literature. It was comforting. I felt like they were much more accepting of me." In the six months that followed, Charlie didn't look at any pornography at all.

At his new church, Charlie has spoken publicly twice about his struggles with pornography. "I never thought I would have done something like that," he says. "To get up in front of all these people whose opinion I care about, who I want to respect me." He pauses. "People's reactions are strange." Some try to high-five him after he finishes his talk, congratulating him and telling him how great what he's done is. It doesn't sit well with Charlie. "Here I am this recovering pervert and they're telling me 'Great job,' " he says, stunned. "I guess it's better than being ostracized."

Recently, as part of his 12-step program, Charlie began the process of making amends to those he wronged while he was using pornography. The most difficult encounter was with one of his family members. Back in the late 1990s, while Charlie was deep into child pornography, his fourteen-year-old niece was having trouble at home and needed help. Charlie's family took her in and she stayed with them for a year. "I came very close to molesting her," Charlie admits. "All that child porn I was looking at, the kind of images I was seeing—it was in my head. I spent a lot of time lusting after her." Charlie takes a long breath. "I felt like such a hypocrite because here she was, coming to us in a moment of need, and I came very close to abusing that trust." The niece, now twenty-one, is still angry at him.

What If Your Child Looked at Pornography?

Despite the prevalence of pornography among minors, parents are still surprised to discover their kids looking at pornography during their preteen and early teen years. In the nationwide study of children ages ten to seventeen, conducted in 1999–2000 by David Finkelhor, only half (48 percent) of kids told their parents they had viewed pornography online; in 44 percent of the incidents, kids didn't report unwanted exposure to anyone. A recent large-scale study by the London School of

Economics found that while 57 percent of British kids between the ages of nine and nineteen had come into contact with pornography, only 16 percent of parents were aware their children had seen it. One-third of the kids said they had received unwanted sexual or nasty comments from people online, but only one in twenty parents were aware of this. Perhaps more alarming, 46 percent of kids said they had given out personal information online; again, only 5 percent of parents knew they did so.[57] In the United States, a study by the Justice Department found that one in five children between the ages of ten and seventeen had received unwanted sexual solicitations online.[58]

Sue Downes, a consultant in Westchester County in New York who specializes in assisting families with their computers, says problems caused by downloaded pornography are rampant and on the rise. Parents frequently ask her to clean up the family computer but often don't want to know what's on there, leaving Downes to do the detective work. "I thought I was unshockable but it continues to shock me," Downes says. Mothers' most frequent concern is how their sons' exposure to hardcore pornography will affect their views of women. "One woman said to me, 'My son knows more about my body than I do. Is he looking at me a certain way now? Is he looking at my relationship with his father a different way?' They're worried about how it distorts their children's view of sexuality and how their children will grow up." Still, Downes says, most parents have no idea what their kids are up to or why their computers become clogged with spam. "They tend to have a lot of faith in their kids. Many are naive. They also cringe at the idea of censorship. I have to explain to them that this is a far cry from *Playboy* magazine."

Stephan, a forty-eight-year-old radio broadcasting executive, is one such parent. He recently learned his eleven-year-old daughter was looking at online pornography when his Internet browser history displayed a number of Web sites that were clearly pornographic, with names like "bigtits.com." The girl's mother confronted her and she denied having looked at the sites. Stephan was "blown away" by the incident. "I can't believe how easy it is for kids to get access to that," he says. "I was also pissed at myself for not having done anything. I'm ashamed to say I don't have blocking software on the computer. I've been meaning to do it." Young people might appreciate the guidance and respect. According to the *Pornified*/Harris poll, eighteen- to twenty-four-year-olds are most supportive of measures to regulate pornography with warning labels and restricting use so that harm is minimized. One in five advocate such measures as the best governmental response to pornography In contrast, only 10 percent of their parents' generation agrees.[59]

Even people who look at pornography themselves are troubled by the possibility of their own children's exposure. Harrison, the twenty-five-year-old graphic designer from Chicago, started on pornography at an early age but has mixed feelings about when children should first view it. "I think there's enough sexuality in our media as it is and kids don't need to be exposed to any more porn," he says. "They've already gotten basic titillation from the media." He cites MTV and Britney Spears, then continues, "There's a very good reason why we protect people under eighteen from buying pornography. I know thirteen-year-olds will be interested in sex. That's when I remember my own sexual desire beginning—my hormones were raging. But that doesn't mean I think it's okay for thirteen-year-olds to be looking at porn."

The stakes have also changed since he was young; kids now see more pornography online than off. "The Internet is out of control," Harrison says. "There needs to be some kind of regulation. I mean, I don't agree that anyone at any age can look at anything with no restriction. It's disturbing." Like tobacco and alcohol—and retail pornography—Harrison believes online pornography should be restricted to adults. "The Internet is the entire reason we've seen the surge in popularity of porn," he says. "Now that more people are partaking, it's edging toward the mainstream. They want to make it more acceptable." Why, he asks, would porn stars show up on VH-1 if porn weren't increasingly popular with and accepted by kids? "The media targets kids whether they admit it or not," he says.

Harrison thinks Internet pornography has a particularly pernicious effect on children. "I remember as a kid thinking what's the big deal about porn?" he says. "Well, okay, if you occasionally sneak a magazine from someone else's house, that's one thing. But with unlimited access online, kids don't realize how detrimental pornography can be, especially for someone who isn't fully developed, physically or emotionally. Porn distorts people's understanding of sex and distorts their sexuality as they're developing." He grows silent with thought. "Earlier, I said I thought porno could be beneficial in that it can create an understanding of sexuality. But in a kid's formative years, when they're establishing their understanding of sex and of their sexual identity, it can be damaging. Just like drugs can be damaging during physical development." Harrison, who would like to get married and have children of his own one day, worries about pornography's impact. "I don't want to classify porn and masturbation in the same category as drugs," he hedges. "But with both, you may as well be honest with your kids." He pauses before he adds, "Though by the time I'm married and have kids, I won't be looking at porn." Nor will he leave pornographic magazines under his bed as his own father did. "I'm not that dumb to think they won't find it." If his son asks whether he looks at porn, "I hope I will be able to say to him honestly, 'No, I don't look at it anymore.' "

Today's users have a hard time reconciling their own use of pornography with what they would like for their own children. "Teens today have so much porn at their fingertips," says Trey, the thirty-one-year-old recently married film editor. "It must be amazing. I wish I had had that much access when I was a kid." Trey attributes his own sexual awakening and comfort level to pornography. Before pornography, he didn't like women to perform oral sex because he felt it was intrinsically demeaning. "Maybe I got that from my mother, who was big into the women's lib movement when I was a kid," he suggests. "Those ideas were definitely reinforced in college. Not until I started looking at a lot of porn was I able to realize what really turned me on."

Trey would like to have at least two children. Yet he had not given any thought to the possibility that his kids might be exposed to pornography. After a moment's deliberation he says emphatically, "I would feel very uncomfortable about my kids looking at pornography before high school. I would definitely want to talk to them about sex before they started looking." He goes on to explain, "I would want to give them a heads up so they understand that that's not what sex is like. In fact, sex isn't like pornography at all. Pornography is cold. There's no feeling or emotion. There aren't people taking care of each other and looking after each other's interests." Trey thinks kids today might have a hard time developing sexually. "Kids have sex so young, especially oral sex," he says. "I guess girls are getting taken advantage of much more often. I wonder what it means for relationships." Trey recalls his own high school relationships as having "real emotion and tenderness." He questions whether today's young romances carry the same impact. "It's certainly disturbing that kids are growing up so quickly," he says. "There was something exciting about not knowing everything about sex."

When they think about it, some men lament their own early exposure to pornography. Kyle, a thirty-seven-year-old from Michigan who hopes to have at least three kids of his own, started looking at pornography at age eleven. "In hindsight, I don't think it was appropriate," he says. "I didn't have a clue what was going on and I had no business seeing that at that age." Kyle gets nervous about Internet pornography when he thinks about having his own family. "It's getting to kids younger and younger, and it's starting to freak me out. The earlier you are exposed, the more likely you are to engage in the activity depicted. Kids should be left to be kids."

Porn Prevention

But how can parents protect children in a pornified world? Internet entrepreneur Daniel Parisi made a tidy sum through his Internet business, pulling in $1 million a year off a single Web site, but after seven years of leasing the site to a European company that handled operations, he wanted out. Parisi decided that what he had originally begun as a "free speech and political site"—which lured very few customers—needed to be sold. The site, Whitehouse.org, was actually a profitable pornographic enterprise, luring many people, often students under eighteen in their mistaken search for the official White House Web site. Thus far, it had attracted more than 85 million visitors. So why the change of mind? Parisi's young son was headed off to kindergarten and his father didn't want him teased or embarrassed by his father's moneymaking ventures. The site is still up and running for children other than Parisi's son to happen upon; of course, one never knows where the Parisi boy will wander online. Who has, and is willing to take, responsibility?

Parents' efforts to quell their children's exposure to pornography may be futile. Porn pops up in the most unlikely places. In Sewell, New Jersey, a couple rented *Home Alone 3* at their local Blockbuster. When they played the tape at home for their four-year-old daughter, scenes from a hardcore pornography video were displayed instead—for ten straight minutes just after the film's opening credits.[60] The Internet is especially difficult to patrol. In the summer of 2004, parents in Grand Ledge, Michigan, were shocked to log on to the Web site for the town's youth football league, a site used primarily by fourth- to eighth-grade athletes and cheerleaders, only to discover a porn Web site in its place. Having forgotten to renew its URL, Network Solutions had sold the site to a Moscow-based man who posted free pornography.[61] Most pornographers, alas, are worse than indifferent when it comes to children or young teenagers consuming their products; after all, they know that product affiliation and brand loyalty begin young. When Hugh Hefner was asked by the *Washington Post* about kids wearing *Playboy*-logo clothing and accessories, he replied, "I don't care if a baby holds up a *Playboy* bunny rattle."[62]

Major impediments to controlling children's access stymie parents' efforts. In 1997, the U.S. Supreme Court struck down the Communications Decency Act, the first federal attempt to control indecent material online. Because the Internet is ubiquitous, the Court ruled that, unlike television or radio, it cannot be regulated without violating the First Amendment. Congress went back to reworking the legislation. Then in 2004, the Supreme Court ruled that the 1998 Children Online Protection Act (COPA) unnecessarily put the burden of regulating children's access to pornography on the producer or distributor, rather than on the user and the user's parents. The ACLU, which fought the bill, argued that requiring adults to punch in the digits of a credit card was a violation of the Bill of Rights. According to the 5–4 majority, COPA's requirement that a credit card be used as a form of adult identification when accessing pay pornography sites online constituted an undue burden on adults who choose to access such material. However, the Supreme Court did not go so far as to rule COPA unconstitutional. At this point, the case has been sent back to a lower court in Philadelphia.

Given the history of challenges, many consider the law to be dead. On the Internet, pornography fans gloated on the day of the ruling. In one pro-pornography chat room, users wrote, "Yay! Another victory for porn!" "LOL,* who even tried to get this law passed?" "This basically helps keep 'free' porn on the Internet!"

With court cases nearly impossible to win, efforts have shifted to a proposal to create a kids' area of the Internet that would be pornography-free or to develop a dot-XXX zone where pornography can be contained, with access by minors limited via filters. Computers would come equipped with filtering hardware so that parents could more readily install available programs. Unlike the television V-chip, which has proven difficult to use and has been poorly promoted, such a system could be user-friendly and actively encouraged. Another group lobbies the cable industry to allow à la carte subscriptions, where a family can pay for the Disney Channel but opt out of Cinemax, Playboy, or other cable stations currently bundled together for subscribers, regardless of their preferences.

In the absence of such laws and programs, the current focus is on improving existing Internet filters. Over the past ten years, filters have become more sophisticated as they attempt not only to limit access to Web sites but to screen content in e-mail, instant messaging, and peer-to-peer networks. More advanced filters are set according to categories, so that in addition to pornography, hate speech and gun and explosives Web sites, for example, are blocked. Some programs allow users to filter out degrees of sexual content, from hardcore pornography to nudity to lingerie. The market for such programs is expected to grow from $360 million today to $890 million by 2008.[63]

Unfortunately, most adults are more adept at punching in credit card numbers than they are at setting up filters. Tech-savvy teens are almost always able to circumvent efforts to block access. Free software downloaded from the Web allows anyone to disable a computer's filtering program. Even if one child's parents set up an effective block or remove Internet access from the home, the next child's parents may not, and

*Common chat abbreviation for "laugh out loud."

children will play wherever they can. "For parents just to install software on their home computers and think the problem will be taken care of itself is denial," said Al Cooper, the late director of the San Jose Marital and Sexuality Center and an expert on Internet pornography. "Not only *can* all children see pornography online, they *will* see it. All kids today will see sexually explicit stuff and they will see it constantly."

Cooper believed the solution is to inoculate kids against the effects of pornography by educating them about sexuality. "When a parent finds a pornographic picture on their six-year-old's computer they need to have a talk with the kid," he explains. "Unfortunately, most parents have the opposite reaction. They get so upset they want to shut the whole thing down. When they do talk to their kids, they often give too little or too much information, without keeping in mind what's age appropriate."

"It's Really Scary to Be a Parent These Days"

Married now for eighteen years, Charlie and his wife have three children—two boys, fifteen and thirteen years old, and a nine-year-old girl. "They say kids pretty much always know what a parent is up to, but at the time I didn't think they knew anything about my pornography," Charlie says. He now knows his kids knew something was wrong—all those hours at the computer, all those hours spent away from the family—but they didn't realize it was sexual. Not at first.

Only in recent months has Charlie talked to his kids—just his two sons, for now—about pornography. He wanted them to understand where he's coming from and to make them aware of the problems pornography poses. His older son says he has never looked at pornography, though Charlie thinks he watches too much WWF wrestling, which he sees as coming close to pornography on occasion. When his younger son asked for an open Internet connection so he could chat with friends on AOL, Charlie was hesitant. "I told him I was concerned because a person doesn't need to look for pornography, it just pops up." His son got upset and asked, "Why do I have to suffer because of your addiction?"

Then, one evening in the spring of 2004, Charlie was coming home from work when his younger son called him on his cell phone. His son was clearly upset. He admitted he had sought out pornography online and had been looking at it. He told his father he had mostly looked at naked women, but he was worried nonetheless. It had been about two weeks since Charlie consented to his son's having unlimited Internet access. To the boy's shock, Charlie didn't get angry. Charlie knew it would be wrong to lash out, and in any case, he was upset more than anything. Charlie explained to his son that it's not that he doesn't trust him, but that he knows how easily a guy can get sucked in. "You may think pornography is harmless now," he cautioned. "But you never know where it can take you." Charlie told his son he was concerned that he might be passing something along.

Badly shaken by what had happened and by his father's frank words, Charlie's son asked his dad to disconnect his Internet service so he wouldn't be tempted again. Elise was distraught, even angry. She wondered if their son was attempting to connect with his father by emulating his behavior. Charlie believes that by telling his sons about what he's gone through and by being honest with them, they'll be honest with him in return. He saw his younger son's coming forward to report his pornography use as a validation of his approach. "It was a humbling experience to admit to my sons my own problems with pornography," Charlie says. "But I think it's brought us closer together. It's added a more transparent aspect to our relationship." And, of course, Charlie no longer has to contend with the secrecy of his former habit.

Though Charlie's daughter is only nine, he worries about her. She's too young to deal with Charlie's own story, so he hasn't revealed to her what he's shared with his sons. "I see pornography portrayed everywhere in our culture, in places where I'm not sure other people even see it," Charlie says. "Catalogs where girls who are seven, eight, or nine years old wear thong underwear. Older girls shaving their pubic hair. . . . How else would you learn that style if not through porn? It's all an effort to look prepubescent."

"Knowing what I know from my own experience, it's really scary to be a parent these days," Charlie says. There is no television in Charlie's house. The family computer has a special filter that requires a designated administrator to enter each individual URL users can visit. Charlie has access to about a hundred Web sites, most of which are work-related, and he cannot link to anything beyond that. Locking down the Internet is essential, Charlie explains. "Any other type of filter can be broken," he says. "Ask any member of a twelve-step program and they'll tell you that. They should know."

7

Fantasy and Reality: Pornography Compulsion

Andy couldn't help it. "I led a complete double life," says the forty-two-year-old Web site production manager from the Pacific Northwest. Married for sixteen years and the father of twin girls, Andy is recovering from an addiction to pornography that began in childhood and has plagued him since. He kept his habit secret from his wife for years, even after they got married. Even after they had children. "I figured I wouldn't use pornography once I was a parent," he says, "but that didn't fix it."

Andy was introduced to pornography by a family friend when he was eleven and become immediately interested. He was already running with a fast crowd; soon they were exchanging pornography among themselves. Andy did all this behind the backs of his seemingly model parents: first-generation immigrants, well-to-do professionals, community-oriented citizens. His father led the local Cub Scouts. His mother was president of the PTA.

Despite his parents' seemly veneer, Andy says his upbringing was far from ideal, full of impossible expectations and emotional abuse. He found himself masturbating compulsively to pornographic magazines throughout grade school, high school, and college. He tried repeatedly to stop, but would always pick up again. One day, shortly after his marriage, Andy's wife, Jane, found him masturbating to *Penthouse*. "What is this smut doing around the house?" she yelled, disgusted. "Get rid of it!" Andy threw it out. "I told her I was sorry and it wouldn't happen again, but I just hid it better the next time," he admits. "I always came back to it. Pornography was my comfort."

His wife caught him again, and often. "Jane felt very betrayed each time," Andy says. "She's a liberal, stand-up woman. She was angry about the objectification of women. She hated the feeling that her body was being compared to theirs. She worried that my porn problem was her fault. After all, she didn't look or act anything like a centerfold. She's blond, green-eyed, very beautiful. But my looking at porn made her feel unattractive." Jane grew depressed because Andy avoided her. Worst of all, Andy says, "I manipulated her trust."

Andy now attends a 12-step program for pornography addiction and avoids porn altogether, though the Internet hasn't made it easy. "It's everywhere—it's not just in porn anymore, either. It's in Victoria's Secret catalogs and on prime-time TV," he says. Nonetheless, Andy is determined not to look at pornography ever again. "I made a pact with myself," he says. "The buck stops here. I will not pass this along to my daughters. I do not want them to be treated the way I treated other women when I was using pornography." Instead, he and his wife talk openly with their girls about sexuality. They point out when they think a woman in a TV show or commercial is being objectified or treated poorly: "We try to educate them."

Andy explains, "I don't think any amount of pornography is okay. Any time you take a human being—a person's soul—and turn her into an object rather than a person who has thoughts and feelings—you're not living a whole life. You're not relating to that person as you would want to be related to yourself. When I was using porn, I treated women like cans of soda pop that I could pick up and drink in. I wouldn't want to be treated that way. Once I came to this realization, pornography depressed me to no end."

Compulsive Pornography

- Do you routinely spend significant amounts of times viewing pornography?
- Do you hide your online interactions from your spouse or significant other?
- Do you anticipate your next online session with the expectation that you will find sexual arousal or gratification?
- Do you feel guilt or shame from your online use?
- Did you accidentally become aroused by Internet sex at first, and now find you actively seek it out when you are online?
- Do you masturbate while online?
- Are you less involved with your spouse because of your experience with Internet sex?

Those who answer "yes" to any of the above questions, from the Center for Online Addiction, may be addicted to cybersex, according to experts. Yet estimating the number of men whose usage of pornography becomes a serious problem is difficult. When does the casual glimpse at *Playboy* become subscriptions to multiple magazines, then become a weekly movie, then become a daily online habit? At what point does pornography become a problem? According to Al Cooper, the late pornography researcher and director of the San Jose Marital and Sexuality Center, any man who spends eleven hours or more per week looking at Internet pornography qualifies as a compulsive user. The National Council on Sex Addiction and Compulsivity estimates that between 3 and 8 percent of Americans are sex addicts of some kind. Conservative estimates claim that 200,000 Americans are addicted to online pornography alone, a number that is rapidly rising.[1] Other studies on online pornography estimate that between 6 and 13 percent of users exhibit sexually compulsive online behavior.[2]

Even those who are able to answer all the questions above in the negative may not be immune to pornography addiction. The line between the compulsive pornography user and the so-called recreational user has noticeably blurred. With pornography so readily available, so anonymous, so easy in its myriad formats, men who may have once occasionally glimpsed at a magazine or rented a movie now consume pornography on a daily basis. Why not? It's right there, just a click of the remote or mouse away. In a pornified world, what once seemed to be a fundamental difference in psychology between users and abusers seems to have shifted into a question of degree.

This shift was borne out repeatedly in interviews, when men who were regular users (of Internet pornography in particular) said they logged on to look at it daily, whereas before the Internet, pornography had been a much more occasional pursuit. Moreover, almost a dozen men—again, self-described "normal" users of pornography—had made efforts to cut down on their consumption, with only limited success, typically hard-won. Almost three-fourths of "normal" users of pornography admitted that they could see themselves become addicted to porn, even if they didn't think they had particular "addictive" personalities. Such observations are not confined to the research conducted for this book. On one humor Web site, with the strangely appropriate name A Pointless Waste of Time, a writer conducted an admittedly informal study of one hundred online pornography users, in which he challenged them to go without looking at pornography, online or offline, for a two-week period. Of the ninety-four subjects who went through with the experiment (six dropped out), fifty-two were unable to go even a week without pornography, and twenty-four couldn't last for three days. In the end, only twenty-eight of the subjects were able to get through the two-week period without pornography. The author observed that, if anything, his "study" understated the problem: "Someone might also complain that a call for a survey on porn addiction would automatically draw people who suspect they are porn addicts (thus skewing the results again)," he wrote. "But you could also say the opposite, that people dependent on porn would tend to stay far, far away from a study that requires them to go without it." He also noted that the study subjects themselves were likely to talk about the test in "addict's terms." As he explains:

> The participants were not strangers to me and were largely people I "know" in an online sense. And while I had heard lots of jokes over time about [them] being alcoholics or hopelessly fat

> or hopelessly poor, I had never, ever heard any of them talk about being porn addicts.
>
> Until we did the study.
>
> From the first hours on, lots of these guys were suddenly talking about "withdrawal" and talking about how tomorrow was going to be a "tough day" with time alone and high-speed access. They were using the language recovering addicts use, which I admit both surprised me and creeped me out a little.[3]

Not only do supposedly "normal" guys talk like pornography addicts, but recovering pornography addicts describe their usage in very similar terms to those who continue using pornography on a purportedly casual basis. The motivations for use are often similar if not the same, the feelings men derive from that use parallel each other, and the steps men go through from interest to satiety, from excitement to boredom, from softcore to hardcore, from fantasy to reality, mirror one another in startling ways.

Today, it's almost impossible to discuss pornography compulsivity without discussing the Internet, which is frequently referred to as the crack cocaine of pornography. Al Cooper believed the vast majority of people who look at Internet pornography are what he called "recreational users"—they see online sexuality as a form of recreational distraction, like picking up a Victoria's Secret catalog or watching reality TV programs. They're not masturbating while looking at it and they look at it for less than an hour a week. Cooper thought this to be the largest category of pornography viewers, yet by this definition, nearly everyone interviewed for this book, including many men who consider themselves casual users, go above and beyond the norm. The second group Cooper called the "sexually compulsive" users, people who had a problem with sex before the Internet and merely transferred it online. The third—and most interesting—category are the "at risk" users: people who would not have a problem were it not for the Internet. "This is an exploding category and very concerning," Cooper explained before his death. The three A's of Internet pornography—access, affordability, and anonymity—have turbocharged the Internet in a way unparalleled by any other media. "People now have access to anything they can imagine and to things they never imagined. All you need are three people with a similar interest and a Web site devoted to midget lesbian wrestling. A new person coming along may not have known that that interests him, but now he's clicking around and it grabs him."

Dan Gray, clinical director of AddictCARE, a Utah-based group of therapists dedicated to treating sex addiction, constantly sees new addicts created by the Internet. "It's common for a man in his forties to call up and say, 'I haven't looked at any porn since I was in high school and even then it was just *Playboy*—until last year when I was sitting in my office and received some porn e-mail or came across porn by accident. It piqued my interest. Soon I was looking at other sites. And now it's been a year and I'm scared I'm addicted. I can't seem to stop.' " Gray thinks more men are addicted to pornography than may be recognized. If men are logging on every night, if they're losing time when they could be doing other things, if they're growing dependent on the endorphins and adrenaline released in the brain when masturbating to pornography, they're likely creating a dependency on that experience. Many addicts refer to the rush of pornography as a "drug," saying they feel "high" on endorphins, adrenaline, orgasm. Pornography is like alcohol, explains Robert Weiss, clinical director of the Sexual Recovery Institute in Los Angeles. Some people don't have a problem; others become alcoholics. The Internet is increasingly drawing members of the former group into the latter.

Men are not oblivious to Internet pornography's seductive pull. In the 2004 *Elle*-MSNBC.com survey, 17 percent of men who had used Internet pornography admitted to having a problem controlling their urge to log on. Eight percent of men who didn't look at Internet pornography at all said they abstained because they were afraid they would lose control of themselves if they even started.

At one 12-step recovery group in the Northeast, the Internet has emerged as a huge problem. Since Liam, a father of four in his forties, entered recovery for pornography addiction in December 2001, the number of older men—men who had never previously had a serious pornography problem but had succumbed to addiction since getting high-speed Internet access—in the program has increased. For the first time as well, young men in their early twenties have joined the group, having suffered from compulsive use throughout adolescence and into early adulthood. "The majority of folks coming now are coming because either the Internet pushed them over the edge or because the Internet itself started the problem," Liam says. Members have come from the corporate world and from respected positions in the community, and also include men who suffer from multiple addictions and might be considered more likely candidates for pornography abuse. A lot of men, he explains, come in with the attitude "I'm strong, I'm self-reliant. I should be able to control this." They think pornography is a normal-guy thing, but that maybe they've taken it just a bit too far. "There's an arrogance," Liam explains. "They've been raised in a very individualistic bootstrap mentality: if you've got a problem, deal with it. There's no reason to seek help from others." Those men tend not to last long in the program.

Almost nobody who goes from pay-per-view pornography to cyberporn imagines they will become an addict. But according to Victor B. Cline, a psychologist who has studied pornography addiction, highly educated professional men tend to be particularly susceptible to the fantasy world of online pornography. "Many of my most intelligent male patients appeared to be most vulnerable—perhaps because they had a greater capacity to fantasize. . . . While any male is vulnerable, attorneys, accountants, and media people seemed—in my experience—most vulnerable to these addictions." Yet when *The New Yorker* film critic David Denby released a memoir in 2004 in which he confessed to briefly succumbing to an obsession with Internet pornography after his wife left him for a woman, it was a scandal. Dan Gray says myths about the typical pornography addict are laughable: "These are regular guys, the men you see at work, in the store, at church. I see feminist men, religious men, professional men, educated men. With some, pornography goes against their very core beliefs." Among the approximately two dozen pornography addicts and their wives interviewed for this book were businessmen, clergy members, engineers, lawyers, members of the media, and a disproportionately large number of people who work in technology. Despite stereotypes claiming otherwise, the vast majority of sex addicts interviewed for this book suffered no early child abuse or molestation. Most went to college and came from stable homes. Most started looking at pornography the way all boys in the pre-Internet era did: flipping through the pages of a girlie magazine—borrowed, bought, or passed down.

Psychologist David Marcus runs several groups for compulsive pornography users in San Jose, California. "This is a burgeoning problem," he says. "Kids and young adults are exposed earlier and more intensely than ever before. It may start off innocuously, and slowly it starts to serve a different function. A kid goes online to explore, checks out pornography for fun or to get off, and then at some point the kid is stressed out and goes online to relieve that stress. Once you use pornography as a way to cope with stress or anxiety, you're exhibiting high-risk behavior. Pornography becomes something more biologically based and can cause real problems. You're no longer going online just for fun."

The Rush

Just as with all pornography users, casual or habitual, fun is generally where it starts. Sex addicts typically describe the feeling they experience as a kind of a trance, a zone where they lose sense of time and place. *Euphoric, high, thrilled, excited,* and *obsessed* are words commonly used to describe the rush induced by pornography. "Once we start to drink in that image, we lose control," explains Tony, a thirty-eight-year-old addict from San Diego, now in recovery. "The consequences often don't stop us." A forty-seven-year-old from Missouri describes pornography as a "powerful drug": "It's mind altering," he says. "More mind altering than alcohol or any other drug I've used. My brain will—it's hard to explain to someone who's not an addict—I almost get the chills. Just thinking about pornography or thinking about thinking about pornography gives me a total rush. Maybe it's just the chemicals in my brain, the release of endorphins." In *A Male Grief: Notes on Pornography and Addiction*, recovered addict David Mura writes: "In pornographic perception, the addict experiences a type of vertigo, a fearful exhilaration, a moment when all the addict's ties to the outside world do indeed seem to be cut or numbed. That sense of endless falling, that rush, is what the addict seeks again and again. . . . Those who stand back from the world of pornography cannot experience this falling, this rush. They cannot understand the attraction it holds. But for the addict the rush is more than an attraction. He is helpless before it."[4]

Many addicts follow a common pattern, using pornography sporadically and then succumbing to addiction when their use transfers online. Kenneth, a consultant from New Mexico, went much of his adult life without pornography. He looked occasionally during high school and college, and as a soldier in Vietnam, but never bothered to buy it. It wasn't until 1994, depressed over his younger brother's sudden death from cancer, that Kenneth began looking at a serious amount of pornography. Not coincidentally, it was at this point that he got Internet access. "I went into a trancelike state," he recalls. "I would be high on porn. In another world, removed. If I was on the Internet for six hours, the time would fly. It would be three in the morning and I had no idea time had passed."

Maybe it was because he was depressed, maybe it's because his father was an alcoholic and addiction ran in his family. Kenneth's not sure why he got sucked in. "In New Mexico, we've had a tremendous expansion of Indian gambling casinos," he explains. "So along with that come the problem gamblers. Why can some people gamble, walk away, and be fine while others become gamblers? Certain people have problems in their lives and are looking for something to make them feel better. Some people get it from gambling, some from alcohol, some from the thrill of looking at porn. The chemicals it released in my brain made me feel better."

Often, men describe the high as a numbness, which is followed by shame, self-loathing, and frustration, particularly for addicts who have tried but failed to stop. Those feelings of anger and self-hatred then drive the addict back to pornography. Getting off on porn—hunt, chase, orgasm, relief—becomes their way to self-medicate pain or disappointment. As the forty-seven-year-old Missourian puts it, "It's a quick fix. For people who are emotionally sick, pornography fills this need. We have this empty hole inside and porn fills it. In the long run, it never works and keeps you coming back, but in the short run, it's a powerful, quick cure."

Not surprisingly, some pornography addicts suffer from other forms of compulsive behavior, frequently with drugs and alcohol. The porn buzz and the drug or alcohol high create a heady combination. When Leo, a forty-two-year-old technology consultant from Dallas, met his first wife, Hayley, at a party during his sophomore year of college, he and a friend, wildly drunk, attempted a three-way. The ménage à trois flopped, but Leo and Hayley launched into a nine-year-long party that encompassed two years of marriage. Their relationship was tumultuous. Hayley would watch pornos with Leo, already a compulsive user, even though she was jealous. She lived in constant fear Leo would leave her. Then there were the drugs. Leo had been smoking pot every night at the end of the day since he was eighteen. During the first year of their marriage, he and Hayley added crystal meth and amphetamines to the mix. With crystal, Leo could have all-night sex parties, whether with pornography or his wife; he would be high for hours on end.

Still, on the outside, they seemed like "normal" people. They held steady jobs, had a nice house, a nice car. Leo attended church fairly regularly. But their private life began to spin out of control. When Hayley became more interested in drugs than sex, Leo decided he wanted "off this train." He decided he wanted to stop doing drugs and Hayley decided instead to leave him.

See the Girl, Play with Her

Relationships with women are often complicated, even destroyed, by pornography abuse. Over time, addicts almost inevitably find it hard to differentiate between the women in pornography and the women in real life. Kenneth, the consultant from New Mexico, struggled with what he was doing. "I had a hard time rationalizing it," he says. "Because even in the midst of it, I knew it wasn't good for me. I knew it affected the way I related to women." In spite of his best intentions, Kenneth, a married man and father of three, began to have trouble relating to women in the real world. "I objectified them," he explains. "It makes sense. If you meet someone and you're preoccupied with women's anatomy because you spend time looking at porn, then in the real world, you spend a lot of time looking at women's anatomy."

Kenneth found it hard to form new relationships with women, socially and professionally. People would drop clues, which he would either ignore or shamefully realize during dark moments. Women would leave the room when he entered; they avoided eye contact. "Part of my denial was that I thought my obsession wasn't obvious to everyone around me, but it clearly was," he says. In one instance, he got a contract to work in Texas. The engineer he was working with turned out to be an attractive woman. She never complained directly to Kenneth. But when the company never hired Kenneth again, he knew he had caused a problem. "I'm ashamed to admit it, but I know I made her uncomfortable," he says. "I was checking her out constantly. I never said anything to her; I was too preoccupied with trying to look down her blouse."

The equation becomes eerily simple: the more pornography viewed, the higher the bar for all women. "Gradually, you need more perfection in terms of the look," Liam, the forty-something father of four, explains. "You're looking for a certain kind of thing, a certain beauty. In my case, it was breasts, but it could have been anything. Literally—and I'm not exaggerating—any woman I would meet in the course of the day, I would first evaluate on the basis of her breasts. That didn't happen before porn. It hadn't happened since I was a teenager. I hadn't been the kind of guy who always had to make a comment on a woman's appearance. But I *became* that kind of guy." Pornography, Liam says, makes an object out of everybody. "It takes a three-dimensional human being with feelings—someone who could be your daughter, sister, or mother—and basically says, this is a creature that is only intended to satisfy your sexual desires. It becomes your natural way of thinking. A very common progression addicts describe is that it gets to a point where you can't even look at a woman without first rating her for her physical attributes. You're no longer conscious you're even doing it. It just happens."

For the addict, pornography becomes the means to "get" someone, to "have" her and control her. Sex is the means to an end, and the woman is a tool who performs the transaction. While the objectification of women is a major topic of discussion in recovery programs (and therefore it's not surprising to hear it articulated by men in those programs), every sex addict was able to offer specific, highly personal descriptions of his own inability to relate to women as a result of pornography. One recovering addict from Washington State explains, "I definitely objectified women when I was using porn. The way I looked at women at the time was, 'What can I get out of you?'—and that was all I cared about. There was no other value in interacting with them." As a result, he felt uncomfortable around women, had no real female friendships for years, and split up with his wife. "There were times when I thought women could tell what I was thinking," he says. "They knew something was wrong with me." Other addicts concur: "I didn't care for women as people." "I found it hard to interact with women in the workplace." "When they had a nice personality, it might make it easier to fantasize about them, but I didn't give a shit about who they were as individuals." "Women all blended together."

You've Seen 1,000 Women, You've Seen Them All

Faced with problems in the real world, addicts find the women in pornography to be a welcome refuge. When Walter, a Texas-based program manager, remarried at age thirty-nine, he experienced a tremendous amount of stress. He had joint custody of his son and daughter from his first marriage, which had ended two years before, and his second wife, Diane, had full custody of her own two kids. Blending the families was a strain, and Walter began drinking heavily and getting into raging fights with his new wife. He felt incapable of handling the complex problems posed by his new family and, at bottom, impotent and insignificant.

Walter had never been into pornography, just occasional glimpses when he was single and a brief fascination with magazines when his first marriage started to crumble. But now he was working long hours and traveling for his job. "Internet porn became attractive to me as a way of medicating," he explains. "I was able to feel wanted by all these women at a time when that feeling was not being presented in my marriage. I felt desired and needed." The lower he felt, the more he looked, the better it made him feel. The women in pornography, Walter says, accepted him. As long as they were looking at the camera and he could make eye contact and pretend they wanted him.

The women in pornography are interchangeable, it doesn't mean anything, addicts tell their wives. *It's just physical.* Their words echo the words of many pornography users, casual and habitual. But despite what wives get told, there *is* an emotional component to pornography—the satisfaction of a need to feel desired, to transgress, to be a man, to fill whatever's missing from the psychological cocktail he equates with happiness. The addict conforms to a twisted logic depending on his current attempt at self-justification or rationalization. *I love women*, he'll boast to himself and to other men. That's why he looks at and admires them. *Those women don't matter*, he'll tell his wife. They're just images.

Looking back, Walter is astonished at the myths he bought into while enmeshed in pornography. Still, many of the men he talks to now don't think that what he did was so heinous. Look, they tell him, it's natural for a guy to look at porn, especially when he's married. He needs variety. Let's face it, they'll say, a wife just isn't enough. But Walter doesn't buy it anymore. "That's a bunch of crap," Walter says. "I'm sorry. Men are supposed to be strong and porn is just a self-esteem weakness. Porn is there to make men feel like men, and women are there to please us. Porn helps men justify all the other things men want to believe about themselves." The truth, according to Walter, is that men don't like to admit the whole reason they go for pornography, which is that they know they couldn't get those women otherwise. "Look at the men in topless clubs," he says. "These are not the kinds of guys who can get a good woman, the women there are generally not worth it, and no real relationships are ever going to come of it. It's an act of desperation."

Yet when men are operating through the veil of addiction, pornography feeds that desperation. Clay, forty-six, from Atlanta, says that with over thirty-five years of using pornography—an average of three hours per day—he has wasted about three years of his life. Work started slipping as Clay felt his ability to concentrate loosen. He couldn't hold steady conversations. "I didn't know how to have adult relationships with anyone," he recalls. "Everything felt shallow. It was as though women were not real people, not individuals. I didn't feel any kind of attachment."

Meanwhile, Clay's wife grew frustrated, having assumed he would stop using pornography once he settled down. For her, Clay's porn signaled the possibility that he might have an affair. In some ways, Clay admits, it was a rational fear; many sex addicts progress that way. But Clay had no interest in realizing his desire with another human being. He had no desire to connect. The more upset his wife grew, the less he desired to be with her. Why bother arguing, having long discussions, struggling to get her into bed, when he could just log on and masturbate? Pornography became his escape. Cold, sure, but easy. He detached himself from what he was seeing. "I would see some young girl in porn and then read a horror story in the newspaper about sex trafficking in eastern Europe, but I just mentally discarded the connection," he explains. "I couldn't let myself feel anything toward these women other than the means to satisfying my desires."

When Clay's wife left him and he went into recovery, Clay retreated even further. Since their separation more than five years ago, he hasn't even gone out on a date. Fearful of his inability to connect with people, Clay believes he's still not ready for normal relationships. The messages he picked up from pornography, the portrait of women he embraced for so many years, the disconnection he feels—none of it has gone away. "I'm lonely," he says with a sigh.

Consistent heavy viewing takes its emotional toll. Men report going through a period of ennui—as excited as they were at the onset, pornography becomes like a drug necessary to maintain a plateau. The highs become harder to achieve. Boredom sinks in. After years of hiding his pornography habit from his wife of ten years and from his four children, Liam felt his sense of self, his whole life, being shut off. He became emotionally distant from his family while growing frustrated, easily agitated or provoked into bouts of fury. The stress of his double life—clean-cut Catholic family man on the outside, pornography addict on the inside—grated against his conscience all day, every day. "I wanted to think I was this good guy," he recalls. But there were these aspects that didn't gibe with the person I wanted to be." Liam felt strangely disconnected. "On the surface, you can describe looking at pornography as physically connecting with other people. But, of course, none of them matter. None of them care about you. None of it is real. It's a very solitary experience." Liam nonetheless was compelled to push on. He wanted to see women getting raped.

Upgrade, Downgrade, More, More

Miles, the thirty-three-year-old military man from Indiana, saw his first nudie magazine at age six and never looked back. When he got the Internet, his tastes shifted to scenes depicting humiliation and degradation. "The specificity online is unbelievable," Miles says. He would look for videos in which a husband watches himself cuckolded by a black man and his white wife. He became interested in rape porn and forced sex and bestiality. ("I didn't like that at first, but then I got into it.") The key to his arousal was finding the "forbidden." Sometimes a video he downloaded looked a bit too real; he wasn't sure if the woman was acting or was truly in pain. "While you're in the middle of watching, it's hard to be rational," he says. "I would try to tell myself, 'Okay, that's not reality. Women don't really want to be victimized.' " Regardless, his enjoyment was very real.

In addition to soaking in online pornography, Miles frequented strip clubs; soon he was paying escorts to strip for him, and ultimately he hired prostitutes. When he got married, he didn't stop. He had affairs with several women and with one man, even though he doesn't consider himself homosexual or even bisexual. There was one particularly worrisome habit. By his late teens, he had begun exposing himself. One afternoon, when he was nineteen, he was at his brother's house watching pornos when he got very excited and wanted to . . . he wasn't quite sure what—something beyond the usual. He went into the garage and began masturbating, deliberately leaving the garage door up, which made it more titillating. A neighbor called the police and Miles was cited for public indecency.

Other incidents followed. One morning during the spring of 2003, Miles, then thirty-two, was driving on the interstate when he felt compelled to stop his car alongside the road, get out, and masturbate. This lasted for a minute or so, then he got back into the car and headed to work. But a passerby had reported the incident and a sheriff 's car began to follow him, accompanied by a fleet of police cars. Guns drawn, the police ordered him out of his car. As he lay on the ground, face in the dirt, hands cuffed behind his back, he thought to himself, "My wife will be crushed. My boss will find out. The military will know. It will be in the newspaper." He was overwhelmed with fear and shame. The rape porn, the violence, the racism, the bestiality—none of it had bothered him the way his own public degradation did.

The heavy user is not likely to think there is anything out of the ordinary about his escalating tastes. As discussed in chapter 3, studies by the University of Alabama researchers Zillmann and Bryant found that prolonged exposure to pornography leads people to overestimate the incidence of almost all sexual activities—particularly sodomy, group sex, sadomasochistic practices, and sexual contact with animals.[5] Max, a thirty-four-year-old investor from Virginia, recalls, "When I was a kid, *Penthouse* would meet the need. But as I got older and porn became Internet-based, I started looking at a lot of amateur pornography with multiple women and group sex. At first, I didn't seek it out. I guess about fifty percent of the time I was looking for something in particular, and the other fifty percent of the time I was just looking around and came across new things. I came across homosexual stuff, and to my surprise, I was curious. Same thing with bestiality and child porn, though those didn't become particular interests of mine. I did get interested in young teen stuff, girls on spring break and that kind of thing. I would tell myself the person was of age while I was looking at it. But I would question it afterward."

Sex addicts are only slightly more likely to escalate to extreme tastes than are "recreational users," but the fetishes, niches, and obsessions they veer toward do not differ substantially from those of the average pornography consumer. Addicts are, however, more likely to take their habits offline. Though regular users appear to be just as likely to visit strip clubs, sex addicts take it further, hiring escorts, attending swingers clubs, exposing themselves in public, and molesting children. For the sex addict, pornography often leads logically into real-world sexual behaviors with other men, women, and children.

Kenneth, the married consultant and father of three from New Mexico, always saw himself as a good guy; he didn't get into pornography until well into adulthood. He liked to find women who didn't seem hardened by the industry, almost as a way to distance himself from the reality of what he was doing. To maintain the illusion of innocence and willingness, Kenneth sought out progressively younger women, girls who looked under eighteen. All the while, he rationalized: "The thing is, I never paid for porn. Maybe it's my Scotch upbringing, but my rationalization was that if I didn't pay for it, I didn't have a problem." Kenneth built up a range of excuses to suit his mood. It's not such a big deal, he would tell himself. I can stop anytime. Everybody's got something they battle.

Eventually, Kenneth was after seriously underage porn. "I was looking for . . . thank goodness I had a hard time finding it, but I was looking for younger girls," he says. Not prepubescent girls, per se, though he came across kiddie porn on one occasion. "It was scary for me because I was turned on and also because it obviously depicted kids who had been abused and tricked," he says. "It's pretty transparent. It's not as if these kids were being paid five hundred dollars a day to pose. You could tell they were stressed out about being naked in front of the camera." The father of a young girl himself, Kenneth became stressed as well. "I knew my relationship with my daughter was at risk."

Desensitization and Dissatisfaction

It's not as if most men intend to get into bestiality, child pornography, or rape reenactments. Desensitization is a major stage in becoming addicted to pornography. According to psychologist Victor B. Cline, the desensitization phase occurs when "pornography which was originally perceived as shocking, taboo-breaking, illegal, repulsive, or immoral, though still sexually arousing, in time came to be seen as acceptable and commonplace. . . . There is an increasing sense that 'everybody does it' and this gave them permission to also do it, even though the activity was possibly illegal and contrary to their previous moral beliefs and personal standards."[6] Even if extremely hardcore material was repugnant upon first, second, or third viewing, after so many hours spent online, reveling in strip clubs, hiring prostitutes, transgressing another step into the forbidden, and tucking yet another secret into their private "other" lives, the forbidden no longer disturbs the way it once did.

When Liam got broadband Internet access in August 2000, things quickly spun out of control. "I was venturing into hardcore things that had scared me in the past," he recalls. "I was starting to scare myself." Though he considers himself a gentle person, Liam became drawn to violent images, particularly of rape. Repulsed and terrified by his curiosity, he nonetheless kept clicking back, and soon started to fantasize about rape even when he was not looking at pornography. "It was impossible to reconcile this with my own conception of myself," he says. "I'd always gotten along well with people. I never treated people violently. Just to think of myself as having these kinds of thoughts was awful." Liam tried to rationalize it. It was stress. He told himself he was just looking. But at night, unable to sleep, he would anesthetize himself with pornography, masturbating at the computer until he was physically and emotionally exhausted.

For some men, venturing into extreme pornography turns into a dare. How far can you go? For others, it becomes a matter of indifference. Donovan, fifty-five, the former CEO of a large international corporation, was between marriages when he confessed to a friend his frustrations with dating. "Why bother?" the friend advised him. "Just go online." He referred Donovan to call girl Web sites. Over the next couple of years, going online and ordering prostitutes became a weekly endeavor. On several occasions, he hired prostitutes to have sex with dogs in front of him, having cultivated a taste for bestiality online. But as his pornography consumption increased, his satisfaction waned. "For me, sex became less and less gratifying," he recalls. "In seeking the perfect experience, I had to go deeper and more degrading. I became depressed and empty." Pornography addiction was like a no-win search for the perfect car or perfect house—you're never happy with whatever you can actually afford. "You're seeing this fantasy physical being and you try to lay that ideal onto an actual human being—who may be more in every other respect than the physical—and you're not satisfied when she doesn't live up to it. You don't see the reality, just the ways in which that human being doesn't live up to the ideal."

Pornography offers an intensity of stimulation difficult to parallel in the world of matrimonial sex. After his fiasco of a marriage with the drug-addled Hayley, Leo retreated to the sanctuary of pornography, looking at magazines and videos for hours at a time, dating only casually. Then he met Abby, one of his coworkers, a divorcée with a young daughter. Leo developed an immediate crush. They had a storybook wedding and began what Leo hoped would be a "normal" life. Early on, he says, he was honest with his new wife. He told her he looked at pornography and showed her a box of magazines in the closet. Leo says Abby was okay with it because she loved him. According to Leo, Abby said, "I'm cool with that."

That's not quite how Abby sees it. Abby, now thirty-eight, had never dated anyone who used pornography before, not that she knew of, at any rate. Before she and Leo bought their first home together, she and her daughter moved into his house. While cleaning it up, Abby came across a closet stuffed with *Playboy*s. She threw them out. "I thought now that he's getting married to me, he's not going to need these anymore." Later, when they moved to their new house, her five-year-old daughter found a pornographic magazine in their bathroom. Abby scolded Leo. It was one thing to hide them in a closet, but it was not permissible for pornography to be lying around for her daughter to see. Still, she tried not to badger him. She even went so far as to watch pornos with Leo. "I thought that was part of the deal at that point," she says. "I figured, if you can't beat 'em, join 'em." Inside, however, she felt "creepy." She realized she must not be enough for him.

Abby *wasn't* enough, according to Leo. He had gotten used to getting something more from his women and quickly became dissatisfied with their relationship. "I went from crazy Hayley to this wild dating and suddenly I was a dad," he says. Having their first baby together dampened the sexual dynamic, and after their second child, sex slowed to a dribble. "I convinced Abby I was doing her a favor. She had no libido, which I felt like was my license to use porn." He used more and more of it as time went on. "What happens with porn addicts is that whatever you looked at three weeks ago is no longer exciting," Leo explains. "I became more specialized. I got into girls around eighteen years old. I wanted to see young girls in their panties." One day, he got up the guts to steal some panties from a friend's house.

"Couldn't You Be More Like a Porn Star?"

Bit by bit, addicts transfer their pornographic expectations to real life. Donovan, the former CEO, lost his job due to pornography and destroyed two marriages during his years of abuse. Both wives were selected solely on the basis of their looks and sexual adventurousness. He introduced his first wife, a model and actress, to pornography, asking her to watch videos and emulate them afterward. At first she was game, but over time, and especially after she got pregnant, she balked. Feeling betrayed, Donovan began seeing prostitutes and other women, watching pornography alone during his free time. The marriage ended after five years. His second wife, whom he met five years after he had turned to the Internet, fit the same mold. "One thing I can say about porn is you get this image of femininity in your head," he explains. "My choice of women to date and ultimately to marry was utterly superficial." When he and his wives or girlfriends went out, Donovan would dress them in provocative outfits. In the bedroom, he kept them well supplied with sex toys and lingerie. He bought breast implants for both wives and for four of his girlfriends on the side and in between marriages.

When not asking women to conform to their fantasies, sex addicts often try to get their women to play along with their fantasies of other women. After four years of marriage, Leo took Abby to a strip club. This was during her "accommodating" phase. They sat down at a table and Leo said to Abby, "See? It's not a big deal." He leaned forward in his chair and watched intently. One of the women came out on the main stage, then migrated to a smaller stage by their table. Leo reached out, touched the performer's leg, and cooed, "You're just oh-so-smooth." At that point, Abby realized his problem wasn't about inanimate objects, as Leo made it out to be. Here was a real person. Abby ran to the bathroom. There, a few strippers asked why she was crying. "Every man who comes in here is dirt," one stripper consoled her, and the others joined in agreement. Abby asked them why they did it. "Because we can take advantage of them and take their money," was their response. When she got back to the table, Leo didn't notice she had been crying. He was watching the show.

Abby started listening to Christian radio, and at her urging, she and

Leo began attending a new church regularly. Leo even became a lay speaker at their church, all the while smoking pot every night and surfing porn for hours. Abby quietly seethed inside, unable to handle Leo's dual nature: good Christian on the outside, porn-frenzied pothead at home. When she reproached him, Leo accused her of being a Jesus freak. So she joined a group for wives of sex addicts. "Over and over you would hear women say, 'My husband is such a good Christian, you just would never think he would do this,'" Abby recalls. "But all these men were into porn, going to strip clubs, lying to their wives, cheating on them."

Then Abby had a hysterectomy, forcing her to abstain from sex for six weeks. Leo turned to pornography for hours on end. "It has nothing to do with you," he told her. "We're just not having enough sex." Abby retreated. "I felt like I was unattractive, uninteresting," she recalls. Their sex life had been good early on, but had steadily gotten worse. Leo became obsessed with various fetishes and scenarios, trying to pull Abby into his world. One day, he was online looking at life-size sex dolls and told Abby he wanted to get one. "When you're not available, I could use this," he told Abby. "I'm being replaced," she thought to herself.

Abby's feelings echo those of other women involved with addicts. Elizabeth, a thirty-eight-year-old pharmacist from Florida, felt terrible throughout her two-year marriage. "I'm not an unattractive person, but he made me feel horrible. I had never been competitive before, but with him I was constantly checking out other women to see who my husband was lusting after and how I measured up. I felt like my arms were too flabby, my butt wasn't hard enough, my calves weren't shapely. I was compelled to exercise all the time." Such feelings are not unfounded. Many men describe a waning interest in their wives and growing annoyance at their wives' efforts to draw them in, subtracting time that could otherwise be devoted to pornography. For those men who hide their habit from their spouses, covering it up requires elaborate efforts. At the very least they'll pretend to be sexually excited by their spouses while closing their eyes and picturing pornography in their minds.

Like many recovering porn addicts, Liam admits that he began to look at his wife differently. It wasn't as though she were unattractive. But she was in her late thirties. "When you're seeking out the perfect woman in a picture, with very particular attributes, it's hard for people to measure up," Liam explains. "You cultivate a taste and the average woman—even if she's your wife—doesn't turn you on anymore." It became difficult for Liam to have sex with his wife without playing an internal movie screen of pornographic images. When that didn't work, he tried to get his wife to copy behaviors from pornography. Obsessed with oral sex, he insisted she swallow his semen and say she enjoyed it—just like the girls in pornography. His wife's displeasure was evident, but irrelevant.

"During that period of my life, sex had nothing to do with expressing love or affection," Liam recalls. "I became more selfish, because with porn, it was all about me—me feeling better, me getting more pleasure, me getting more excited. It was completely self-centered. After all, porn wouldn't make any money if it weren't effective. Where would the money be if porn was about giving to others and behaving selflessly?" The self-centeredness pervaded all areas of his life, psychologically, spiritually, emotionally. "My entire orientation became focused inward," he says.

Porn Sex vs. Real Sex

The majority of sex addicts eventually turn off their wives or girlfriends altogether or tune themselves out. Rachel, a thirty-four-year-old mother of three from Michigan, describes sex with her husband as oddly disconnected. "I obviously knew where his body was," she says, "but where was his mind? He would sort of be there at first, but then I didn't know where he went. I don't want to sound wacko, but he was just not there with me. Especially leading up to orgasm and during orgasm. At a certain point, I realized I was just a tool. I could have been anything or anybody. I felt so lonely, even when he was in the room." Elizabeth's husband became obsessed with mutual masturbation. After a while, she didn't want to rely so heavily on what seemed to her like a disconnected act. "Why should it be him getting himself off and me taking care of myself when we're together?" she wondered. "It takes all the intimacy out of the experience." When they did have sex, her husband insisted on ejaculating on her body rather than inside her. "Just the way they do in porn films," she says. "Ironically, he thought he was the greatest lover ever. He saw himself as this fount of pleasure."

Rachel's and Elizabeth's experiences are common. Psychiatrist Jennifer

Schneider's study of ninety-one women and three men, all of whom had spouses or partners seriously involved in cybersex, found that discovering a partner's online sexual activity results in feelings of hurt, betrayal, rejection, abandonment, devastation, loneliness, shame, isolation, humiliation, jealousy, and anger. More than one in five of those surveyed had separated or divorced as a result of their spouse's cybersex addiction. Half reported their spouses were no longer sexually interested in them, and one-third said they were no longer interested in sex with their partner.[7]

For Miles, the exhibitionist, pornography fantasies and his sex life began to overlap. After looking at fetish sites for flashers, he became convinced that every woman who passed him on the street would expose herself at any minute. Driving down the freeway, he would find himself thinking, "Some woman is going to lift up her shirt." The idea became all-consuming. At his workplace, he would tell himself, "Okay, I've been working with this woman for three or four years now. I bet I could get her into bed." Every thought he had was about sex. Every thought was about women wanting to do something sexual. Every thought was about getting them to do what he wanted them to do.

He and his wife had an active sex life, but he was keen to integrate pornography, especially the humiliation and degradation he enjoyed online. He would ask his wife to verbally abuse him while they were making love, to talk about having sex with black men instead of with him, to taunt him that his penis wasn't large enough. For a while, his wife played along. She would tell him that she wished Miles were black, she wanted black men more than she wanted him. But one night, after the usual routine, his wife said, "Miles, I don't know why you want me to talk about other men and specifically black men, but I want to have sex with *you*." Only Miles wasn't making love to his wife. "I was just masturbating with her," he explains. "All the while I was thinking either about porn or trying to make her say things she didn't want to say. I was really just using her—she was like a masturbatory accessory."

Omission and Deception

Wives and other family members are frequently kept in the dark until an addict reaches a breaking point. Many compulsive users deny their problem even to themselves up until they enter recovery, and some deny it during relapses. A number of men who had never paid for pornography, always borrowing videos or looking at free porn online, used their lack of expenditure as an excuse: "If I never spend money on it, I can't be an addict." Others felt as long as they didn't "hurt" anyone, there couldn't be anything wrong. They would tell themselves they were just being more open and honest about the sexual nature of man than all the hypocrites, even as they made attempts to hide their habit from spouses, colleagues, and themselves. The majority admit to compartmentalizing their addiction, whether unconsciously or through careful deliberation. "I would separate it out," recalls Clay, the forty-six-year-old recovered addict from Atlanta. "For me, it was like balancing the scales. I'm doing bad stuff, but I'm also doing good. I started volunteering in the community for the local AIDS organization, while at home my wife had left me because I was spending hours a day looking at pornography."

Addicts work out rationalizations or alternate between denial and justification. Time and again, Leo promised Abby he would quit looking at pornography. "It's been difficult to stop," he confesses. "I'd go for long periods without it. I would purge—no magazines, no nothing. White knuckling." Abby would begin to trust him again and then wham! he says—she would find something on his computer. "The Internet is the source of all evil for a porn addict," Leo explains. "You'll be on eBay and then suddenly you realize you can type in XXX. You can be off it for ten months and it'll take ten seconds to lose it. 'I'll just check it out,' you'll say."

When Abby left Leo the first time, he called some friends from church to seek advice. "Oh, that's just normal guy stuff," they told him. After that, Abby didn't want those friends hanging around their house anymore. Leo even went and told the pastor about the source of their marital problems. "She'll just have to learn that all men struggle with pornography," the pastor advised. Abby quit the church. "It truly bothered me that all the while, Leo continued to go up there and give sermons and I kept hearing from people, 'He's so wonderful, he's such a great Christian,'" she says.

"This is what our relationship had become. Him hiding and me searching. When he was at work, that's what I'd be doing—looking through his car." Abby laughs bitterly. "Tell me that's not unhealthy. There was no trust at all." She felt dead inside. She couldn't be intimate with her husband. " 'Who *is* this man?' " she would ask herself. "When somebody has this secretive nature, you realize you don't know them and so how can you give to them?"

One day, Abby discovered a box of diskettes in the closet. She went through the entire stash and found pictures of little girls. "I was so freaked out, I didn't know what to do," she recalls. "At this point, he had stolen women's underwear and I had found them hidden in his suitcase." She called Leo at work, screaming with rage. She told him he was lucky she wasn't calling the police. "It's no big deal," he told her, and offered a litany of excuses. Abby was in shock. She went to Barnes & Noble in despair, trying to find books to explain what was wrong with her husband. "I didn't know what to do or who to call," she says, sobbing at the recollection. "I felt like I was having a nervous breakdown." She got back into the car, drove home, picked up the kids from school, went directly to her parents' house, and told them everything. Her parents were astounded. A week before, they had heard Leo give a sermon in their church. Her father, a retired postal inspector, had witnessed multiple arrests for child porn. Abby's parents were no innocents, but they had never imagined Leo's hidden life.

Slipping into a hide-and-seek world, afraid that a spouse, colleague, boss, or child will discover what he's up to, the addict withdraws from normal life. "Sex addiction is a mental illness of isolation," explains Liam. "It's using something to escape, like any addiction. With pornography, you enter this fantasy world where there are no consequences for your actions." But the stress of hiding pornography from loved ones can become overwhelming. Just as the gambler flees problems and conflicts, turning to the card table to assuage pain, so does the compulsive pornography user turn to pornography. Hours go missing, basement doors locked, questions left unanswered. Many wives describe their husbands withdrawing physically and emotionally from their families, friends, and communities.

For as long as he can remember, Miles felt compelled to hide his pornography. Growing up, his parents had told him looking at pornography was wrong; his father called it "poison." The fear of getting caught, the embarrassment when discovered, the constant hiding weighed on him. Though his wife knew when they met that he looked at pornography, he soon felt it necessary to hide it from her as well. She had watched videos with him when they were dating, but after a while she became uncomfortable, and began to believe his pornography constituted cheating. "It became a game of me sneaking away to look at porn," he recalls. Before the Internet, he would steal away to video stores and watch movies when she wasn't around. He was often irritated when his wife proved to be an obstacle. "Other times, I felt guilty because I knew she didn't approve," Miles says. "I knew it was wrong, but there was also a fire inside me, and her feelings just didn't matter enough." In retrospect, Miles says, his reasoning seemed off. His mind was blurred.

The Blur

When an addict tries to stop using pornography, his recovery is as slow and convoluted, as rife with relapses and failures and ongoing challenges as any drug addict or alcoholic. *I'll stop once I get married,* the pornography addict tells himself. *I'll stop once I get involved in church. I'll stop once I start that new job. Once we have kids, I'll stop. I'll stop when the kids are old enough to use the computer. . . .* Shortly after Tony, the researcher from San Diego, decided to stop using pornography in 1995, he got Internet access at work. His work made it impossible to avoid going online and he relapsed, despite attending 12-step meetings. "It was all free and could be done privately," he says. "I didn't have to go to a store or deal with the social consequences of somebody seeing me. I didn't have to constantly search for the right videos. Now, anything could be found online. The first porn I had ever seen had been women having sex with young boys and animals. I became obsessed with finding that again." Losing days and nights to pornography once more, Tony redoubled his efforts at recovery. He got rid of the Internet at home and cut down at work. But two weeks later, he found himself in an adult bookstore. He reinstalled the Internet, but with filters. But it seemed that no matter what he did, something popped up to provoke his compulsion. He'd be watching CNN and an advertisement for the *Sports Illustrated* swimsuit show would appear. He'd catch a glimpse of *Maxim* on the newsstand. These days, Tony only watches programs with TiVo so he can fast-forward through commercials, which often border closely on pornography and are liable to send him searching for something harder.

Cycling through use and abstinence, promises kept and broken, admission and denial, many compulsive pornography users take their wives, families, and colleagues along for a months- or years-long roller-coaster ride of hope and betrayal. After yet another relapse, Abby gave Leo an ultimatum. In May 2003, back together after a separation, Abby was ready to move to another city. For several months, Leo had been working there during the week and flying back home on weekends. They had just put the house on the market. Leo had tried to stick by his promise, but after seven months of self-professed sobriety there was an incident. "My stepdaughter found something on the computer," he says vaguely.

Abby remembers that afternoon well. She and her fourteen-year-old daughter were home with the flu while Leo was attending his weekly sex addict meeting. Suddenly, Abby heard a shriek from the family computer room. Her daughter came running into the room screaming. "I thought someone had stabbed her," Abby recalls. Abby went to investigate the family computer. On the screen were photographs Leo had taken of himself dressed in her daughter's underwear. "Try explaining that to a fourteen-year-old," Abby says tearfully. "She was so freaked out. All I could think was, 'Why did she have to find this?' " Abby told her daughter to go upstairs and pack while they waited for her and Leo's three sons to get home from school. She then called Leo to confront him with what the girl had found. "I deleted all that," Leo protested. "There's no way she saw that." Abby insisted he not come back to their house. When Abby went up to her daughter's room, she found her there sobbing, cutting her underwear into tiny pieces.

Months later, her daughter, consumed with anger, is in therapy. She stopped going out and avoids her friends. How could she tell them, "My dad doesn't live here anymore because I found pictures of him in my underwear?" Though she viewed her stepfather as a father figure and had lived with him since the age of four, she doesn't want to see him again. For Abby, this was the breaking point. "I had found gay porn, child porn, and now he's taking pictures of himself in my child's underwear. What am I waiting for? How many chances am I supposed to give him? How big a disaster does it have to be? I don't think this is what God intended for me."

Often it takes a real tragedy to compel compulsive users into recovery—the total conflation of pornographic fantasy and the reality of addiction—the end of a marriage, loss of a job, or violation of the law. On a family vacation, Kenneth, the consultant from New Mexico, found himself propositioning fifteen-year-olds. "Whatever denial I had been maintaining, this pretty much blew my cover. I knew I was totally out of control." Though he managed to leave his daughter alone, he began molesting his children's babysitters—girls in their young teens. No charges were pressed, but his wife found out. "It pretty much destroyed her trust in me," he says. "After that, she had a very hard time relating to me sexually. She saw me as a predator."

"I know it sounds like an excuse, but I do not think this would have happened had I not been looking at porn. I think there's a real connection and I feel strongly about it. After a while, the line between fantasy and reality became very blurred to me. Here all these women in my fantasy world were pretending to be anything I wanted. I was in control. My fantasies were their command. Before long, I got the impression that all that women were interested in was having sex with me." Kenneth doesn't want to make excuses. "It doesn't mean I'm not responsible," he says. "But using pornography can definitely get men into big trouble."

Ironically, Kenneth was a longtime supporter of pornography, not only on an individual level but for society at large. A progressive Democrat, Kenneth considers himself a dedicated defender of civil liberties. He followed Larry Flynt's battles in court because, he says, "I thought he was fighting the good fight." He admired Hugh Hefner and lamented any impingements on free speech. "Now I don't know," he says. "It's not that simple. My views on pornography have changed." He pauses and sighs. "I don't think prohibition is the way to solve social problems. But we have to find some better way to deal with this."

8

The Truth about Pornography

> Please read and comply with the following conditions before you continue:
>
> I am at least 21 years of age.
>
> The sexually explicit material I am viewing is for my own personal use and I will not expose minors to the material.
>
> I desire to view sexually explicit material
>
> I believe that as an adult it is my inalienable right to receive/view sexually explicit material. . . .
>
> All images and videos within this website are nonviolent. All performers on this site are over the age of 18, have consented to being photographed and/or filmed, have signed model release and provided proof of age, believe it is their right to engage in consensual sexual acts for the entertainment and education of other adults and believe it is your right as an adult to watch them doing what adults do.
>
> The videos and images in this site are intended to be used by responsible adults as sexual aids, to provide sexual education and to provide sexual entertainment.
>
> —*Welcome page on a pornography Web site*

Once those "21 or older" who choose to comply get inside this Web site, which bills itself as "The Home of the Asshole Milkshake," it blares, "The most extreme shit you'll ever see. See why the U.S. government is after us!"[1] Viewers are "educated" as to how multiple men can anally penetrate a woman and then force her to drink the ejaculated semen extracted from her own anus. Others can be "entertained" by viewing *Forced Entry*, a video simulating vivid rape and murder scenes of women. Despite the site's self-professed renegade status, it does not differ substantially in content or tone from vast numbers of pornographic Web sites, and it's only a click away from "softer" sites. Moreover, nothing prevents minors from making the transition. In a study by the Pew Internet Research Center, 15 percent of boys twelve to seventeen (and 25 percent of boys fifteen to seventeen) have lied about their age to access a Web site—surely a lowball figure. The Internet and other technologies have changed the rules of the game, obscuring the boundaries between softcore and hardcore, upgrading customers to harder, faster—more quickly than ever before.

Incidents that muster outrage in the "real world" elicit little response when supposedly relegated to the realm of pornography. In a coffee-table book of photos of porn stars and related essays, Salman Rushdie claimed that, though pornography is particularly popular in Muslim countries due to the segregation of the sexes, a free and civilized society should be judged by its willingness to accept pornography. Given the popularity of porn in America, what does this say about our country? Are we sexually repressed or are we free? Moreover, such seemingly liberal observations ignore the similarities between the sexual repression outside pornography and the repression within it. As a prisoner tortured and photographed pornographically at the Abu Ghraib prison in Iraq explained, "We are men. It's okay if they beat me. . . . But no one would want their manhood to be shattered. They wanted us to feel as though we were women, the way women feel, and this is the worst insult, to feel like a woman."[2] For the prisoner, to be made into pornography—to be pornified—was to be dehumanized; yet when presented in the context of pornography proper, it's acceptable, even entertaining, for people to be treated as such. In the United States, the outrage over the actions at Abu Ghraib was accompanied by a strange hush regarding the inspiration of those acts and images, which are perpetrated in pornography, in this country as elsewhere in the world, every day. Few people think to question, let alone fulminate over, the messages sent by "legitimate" porn.

We have entered the twenty-first century immersed in a new pornified culture with little language to describe or decry it. Instead, there is silence, nervous laughter, ignorance, and outdated arguments. We shrug or nod when told that pornography is natural. Masculine. Empowering to women. Harmless. Progressive. Necessary. It's time to start questioning these assumptions.

The Porn Imperative?

A common assumption prevails that pornography is natural, an eternal component of male biology and the human sexual landscape. Advocates cite the "porn has existed since cavemen" argument, pointing to cave wall drawings and early sculptures of naked women to prove the timeless appeal of pornography. Man, we are meant to believe, was born for porn. Yet those sexual representations were paltry, tame, and ultimately insignificant compared with the quality and quantity of pornography available today. An unadorned Greek statue is a far cry from Meatholes.com, or even *Maxim* magazine.

Pornography proponents not only deliberately conflate art and pornography; they equate human sexuality with pornography consumption, drawing a causal link between man's instinct to look at other people with admiration or desire and his use of pornography. According to such a view, because men like to look at naked women, they will inevitably look at pornography; to be a man is to be a pornography consumer, simply by dint of one's manhood and sexuality. It's a view championed in the media and in popular culture. Dan Savage, a sex columnist, has said, "I get a lot of questions from women who are upset because their partners or their husbands look at pornography still or go online and look at pornography and why not just look at them since they're there. And my answer is always, you know, men look and men will always look. And women look too, they're just slyer about it. I think, better at it. And if you want to be with someone who doesn't look at others and lust after others, you should get a dog or girlfriend or a plant or something besides a husband."[3] But there's a vast difference between sexuality and its artistic representation, and pornography, a commercialized means to arousal. To pretend they are equivalent is nothing short of deceit. And to blithely declare that admiring an attractive woman at a cocktail party and spending hours at the computer using Internet pornography are the same thing is ludicrous.

Still, the idea that pornography is "natural" and biologically inevitable has its defenders, the latest armed with scientific data. Evolutionary psychologists have joined the cause of tracing pornography back to our genetic ancestors, providing anecdotes about certain subspecies of birds and earlier stages of humankind to prove man's need for sexual variety and pornographic release. But these true believers in the biological imperative for pornography fail to differentiate between science and culture, between causation and correlation, between cause and effect. "There's this whole argument that men are more visual than women, but it's fruitless," says psychologist Gary Brooks. "It may be partly biological, but men are also *taught* to be more visual. They're taught that that's what it's about and it's made worse by pornography, which has a money-vested interest in getting men to think this way. That men need pornographic stimulation is one of the lies pornography has perpetuated." Boys become conditioned to these kinds of images, according to Brooks. "For example, pornography has made American men very breast-centric. Even though, from a biological standpoint, breast size has no relation to women's reproductive ability or health status. Evolutionary psychologists argue backwards, trying to explain what already exists."

The desire to find a scientific justification for pornography is understandable. In a world in which sex roles have changed dramatically during the past thirty years, our cultural understanding of masculinity and manhood is in flux. To find some kind of firm grounding might ease the discomfort these changes have wrought. In a culture that has become unsure of how manhood is defined, the closer one comes to *The Man Show*, *Maxim*, and the *Playboy* mentality, the more one's masculinity is ensured. With women becoming more powerful professionally, financially, and emotionally, pornography is still an arena in which men hold all the chips. Whether they use science or religion to justify their beliefs about pornography, men cling to old stereotypes because they serve their function: "Dear Amy," writes "Bob from Setauket" to the *Chicago Tribune* advice columnist in response to a column she wrote that was critical of pornography, "Get real, lady. Men enjoy looking at beautiful women. They are either honest about it, or they lie about it. It is normal and God made us that way. It is an utter turnoff for a man to be told that the only woman he can look at is his wife. Maybe you need to check a man's point of view. . . . We are different and we see things different. Accept it."[4] It's no surprise that many men are more than a little frustrated, even angry, about redefining their role as men and having that role judged by women and by the rest of society.

It's easier to say, "I can't help it. I'm a man," than to delve into the reasons behind the consumption and proliferation of pornography. Yet human biology and zoology cannot explain it all away. Biology as viewed through an evolutionary psychologist's lens does little to explain women's increasing use of pornography, for example. Nor do evolutionary psychologists make an effort to winnow biological roots from cultural influences or to vest culture with the power to influence biology. By claiming something is "natural," any debate to the contrary is effectively stifled as the antiquated whinging of those opposed to science, biology, and the sometimes unpretty realities of human sexuality.

But the prevalence of pornography, and in particular its surge and transformation over the past ten years, simply cannot be adequately explained by evolutionary psychology. The standards of pornography itself often belie such theories. For example, despite the evolutionary psychology myth that men are necessarily more sexually voracious and aggressive than their female counterparts, women in pornography are frequently portrayed as sexually insatiable. They are often the aggressors, wantonly tempting men, indifferent to emotion, and apt to bed multiple partners of both sexes. As Dolf Zillmann notes in his studies on pornography, "The massive exposure of men to portrayals of women as sex-crazy creatures who move from partner to partner is thought to make women seem unworthy of attention and care in an enduring relationship."[5] Is it biology dictating pornography or the porn itself that conveniently adopts male-centric beliefs about women's role and inherent worth? Even if pornography didn't send conflicting messages about the "nature" of man, no convincing evidence supports the idea that men are naturally predisposed to, or may even require, pornography. Those who conflate looking at pretty pictures with masturbating to pornography usually have an agenda behind their theories. They have something to prove.

Being Progressive about Porn

But it's not just unreconstructed chauvinists, evolutionary psych theorists, and those who believe God created porn for man who are out to prove pornography's legitimacy. In today's polarized cultural debates, supporting pornography has become the default liberal, moderate, and civil libertarian position. Speaking out against pornography has become a reactionary cause rather than a progressive one—even though acceptance or approval of pornography shouldn't be any more an indication of one's liberal bona fides than denouncing it should be of proving one's conservatism.

The drawing of political battle lines over pornography dates back in large part to two conflicting federal reports designed to study and address the issue. In 1968, the United States President's Commission on Obscenity and Pornography was charged with understanding the effects of pornography "upon the public and particularly minors and its relationship to crime and other antisocial behaviors." After two years of research, the commission issued a report that concluded, "In sum, empirical research designed to clarify the question has found no evidence to date that exposure to explicit sexual materials plays a significant role in the causation of delinquent or criminal behavior among youths or adults. The Commission cannot conclude that exposure to erotic materials is a factor in the causation of sex crime or sex delinquency."[6] The Nixon administration promptly denounced the report. Sixteen years later, the Reagan administration commissioned what later came to be known as the Meese Report (for the Attorney General's Commission on Pornography), which came to the exact opposite conclusion. Pornography, the Meese Report explained, leads to sexual violence, rape, deviation, and the destruction of families. Yet while the earlier report exonerating pornography was widely distributed and published by a commercial press, the Meese Report was difficult to track down, unpublished commercially, and immediately distorted and vilified in a popular pro-pornography book published by *Penthouse* and distributed on newsstands everywhere.

As a result of these two contradictory reports, many Americans, especially liberals and moderates, came to the conclusion that the first report was accurate while the second was politically motivated hackwork, created by religious zealots to crack down on the absence of family values and promulgated by a man who was himself under investigation for corruption. Who was *he* to talk? While there may well be some truth to the political motivation behind the second study, concluding that the results were therefore inaccurate unfairly distorts the report's findings. In truth, the second report contained a good deal of valuable, nonpartisan data from reliable academicians and social scientists. Jennings Bryant, a liberal professor of communications and the coauthor with Dolf Zillmann of one of the major studies depicting the harm wrought by pornography, witnessed the rampant politicizing of his study's conclusions and recommendations; in the years that followed the study's release, he became the target of vicious attacks by pornography supporters. Meanwhile, social scientists who supported pornography were co opted by the pornography industry and ferried about to pro-pornography lectures and conferences worldwide.

Regardless of the motivations behind and differing conclusions of each of these two major reports, it's hard to argue against the fact that both reports are outdated. The first report was generated back when *Playboy* didn't even include full-frontal nudity and before most hardcore magazines had been launched. Penetration shots were rare. *Hustler*, for example, wasn't created until four years after the first presidential commission issued its final report. Not only was the magazine world relatively tame at the time of the 1970 report, but both it and the Meese Report were written before cable television, the VCR, and especially the Internet took pornography to a whole new level. Furthermore, the 1970 report's goals were narrow—trying to forge a link between pornography and sexual violence—without exploring the vast area of influence that stops short of violence. There was no effort to study or document other negative effects of pornography on men, women, or children, an area that the Meese Report took up to a greater, though still far from complete, extent.

In the wake of the two reports and their distortion in the popular media, pornography became a politically progressive cause, a convenient tool in the culture wars. Pornographers successfully fomented a bogus fight between Victorian prudishness and modern sexual freedom that has been taken up by everyone from libertarians to Web-heads to feminists to liberal Democrats—and the battle line hasn't budged for decades. As Marian Salzman, chief strategy officer at advertising agency Euro RSCG Worldwide, noted in January 2004, "It's a way to prove your liberalness not to be freaked out by porn."[7] The next generation of pornography consumers has been effectively won over, often unaware of the political machinations that preceded this new "consensus." Today's teenagers and twenty-somethings view "their" pornography as something to defend against government intrusion. An undergraduate student at the University of Houston recently complained in his school newspaper about former attorney general John Ashcroft's efforts to combat pornography by claiming the effort was there only "to satisfy the fraction of Americans who think Michael Savage isn't crazy." He ends with the exhortation, "Let Ashcroft know what you think of his priorities: Go rent *Debbie Does Dallas* and enjoy it."[8]

Not surprisingly, given such politicization of the issue, Americans' points of view on pornography these days often lines up with their political philosophy. While people identifying themselves as Republicans or Democrats show little difference in their opinions about pornography, those who self-identify as liberal are more likely to support pornography than those who consider themselves conservative. For example, liberals are more likely than conservatives to believe that pornography improves people's sex lives and less likely to believe that pornography changes men's expectations of how women should behave. In the *Pornified*/Harris poll, 54 percent of conservatives say pornography harms relationships between men and women, and 39 percent see pornography as cheating, compared with 30 percent and 15 percent, respectively, of liberals. And when it comes to measures to control pornography, conservatives are more likely to advocate reforms: 45 percent of conservatives believe that government should regulate Internet pornography so that kids cannot access X-rated Web sites, compared with 32 percent of liberals who champion such measures. To condemn or even question pornography these days is, ironically, seen by liberals as a sign of closed-mindedness.

Moreover, in our pornified culture, pornography is typically seen by the Left and by libertarians as a right and a vindication. Pornographic

Web site links are included on hipster blogs alongside serious and offbeat news stories—just another form of infotainment. Online, men fulminate over any attempts to "suppress" their right to pornographic freedom and academics dissect the "sex positive" aspects of pornography. At the hip private club Soho House in New York, members can work out to a selection of pornographic DVDs provided by the gym library, and watch them on screens attached to their treadmills for everyone else to see. Pornography is viewed as another form of cool entertainment, and people should be allowed to amuse themselves as they please. "Porn is where hip hop was ten to fifteen years ago," Cobe Chantrel, vice president of marketing at Hollywood talent management company The Firm, has said. "It's very rock and roll. There's a rebellious, edgy attitude to it."[9]

But were pornography truly so sexually liberating, there would be little that is outré or taboo about it all. Hypocrisy and guilt still dominate sexuality in many ways, and pornography isn't the cure for Puritanism or the sign of its defeat—it's an emblem of its ongoing power to isolate and stigmatize sex. A truly liberated society would be one in which there were no need to "rebel" via commercialized images of sex. And pornography is hardly revolutionary. Indeed, porn may be the ultimate capitalist enterprise: low costs; large profit margins; a cheap labor force, readily available abroad if the home supply fails to satisfy; a broad-based market with easily identifiable target niches; multiple channels of distribution. Pornography is big business, and it's out to protect its interests against what it sees as excessive governmental and societal interference. The industry even has its own lobbying arm, whose head, a former defense industry lobbyist, told *60 Minutes,* "Corporations are in business to make money. This is an extremely large business and it's a great opportunity for profit for it. . . . When you explain to [legislators] the size and the scope of the business, they realize, as all politicians do, that it's votes and money that we're talking about."[10] Pornographers distort pornography into an issue of progressivism and civil liberties precisely because they have millions of dollars of profit on the line. The industry—which likes to position itself as just another all-American enterprise trying to earn an honest dollar despite government interference, excessive regulation, and taxation—isn't any different from any other large corporation, be it Halliburton or GlaxoSmithKline. The idea of "progressive" Americans lining up to defend a notoriously corrupt and abusive industry would seem implausible.

But there's more to the pro-porn rebellion. The latest wave of pornography crusaders is not only railing against moralizing on the part of the government and organized religion, the argument that dominated the family values–obsessed eighties. Nor is it just about a libertarian or free-market fight against government regulation. Today, pornography advocates are also and perhaps equally rebelling against what they view as the excesses of liberalism and feminism of the early nineties, in particular, the extremes of political correctness. Defending pornography seems to have become a way for people who think of themselves as progressive, liberal, and open-minded to revolt against the close-minded, PC police of university campuses and corporate human resources guidelines. Denouncing pornography is akin to mocking what is derisively referred to as "sexual correctness."

But no matter how distasteful knee-jerk political correctness may be, it's hard to ignore the equally illiberal nature of porn itself. Certainly, it's hard to find anything more retrograde, repressive, or closed-minded than the sexual clichés peddled by pornography. Rather than a mark of escape from the past, the dominant morality of pornography reeks of Puritan and Victorian prudery; it creates a world populated by virgins and whores, by women who are used and shamed for being sexually voracious. Their degradation is deserved, according to the prim sexual vision of the pornographer. Even when the woman isn't overtly degraded, she is deemed less than the man watching her by dint of being paid to please him sexually in a public forum. Even when pornography is made specifically "for" women, as in the case of "indie" magazines like *Sweet Action,* the model often replicates that experience, unthinkingly substituting men's bodies for women's along the same old porn patterns. In pornography, sexuality frequently accompanies or provokes disgust and hatred—something to be done quickly, and just as quickly disposed of. In the world of pornography, sex is generally dirty, cheap, and—in the end—not much fun. Surely it is this pornified version of sexuality that deserves denigration, mockery, and rebellion.

Pornography: A Right or Wrong?

But rather than fight for people's right to speak out against pornography, Americans have instead fought for the right of pornographers to distribute their product without regulation and for consumers to lap it up unhindered. "Isn't it our right to look at and read and masturbate to whatever we want?" has become a rallying cry. "What right does the government have in our bedrooms?" Businesses have made a fortune by linking pornography with civil liberties, arguing that to use pornography is to turn one's nose up at the Ed Meeses and the hypocritical reactionaries. They've managed to equate the use of pornography with a defense of the Bill of Rights, convincing an entire generation that pornography is not only okay, it's the American citizen's right. Today, according to the *Pornified*/Harris poll, 23 percent of Americans believe that whether one likes it or not, people should have full access to pornography under the U.S. Constitution's First Amendment. Democrats were only slightly more likely (24 percent) than Republicans (20 percent) to take this position. Not surprisingly, those of the baby-boomer generation and younger are nearly twice as likely to believe pornography is protected speech than Americans age fifty-nine and older, and men are more than twice as likely as women to consider pornography a political right.

The major pornography lobbying group calls itself the Free Speech Coalition, much in the spirit of anti-environmentalist groups that adorn themselves in leafy labels like the Blue Skies Society to obscure their true agendas. The rhetoric of the pro-pornography movement also bears a striking resemblance to the gun rights movement. Each popularizes the idea of a Big Brother federal government tyranny out to strip Main Street citizens of their fundamental rights. Just as the Second Amendment was never intended to encourage the sale of semiautomatic military weapons to ex-cons, the First Amendment was never meant to sanction the dissemination of speech that is free of social merit, artistic quality, or political purpose. In a country obsessed with the Founding Fathers and their vision, little thought is given to what they would make of the current application of the Constitution's free political speech.

In the fight for freedom of porn, Larry Flynt—who once yelled at the Supreme Court, "Fuck this court! You're nothing but eight assholes and a token cunt!"—positions himself as the Martin Luther King, Jr., of free speech, waging a battle for civil rights by endlessly contesting obscenity prosecutions on the basis of the First Amendment.[11] He conveniently has the right set of enemies to rally his followers to the "liberal" cause. By going up against people like the Reverend Jerry Falwell of the Moral Majority, Flynt has turned himself into a martyr for supposed progressivism and "true" patriotism. The cover of Flynt's book *Sex, Lies, & Politics: The Naked Truth* features him posed in front of an oversized American flag. Meanwhile, his magazine *Hustler* has depicted violent and senseless forms of hardcore pornography, with one infamous spread depicting a woman shaved, raped, and apparently killed in a concentration camp–style setting.[12] Those who refuse to play along with Flynt's constitutional ploy are ridiculed as reactionary and prudish. Yet even free speech advocates like *Harper's* editor Lewis Lapham, who originally intended to lend his signature to a joint letter in support of Flynt against obscenity charges, withdrew his offer after viewing a copy of *Hustler*. "I'm not sure this was quite what Jefferson had in mind," he noted at the time.[13] Flynt isn't the only businessman eager to equate his enterprise with constitutional freedom. The Playboy Foundation, for example, bestows an annual award loftily entitled the "Hugh M. Hefner First Amendment Award" to high school students, lawyers, journalists, and educators who protect Americans' right to free speech. Certainly people like Bill Maher and Molly Ivins, both recipients of the twenty-fifth anniversary award, deserve recognition for their efforts to promote free political speech, but the irony of an organization that disregards the rights of women giving such an honor is lost in the limelight of the celebrity-studded event. Those who defend pornographic images that denigrate women would be loath to defend *Little Black Sambo* books or Nazi artwork. But such hypocrisy and oversights are ignored on today's political battlefield over porn. Just what are we willing to tolerate in the name of "tolerance," and why?

Rather than deal with the reality of pornographic material, there is a willful attempt on the part of pornographers and their defenders to portray pornography as something it clearly is not: a useful sexual education tool, a harmless form of recreation, open communication about sexuality. Lawyers for the ACLU frequently refer to "speech about sex" or "sexually oriented expression" instead of "pornography" when fighting measures intended to curb pornography. They argue that children will be prevented from accessing harmless and informative content about contraceptives and sexually transmitted diseases, that adults will be unable to read sexual material, such as sexually explicit essays or how-to guides on increasing sexual desire or skill. In the aftermath of the Child Online Protection Act's defeat by the Supreme Court, Ann Beeson, the ACLU's associate legal director, said, "By preventing Attorney General Ashcroft from enforcing this questionable federal law, the court has made it safe for artists, sex educators, and Web publishers to communicate with adults about sexuality without risking jail time."[14] Perhaps sex educators, artists, and legitimate Web publishers *were* unfairly included in COPA's targeted web, but many legal experts disagree with that analysis. And were that the case, the law could have been rewritten so as to confine its targets to pornography proper, allowing other sexually explicit forms of art and information to flourish. Instead, the law's opponents, including the ACLU, rushed to defend the right to free speech but neglected to differentiate between pornography and other forms of "sexual expression." As a result, what was once considered harmful, obscene, and dangerous is now exalted as free political speech. To call it "educational" or "speech about sex" smacks of legalistic semantics and intellectual dishonesty.

By defending pornography as free speech, so-called advocates could actually be seen as threatening its foundations, as the Supreme Court noted in the 1973 *Miller v. California* obscenity case, the federal court's last major ruling defining pornography: "In our view, to equate the free and robust exchange of ideas and political debate with commercial exploitation of obscene material demeans the grand conception of the First Amendment and its high purposes in the historic struggle for freedom." According to the decision, obscenity—which is not protected by the Constitution's First Amendment—is material that a judge or jury finds is, as a whole, appealing to a prurient interest in sex, depicts sexual conduct in a patently offensive manner, and lacks serious literary, artistic, political, and scientific value. Using that definition, would *Gag*

Factor 15 pass muster? How about the online how-to guide to creating an Asshole Milkshake? Until very recently, no one even conceived that the First Amendment would apply to pornography, which was considered by common consent and by law to be unworthy of protection. Not only do pornographic images stretch the definition of "speech" but, as disseminated in the marketplace, they have a similar demonstrable effect on women as a white person making a threatening and vulgar racial epithet toward a black man or woman, which courts have already ruled to be unprotected by the First Amendment.

Moreover, rather than impose some kind of nationwide dictum, as its opponents suggest, the law in question gives considerable freedom to local communities to decide what's permissible. According to *Miller v. California,* localities are allowed to apply a "community standard" to make their own decisions about "obscenity" based on contemporary mores. A town can determine what kind of storefronts they want visible on Main Street or whether they want billboards advertising pornographic materials on their highways. Of course, the idea of "local community" shifted radically following the introduction of satellite television and the World Wide Web. A pornography shop operating on the wrong side of town can be easily opposed by a town council, but a Moscow-based Internet entrepreneur or even a San Fernando Valley pornography empire beaming their goods worldwide online does not easily fall under any local jurisdiction. But just because the community standard doesn't fit this new paradigm does not mean we should give up on it altogether.

A large majority of Americans aren't ready for defeatism either. According to a 2004 nationwide poll by Wirthlin Worldwide, 79 percent of Americans agree that laws against distributing obscene materials on the Internet should be vigorously enforced.[15] (Democrats are as likely as Republicans to agree.) Despite the limitations of the community standard, a significant number of Americans (37 percent) believe pornography should be illegal to all and a majority (60 percent) believe it should be illegal to anyone under the age of eighteen.[16] Surprisingly, men are significantly more likely than women to want pornography illegal for minors (69 percent of men versus 52 percent of women). Furthermore, *only 4 percent of Americans believe pornography should be legal for all.* If the local community doesn't exist on the World Wide Web, then perhaps we need a new standard, one that may not wipe out the world's pornography but could control its excesses within our nation's borders. In America today, it is easier to get pornography than it is to avoid it; we have protected the rights of those who wish to live in a pornified culture while altogether ignoring the interests of those who do not.

Some argue that what goes on in the privacy of an individual home isn't subject to any kind of community standard and therefore the Supreme Court's ruling doesn't apply. This argument, too, is shaky. Pornography affects not only the individual user but the user's family members, colleagues, and peers, as well as strangers and acquaintances with whom the user interacts every day. The effects of pornography extend well beyond the privacy of a single person's household. Moreover, what goes on inside a private home isn't a free-for-all. Husbands beat their wives inside the privacy of the home and kids are sexually molested and abused; though using pornography shouldn't be equated with such crimes, the common link is harm. Pornography need not be criminalized in order for it to be condemned.

But once again we spend far less time criticizing pornography than we do in ensuring its existence and dissemination. People speak of Internet accessibility in hushed terms, as if an unfettered right to online material is the divine and essential right of man. Yet entertainment and information in all other media contain barriers to entry: Movies require the purchase of a ticket. Television is regulated in terms of what can appear: the language used on network sitcoms is restricted, and the programming a six-year-old is liable to encounter when he tunes in to cartoons on Saturday morning is clearly outlined by the federal government. Public libraries require people to apply for a library card, giving up "personal" information as a prerequisite for checking out material. Marketers are prevented from making unsolicited telemarketing phone calls to people who sign up for the Do Not Call registry, a regulation recently upheld by the Supreme Court.

Still, defenders of pornography argue that people have a constitutional right to access pornography on the Internet and requiring a screening process violates that right. "Screens drive away users," the ACLU has said. "Users don't want to give their credit card [numbers] in order to see material that is meant to be seen for free on the Web."[17] But the "burden" of asking a person to use a credit card number in order to access materials is far from censorship. Rather, it is a small inconvenience, surmounted in a matter of seconds. If adults are rankled by the requirement, then they don't have to visit the pornography site, and can access pornography through other media—media that, incidentally, *are* restricted. Second, there's the false claim that such materials are "meant to be seen for free." Meant by whom? What omnipotent force deemed this the right of all citizens? True, pornographers offer free material to entice users into purchasing harder content. True, pornographic content may be pirated and offered for free to users, violating copyright law and ethical business practices, but that does not ensure that everyone necessarily must have the "right" to view pornography for free.

More than a form of speech, pornography is a commercial product, manufactured and distributed by companies from one entrepreneur to huge corporations, and subject to the rules and ethics that govern commerce, not communication. Is oil censored? Are guns censored? Pharmaceuticals? Name a business in America that is not subject to trade regulations, taxes, zoning restrictions, pricing controls, distribution limitations. Asking an adult to punch in credit card numbers in order to access material is as much censorship as asking a youthful-looking adult trying to purchase cigarettes for proof that he or she is over eighteen. When people are carded at the movie theater for trying to enter an R-rated movie, nobody fights against it, championing their access to "free speech." The fact is, censorship already exists, if that's what one chooses to call it.

There are no convincing reasons why pornographic material should be limitless on the Internet while it is clearly limited elsewhere, but there are convincing arguments in favor of requiring credit card identification to gain access to pornography online. Perhaps punching in those numbers will offer consumers the opportunity to reconsider what they're doing rather than mindlessly looking at exploitative material. Take the case of Andy Bull, the former online editor of *The Times* of London, who became an Internet pornography addict while conducting research for a book about the Internet. Bull ultimately served three months in prison for child pornography use. Before his pornography problem developed,

Bull was a devoted believer in the World Wide Web. "I had the zeal of a convert," he recalled recently in an essay published in *The Times*'s magazine. "It seemed obvious to me that the cyber-dollar would become the international currency, English the international language. The Internet could make true, grass-roots democracy realizable for the first time. . . . I was also struck by the libertarian ideals of those who created the World Wide Web. They decreed that the Internet must be free: free of imposed values, morals, restrictions. They did not recognize intellectual property rights any more than conventional sexual mores. Online, no one should have to pay for anything. Like revolutionaries down the ages, they spurned censorship of any kind." Bull's book was meant to document this phenomenon, which he called the "Virtual Eden"—a place where it was "down to the individual's conscience what they do and do not look at and delve into." Conscience notwithstanding, soon Bull was regularly looking at pornography online. His slip into child pornography was gradual—it didn't begin until several years after he began looking at cyberporn, and it started the way it begins for many others: first the teenage girls, then the pubescent girls undressing, etc. Soon he was looking at popular "schoolgirl" magazines downloaded from Japan. Four years later, still "researching the book," Bull was arrested at home in front of his shocked wife of twenty years, fifteen-year-old daughter, and twelve-year-old son. As a result of his experience, Bull believes online anonymity must end:

> Just as when we travel the real world, we must carry a passport, so we should carry an online passport. Technically it could be done—if there were the will. . . . Surely there will be at least a niche market for an ISP that guarantees its search engine will not list illegal or dangerous material, that insists that your ID is visible to the proper authorities when you surf, and which will monitor activity on your account. . . . There are companies who are looking hard at Internet security, but all too often their products are designed to protect the criminal, not the victim. The most blatant have names like History Kill and Evidence Eliminator. They promise to cover your tracks online.[18]

Such measures are tough to pass. Opponents of the courts' efforts to limit pornography raise pointed questions about just what would be included under "indecency" laws. What is "patently offensive," they ask, arguing that one person's standard might differ so radically from the next person's that it would lump committed homosexual coupling with hardcore images of women being brutalized. What lacks "serious" value? One person's estimation of offensive hardcore pornography might be the next person's erotica.

Certainly, to get the government involved in people's private sex lives is a scary proposition. What's deemed dangerous by one person may be normal, even pleasurable to another. Reasonable people might assume that it's "obvious" what we mean by obscenity—a definition that would likely include violent pornography, scatological porn, bukkake—but it takes just one government administration to decree that all homosexual acts are obscene to understand why obscenity is an uneasy standard to enforce. Most Americans are probably like Justice Potter Stewart when they say that while they cannot define pornography they know it when they see it. To pretend that the line between an R-rated film with depictions of sexuality and a XXX movie with hardcore double penetration and "money shots" is anywhere close to being blurred is willfully obtuse and plays into the worst fears of those who might otherwise naturally oppose pornography.

Nonetheless, we have to be able to draw a line somewhere; throwing up our hands, or defending the indefensible because the dilemma poses difficulty, is not the answer. The vast majority of Americans support the First Amendment, but pornography is not solely or even primarily an issue of free speech. Nor should one interpretation of the First Amendment be the only guideline, the only right, the only moral that matters. Just as pro-choice Americans can advocate fewer abortions while defending the right to have abortions, surely Americans can find practical ways to limit and regulate the pornified culture without challenging our constitutional foundations and rights. We shouldn't just worry about the consequences of banning pornography; we also need to worry about the consequences of letting porn proliferate unfettered. Pornography should move beyond a discussion of censorship and into one of standards.

Out with the Old

Just as there are problems with the arguments in favor of pornography so are there with existing arguments in opposition. To date, the outcry against pornography has predominantly come from otherwise distant corners of the political spectrum. Religious opponents deem pornography a sin, a moral offense against God, and a desecration of the holy bonds of matrimony. Right-wing political opponents cite the frequent abuse of pornography among pedophiles or noted serial killers like Ted Bundy and Jeffrey Dahmer. And many feminist and legal opponents argue that pornography leads to rape and that all sex is violence.

To date, the federal government's response to pornography has made it easy to ignore or oppose. John Ashcroft's efforts in the first Bush administration could be easily lumped with his Patriot Act tinkerings with civil liberties or with his intolerance for a nude sculpture of Justice in a government building. Asked about Ashcroft's efforts to clamp down on pornography, Hugh Hefner blamed the religious Right, telling CNN, "We're dealing with religious fanaticism overseas . . . and at the same time, we're allowing a certain amount of religious fanaticism to do the same kind of foolish things at home."[19] Proponents of pornography, not surprisingly, find it easy to defang these brands of opposition through mockery and exaggeration.

One of the main problems with the conservative and religious opponents to pornography is they tend to oppose the very thing that would help alleviate the problem: sex education. For example, Patrick Fagan, formerly of the Child and Family Protection Institute and currently a Heritage Foundation fellow, has said, "Pornography can lead to sexual deviancy for disturbed and normal people alike. They become desensitized to pornography. Sexual fulfillment in marriage can decrease. Marriages can be weakened. Users of pornography frequently lose faith in the viability of marriage. They do not believe that it has any effect on them. Furthermore, pornography is addictive. 'Hardcore' and 'softcore' pornography, *as well as sex-education materials,* have similar effects."[20] Sex education is a far cry from pornography; only such pornography opponents—and, ironically, pornographers—fail to see a distinction. Yet sex education could help clarify the differences between pornography and other forms of sexual expression. The solution to pornography's insidious message to men, women, and children is not isolating the information available, but ensuring that people have context. For children to understand why pornography is wrong, they need sex education programs that explain healthy sexuality and demonstrate why pornography is fundamentally opposed to the exercise of positive sexual pleasures. By perpetuating the idea that all sexuality is "taboo," conservative opponents only encourage and legitimize pornographic rebellion.

Many conservative opponents lump pornography with what they deem to be other forms of sexual deviancy, such as homosexuality and extramarital sex. Opponents use pornography as an easy opportunity—who wants to come out in favor of smut?—to legislate other forms of sexual behavior, such as homosexuality and birth control education. Such arguments against pornography create a problem for all of pornography's opponents by giving substance to fears of a slippery slope. Similarly, on the civil libertarian side, where many liberals dislike or disapprove of pornography, advocates bundle the issue with sex education and classic erotic novels, deliberately blurring the lines to win liberals to their side. On both sides, deliberate obfuscation is the way the game is played.

As for what would seem to be an expected female opposition to pornography, women have largely silenced themselves on the issue, not having made much of a peep since Gloria Steinem donned her bunny ears more than thirty years ago.* Many women seem to have bought into the idea that they should either accept men's involvement with pornography or get in on it themselves. The only arguments against pornography from women come from conservative hothouses like the Eagle Forum and Concerned Women of America and from feminist hardliners Andrea Dworkin and Catherine MacKinnon, making for strange bedfellows. Cultural conservatives argue that pornography subverts the biblical view of womanhood, while legally oriented feminists argue that pornography endangers real-life walking and talking women. Cultural

*Steinem worked undercover as a Playboy Bunny and then wrote about her experience in *New York* magazine.

conservatives argue that pornography is one of several threatening sexual perversions, while feminists typically defend and support homosexuality. Cultural conservatives oppose the dissemination of sexual information, while feminists are the authors of *Our Bodies, Ourselves*.

The result is that both sides have lost what may otherwise be a natural, broad-based following among women. Those on the Right moralize about sex and erotica and the state of the family in general, thereby alienating women who want to celebrate their sexuality while rejecting pornography. Meanwhile, women on the Left focus their sights on a legal battle against pornography, and in gathering their arguments and their statistics ignore anyone who rejects the idea that all women are victims and that all sex is rape. While pornography does exacerbate discrimination, the legalistic attack on pornography has been forced into an untenable position. "Harm" legally must be proved, thus opponents spend their time trying to show that pornography *inevitably* leads to violence, that pornography *causes* men to rape. The backflips of logic and evidence required to make that point strike most people, and most courtrooms, as unpersuasive. Meanwhile, all other feminist, liberal, and moderate arguments against pornography have gotten lost.

When pressed or questioned, most people—even those who dislike pornography—bleat out defenses of pornography like recordings, falling back on legalistic jargon and irrelevant abstractions. But the bottom line is that none of the old arguments about pornography reflect how it affects people's lives and infiltrates their relationships today. Nor are there proposals to contend with the new reality of our pornified culture. In fact, most people don't talk about whether they're "for" or "against" pornography anymore; the cultural consensus seems to consider the matter beyond debate. Through complacency and carelessness, the majority of Americans shrug or laugh off the issue as inconsequential and irrelevant to their lives. But as we have seen, the costs to our relationships, our families, and our culture are great, and will continue to mount. Clearly, we need to find new ways to approach the problem.

Conclusion: The Censure-Not-Censor Solution

To date, arguments against pornography pass over the huge, muddled middle ground where most people actually experience its effects. For most people, pornography wreaks a subtle but real emotional, and in some cases physical, devastation. One need not oppose pornography on religious or political grounds, nor does one need to oppose any and all sexual expression to nonetheless be troubled by the pornified culture.

Even many of the people who use pornography themselves are distressed by the ways in which it has infiltrated people's everyday lives. Men are embarrassed to find themselves masturbating to their computers for hours on end. They question the influence pornography has on their sexual functioning. They worry they're wasting their time and losing themselves in the process. Pornography not only damages relationships and interactions between men and women personally, professionally, and socially, it also makes women feel inferior and cheated, incapable of living up to airbrushed and surgically enhanced perfection. Women are baffled that their husbands and boyfriends feel drawn to submissive or unrealistic images of female behavior. They fear they can't compete with the barrage of easy orgasms that their mates can attain anytime, anywhere to the images of other women—and without their knowledge. And they lie in bed at night wondering why their sex lives have gone sour, their husbands seem distracted, and Viagra is suddenly necessary for their boyfriends at age thirty-six. Both men and women fear the influence that pornography has on their children and the way a pornified culture colors the way young people come of age sexually in this country.

Despite widespread denial and the pervasiveness of outdated rationalizations, many Americans have a problem with the rampant spread of pornography. According to the *Pornified*/Harris poll, when asked what the main thing the government should be doing to address pornography, 42 percent of Americans said the government should regulate Internet pornography specifically so that children cannot access X-rated material online and 13 percent said the government should regulate pornography in a way similar to cigarettes—with warning labels and restrictions to minimize harm. Interestingly, young people (ages eighteen to twenty-four) are most supportive of such measures, yet people in households with children were no more likely to favor them than those without kids around. Moreover, liberals and conservatives were equally likely to favor the regulation of pornography. Finally, only 1 percent of Americans believe the government should fully legalize all forms of pornography, and only 10 percent of Americans believe the government should have no role with regard to pornography. Clearly not everyone favors a laissez-faire approach to the problem, and there *is* room for consensus.

What, then, can be done? In the absence of meaningful government action, the private sector could be mobilized. Yet companies that distribute or sell pornography do little or nothing to cut back, and no meaningful citizen lobby compels them to do so. On the corporate side, disincentives against taking action are strong. First, pornography is big business and growing; in a solid and competitive market, there's money to be made, and lots of it. Second, companies cite the risk of putting self-imposed limits on the supply of pornography; in our litigious society, a company could land in court for years fighting charges of free speech infringement. Third, companies argue that, in today's cutthroat global business climate, if one company—or even all companies in one country—stop supplying pornography, the competition will spring to fill the gap, supplying it no matter what other companies do, even if it means the pornography supply moves underground or overseas. Finally, and not to be underestimated, the pornography industry has done a very effective job keeping our attention off the harm their products inflict. Compounding all these challenges, the reach of pornography, driven by technological changes and cultural acceptance, has dramatically increased in the last ten years. Most Americans have no sense of the damage being done.

Accepting the Reality of Pornography

And real harm is being done. For years, another industry insisted their products did no harm. Corporate owners, employees, and consumers scoffed at studies showing tobacco's links to cancer and emphysema. Industry leaders stood in front of Congress and testified that tobacco was not addictive. All Americans, they said, should be allowed to choose to smoke. Nothing should stand in the way of that freedom. Cigarettes, they explained, were harmless; therefore companies that manufactured them were not in the business to communicate deleterious effects. Later, in the presence of overwhelming public outcry and governmental and grassroots action, they made concessions: Perhaps tobacco *was* harmful to young people. Perhaps children *should* be educated about the potential for damage. Perhaps there *should* be some age limitations on the purchase of tobacco. All the while, hedging and budging, bit by bit. Not that there's anything wrong with tobacco, they continued to insist.

The industry could just as well be pornography. Pornographers consistently deny the harm inflicted by pornography—on its users, on relationships, on society overall—and the industry escapes regulation. When debate does stir up, they focus attention on children (and their parents), skipping over pornography's other targets, adult women and men. And they happily ignore the broader implications of a pornified culture.

Pornography has burst out of the container that civilized society once placed it in for the good of both adults and children. But while its place in American society has shifted radically, nobody—not the government, not the private sector, not society or our cultural institutions—has done anything to address the change. We have relaxed the social, practical, and cultural restrictions once placed on pornography and it has wended its way into our daily lives, playing a more central role than ever before.

Many things we dislike and decry are nonetheless still made available in a free market and a free society. Even things we know cause harm: high-fat food, alcohol, cigars. Banning pornography would be like banning stupid television shows with ridiculous story lines and unlikable characters who say foolish things. Sure, we would all be better off not watching such drivel, but should it be outlawed altogether? Of course not. Just as most Americans, particularly nonsmokers, deplore cigarette smoking, they nonetheless believe adults should have the right to choose for themselves whether or not they want to smoke, and to suffer the consequences if they do. Nor should we necessarily demonize everyone who has looked at pornography. Most people condemn tobacco *the product,* not the people who consume it. Just as with tobacco, there need not be absolute judgment and denunciation, extremism and abolition when it comes to those who use pornography. But likewise, there should not be absolute judgment or denigration toward those who object to pornography and to its influence.

Whatever one's personal use of pornography, we as a society need to confront and understand its broader effects and make efforts to contain them. As with alcohol, cigarettes, and even fast food, pornography can and should be discouraged. Those who don't mind—or even enjoy—overt displays of pornographic magazines on public newsstands might ask themselves how they would feel if their seven-year-old were seeing them. They may think pornography is okay in the abstract, but not when their own husband is poring over Internet pornography late at night. They might think about the fact that pornographic spam hits not only their own e-mail account, but also the inboxes of their children and their nieces and nephews—and that while they themselves might delete the spam without a thought, children may unwittingly (or wittingly) click on those links. They might consider pornography fine when they make their own first stop at a free softcore Web site, but rethink that stance when they find themselves preferring the company of their computer over that of their wife or girlfriend. They might rethink that stance when they consider how pornography affects their wife or girlfriend, and how it colors their relationship as a consequence.

It should be simple in these cases to find a suitable response. In some instances, it's just a matter of limiting personal consumption, in others of enforcing existing restrictions. Magazines could once again get brown-paper wrappers and back-of-the-store or behind-the-counter placement. Better technology could provide effective filtering systems that would make it harder to access pornography online. Thus far, the pornography lobby has made regulating the supply difficult. As industry analyst Dennis McAlpine explained on the PBS show *Frontline,* when it comes to enforcing obscenity laws on cable operators, "It's a lot easier to get somebody when they first go over that line than when they have been over that line for five years and nobody said anything, because that line has then been moved. As you keep moving the line and it becomes accepted, it's a lot tougher to go get them. . . . Going back is a lot tougher to do. They can keep moving it forward. And the longer that nobody tries this in court, the more likely they've got a case that it is acceptable."[1]

Still, once enough people are awakened to the reality of life in a pornified culture, once they realize that the consequences are much more dear than an embarrassed chuckle over seeing Janet Jackson's breast, the difficulties of regulating pornography will not seem so insurmountable. People might bring enough pressure for politicians to buck lobbyists and take action. They might even get the court system to uphold regulatory decisions made long ago but subsequently ignored or overwhelmed by spurious challenges from the pornography industry. Indeed, a number of new regulatory measures have been floated in recent years. One suggestion put forth on the *New York Times* op-ed page by Jonathan A. Knee, director of the media program at Columbia Business School, is to criminalize the giving and receiving of payment to perform sexual acts, which would make the laws against pornography consistent with those of prostitution. Such a proposal, he suggests, would skirt the First Amendment issue while not requiring new leaps in the law. After all, he points out, "society objects on principal to the commodification and commercialization of sexual relations, even between consenting adults."[2] Other efforts aim to regulate the distribution of pornography, particularly in countries such as Australia and Britain. In the United Kingdom, one mobile company, Vodafone, recently blocked handset access to sex, dating, and gambling Web sites unless users could prove their eighteen-or-over age status and opt in to receive such services.[3] In Israel, cell-phone pornography has been banned.

But while much of the blame for pornified culture lies with an unfettered and out-of-control supply, it is in the demand for pornography that the most practical and effective solution lies. Consider a taping of *Girls Gone Wild*. A bunch of drunken college women on spring break decide it's cool and funny to lift up their shirts for the ogling crowds. They're encouraged by the hooting cries of college guys surrounding them on the beach, yelling at them to just "go for it." They're urged on by the cameramen and producers from the *Girls Gone Wild* team, who need the footage to justify their paychecks. Who started this and who is to blame? Is it the women's fault for not having enough self-respect and courage to mock the jeering crowds and walk away? Is it the men's fault for encouraging the women to behave like fools? Or are the cameramen and producers to blame, cynically exploiting young men and women in order to make a buck? Perhaps some reasonable blame could be assigned to all three. But none of these people would be doing any of this if there weren't a considerable demand for *Girls Gone Wild* videos among viewers at home. If demand didn't exist, the product wouldn't sell—and would disappear. There may be fault distributed across the board in the production of pornography, but the most consequential players are the men eager and willing to pay for it.

While the supply of pornography can be effectively limited, the greatest potential for change lies with the demand, and it's the demand that may well prove to be the easiest, most efficient target for effecting change. The government and the private sector, the media and the popular culture, private citizens and public institutions could all work to quell consumer demand. Just as cigarette smoking was glamorized and encouraged in popular culture throughout most of the twentieth century, and then discouraged and regulated once its harm became clear, Americans need to be informed about pornography's negative impact—about how its unabashed acceptance is not a step forward for women, nor a harmless diversion for men, nor a step toward a more open and liberalized sexuality.

What we need is a mind-set shift, one that moves us from viewing porn as hip and fun and sexy to one that recognizes pornography as harmful, pathetic, and decidedly unsexy. Once pornography becomes discredited and derided by both men and women, consumption will become less brazen, and will eventually decline. Imagine a public service TV spot: "Think porn's sexy? Ask former porn star Lara about the director who sexually harassed her. About the fact that she can't get any other jobs that pay nearly as much. How bruised and sore she is, how fearful that she can't have more children. Growing up, Lara wanted to be a lawyer, then an actress. Instead, she's trying to support her three-year-old son while hiding where she gets her money. Sure, porn's sexy—if you like your women desperate, depressed, and defeated." Once people learn how a girl like Nora Kuzma grew up to become exploited pornography star Traci Lords, once they realize that the pornography trade isn't all about seedy-cool *Boogie Nights,* people will choose not to buy into the porn world's conception of sexuality. In her memoir, *Underneath It All,* Lords complains, "Today porn is everywhere I look. I find it in the junk mail folder on my computer . . . porn stars play themselves on television shows, appear on billboards, and give interviews about how 'liberating' porn is for women. Well, I believe it's anything but."

The difference individuals can make via their own behavior and standards should not be underestimated. Imagine if one man, a good friend of the groom, were to say to the departing bachelor, "Actually, I don't think going to a strip club for your bachelor party celebrates your impending marriage. It's not respectful to your wife or to women in general, and I don't think it reflects well on you or on any of us. And while I support your marriage and am excited to celebrate with you, this isn't the way to do it." Imagine if women were to speak out about their discomfort and dislike of pornography, about how their partners become distant, disconnected, and lonely, rather than pretend to be game and go along. Imagine if women who pursued pornography themselves because it was deemed hip or sexy or fun decided instead that it was hipper and sexier and more fun to actually have sex with another live, completely engaged individual.

Men and the Reality of Pornography

Men have been sold on the idea that pornography is a harmless amusement and a natural pursuit, both a right of passage and a man's right. Not surprisingly, this message has come courtesy of the industry itself, put forward in the earliest pornographic magazines and pounded home through the years. When objections to pornography were made, men were to understand that those cries came only from women, and that, naturally, women couldn't understand. When questioned, most men readily concede that pornography probably isn't the greatest thing for women. But few men have stopped to consider what pornography does to men.

It's time they took notice. Pornography has a corrosive effect on men's relationships with women and a negative impact on male sexual performance and satisfaction. It plays a rising role in intimacy disorders. More than ever, it aids and abets sexually compulsive behavior in ways that can become seriously disruptive and psychologically damaging. Men who become addicted to pornography feel helpless and degraded, often losing themselves and their loved ones to the habit. Even men who use pornography regularly, but not compulsively, question the effect it has on their lives. For married or otherwise monogamous men, pornography often signals discomfort or uneasiness in a relationship. They hide their porn from their girlfriends and wives, make light of it with other men, and even lie about it to themselves—underestimating their consumption, writing off the impact, telling themselves they only ended up looking for two hours because they were stressed, tired, bored, or annoyed. Men caught with pornography by their bosses or their wives often feel humiliated and pathetic. They get defensive and angry, alienating the people who matter most to them. They can lose their jobs and jeopardize their careers. They can weaken or destroy their marriages and isolate their children. What titillates in the short term hardly merits the long-term costs.

Pornography is degrading in its own way to men. In interviews, porn stars and strippers typically say they view their male patrons with revulsion and disrespect. They see men who frequent strip clubs as pathetic, egotistical, women hating, superficial, stupid, out of control, predatory, or just plain rude. Yet men who use pornography have been stamped by the pornified culture as manly, virile, powerful, suave, and confident. They have been told that they're "getting" women through the pages of magazines, the purchase of lap dances, the downloading of images. In reality, they are most certainly *not* getting any women while engaged in such pursuits. So why should men allow themselves to be manipulated in this way? And why shouldn't men be allowed to speak out? If a man chooses not to go to a strip club for a bachelor party, not only out of respect for women but out of self-respect, he should be commended rather than mocked for his actions. If enough men did so decisively, pornography would no longer be fated for mass acceptance.

One of the greatest myths spread by the pornified culture is that all men look at pornography. Yet the *only* men who believed this to be true in interviews happen to be the men who looked at pornography themselves. According to the *Pornified*/Harris poll, only 27 percent of Americans agreed with the statement "All men look at pornography." The truth is, despite what fans tell themselves about the ubiquity and necessity of porn, many men do not look at it, and their disinterest isn't necessarily about religion or politics. Many men who do not look are neither asexual nor repressed, neither afraid nor unaware of pornography's "appeal." Yet expressing distaste or disinterest is considered shameful or foolish in a pornified culture. Those who oppose pornography are branded as pussies or wimps, cowed by women or afraid of their own sexuality. This is startling when you consider that, given most men's preference for actual sex to pornography, to use pornography is to declare oneself amorously inept or impotent, unable to relate to women, socially and emotionally immature, unwanted, or lonely. If men truly prefer sex to porn, they should be allowed and encouraged to act that way.

The humiliation of using pornography back when it was a lot less anonymous and accessible wasn't exclusively about religious guilt. It was about the embarrassing reality that using pornography denotes a lack of confidence in one's manhood and insecurity in one's sexuality. Women in pornography exist to tell men, "We want you"—we women of the Ivy League, we Hollywood starlets, we girls next door, we the blonde you could never get. A man's sense of manhood is affirmed only by his acquiescence to the idea that he cannot get this woman in the real world, but needs to feel as though he can. Why should men be considered so pathetic as to need these forms of self-esteem trickery? Pornography is sold as something manly and adult, even though pornographic fantasy often stems from sorry episodes of adolescent rejection. It's not just for their nubile beauty that men use pornography to get off on women who look like teenagers. It also serves an emotional need to prove themselves, to be able to say, "Look at me now, I can have you if I want." Many men use pornography as a way to get back at the girls who rebuffed them during their adolescence—they still want to "get" the high school prom queen. Pornography allows men to feel better and stronger and more powerful than those women/girls, mirroring and mining their adolescent fear of emotions and vulnerability. Pornography allows men to fall backward into an arena in which sex is devoid of emotions and fear and risk. It coddles the grown man, then tells him to feel "manly" about his own regression.

In asking men to buy into its myths, pornography underestimates and assumes the worst in men. Most men are intelligent enough to distinguish material that celebrates women from material that denigrates women; they can recognize images that depict healthy sexuality and humanity and images that ridicule and cheapen sexuality and deprive participants of their humanity. It's disrespectful of men's capabilities to expect them to condone viewing pornography that quite clearly shows women in a negative light, doing things that men presume most women would not want to do—gag on semen, get doubly penetrated to the point of pain, be ejaculated on in derogatory ways—treated in so many ways like something less than human.

The pornography user might ask himself how comfortable he would be viewing such material with his teenage daughter or his mother, his sister, or his wife. There's a reason for uneasiness that extends beyond the fact that for most men, as for women, sexuality and masturbation in particular are private matters. The material itself adds an unendurable aspect to public sharing. Few men want their wives to know precisely what they've become accustomed to getting off to. It's usually a far cry from shared fantasies over pillow talk. Most men would not want their female boss at the office to know they spend evenings at home fantasizing over the humiliation of countless interchangeable female bodies. Most men take great pains to deny or rationalize it themselves. What if the lonely, isolated individual clicking away on his Internet browser were to log off not because he was forced to nor because he felt a sense of religious or puritanical guilt, but because he knows to stay online is self-defeating?

Women and the Reality of Pornography

Men are not the only ones who have been taught to seek a false sense of empowerment through pornography. Liberal female college students, third-wave feminists, and even female conservative realists of the "boys will be boys" school now argue that women deserve pornography, too. They claim that to "own" pornography is to make it theirs and that women empower themselves by harnessing their sexual wiles and using it to their advantage. In the same way that certain women's groups have rallied behind prostitutes, demanding they be called "sex workers" and accorded labor rights, the pornography-as-empowerment movement sees no problem with women being bought for their bodies—as long as *they* are making the profit.

Indeed, pro-porn women are most definitely in favor of women raking in money for sex, and they angrily denounce those women who would have it otherwise. Pro-porn women such as Melinda Gallagher, founder of CAKE, accuse feminists of squelching women's sexuality: "The imperialistic mentality of the anti-porn feminists, who came into women's lives and said, 'You shouldn't like this and that's bad and we're gonna draw that line,' created a lot of damage. CAKE is not going to buy into that mentality."[4] Tristan Taormino, a writer and director who bills herself as a "feminist pornographer," travels to college campuses to speak out about women's right to "pornify themselves." At the first international conference on pornography in 1998, advocates on a panel called "Women and Pornography: Victims or Visionaries?" theorized that anti-porn women were more responsible for driving men and women apart than were their pro-porn counterparts. One went so far as to lay derogatory hardcore pornography at the feet of women who oppose pornography. "You've got them so scared sexually that they're mad!" said Nina Hartley, a porn star who was featured in the film *Boogie Nights*. "They can't get laid! They can't get blow jobs! They can't cum! That's why you're seeing more of these women getting dragged on their faces, and spit on, and having their heads dunked in the toilet. Men are mad!"[5]

When they're not accusing anti-porn women of generating hardcore male pornography, many of the new feminist pornography purveyors claim to be subverting "patriarchal porn" with their own version of "alterna-porn." Missy Suicide, the founder of the female-operated pornography Web site Suicide Girls, explains, "Sex and sexuality is [*sic*] nothing for a woman to be ashamed of, but for a long time it felt that way, even in feminism. It's that old attitude that any time you take your clothes off you're being objectified or exploited. I think the women on Suicide Girls are brave in saying, 'I'm confident, I'm intelligent, and I don't have a problem sharing my sexuality with the world. This is what a real body looks like, and it's beautiful.' This is what should be celebrated."[6] Of course, it is unclear where amid the naked poses women can be heard expressing intelligence or confidence. Nor is it clear that their message is getting through amid the barrage of male-oriented pornography out there. There is something almost futile about the new alterna-porn sites, which, in featuring women who are less attractive to the mainstream man, are also vastly less popular than more stereotypical pornography Web sites. This lesson was learned the hard way when the Suicide Girls site was linked to Playboy.com for several months. Playboy.com members greeted the Suicide Girls' untraditional bodies, piercings, and hipster hairstyles with anger and disgust.

Is it even desirable for women to become producers and consumers of pornography? Certainly there is no advantage to women's sexuality becoming more visually cued so that women judge potential partners by their physical appearance to the same extent men do. Equality should come from elevating women to where men hold an advantage, not lowering them to share the costs of pornography with men. Even men who enjoy pornography recognize its degrading nature. One thirty-five-year-old who works in the used-car business and looks at pornography weekly said almost impatiently, "*Of course* pornography is degrading to women. They're being used and that's why I don't like seeing porn where you can tell that they're not enjoying it. If it seems like they're enjoying it you can rationalize in your head while you're looking at it that they're enjoying it as much as the guy is. . . . I guess it's *possible* she's enjoying it, but I highly doubt it. Still, when you're looking at porn, you just try not to pay too much attention to what the woman is thinking and what's going beyond the scenes. Otherwise, you just won't enjoy it at all." By co-opting pornography, women will sink into the same pattern of denial and rationalization.

So why are women so eager to embrace porn? The women's movement during the sixties, seventies, and eighties was accused of being elitist and of not understanding the needs, pressures, and desires of average American women and, in particular, poor, uneducated women. Part of the female pro-porn movement stems from an attempt to correct this alleged attitude. In their effort to be "nonjudgmental," many younger feminists have become uncomfortable condemning pornography when its participants and stars are largely women who choose their work out of financial desperation. Embracing pornography has become almost a new form of political correctness—heaven forbid that someone might appear to "denounce" another person's sexuality or "chosen" profession. Commenting on the university administration's acceptance of Harvard's pornographic magazine *H Bomb,* one of its female founders explained, "I guess they got past their fear of porn." Such phrasing is carefully chosen. Rather than be opposed to pornography for ethical, feminist, or humanist reasons, the only opposition one could have to pornography is fear—that is, phobia as in homophobia. Pornography proponents have even taken to calling their opponents "pornophobic." In other words, to disapprove of pornography is to be intolerant of other lifestyles, and people who disapprove of pornography are just as bigoted as homophobes. And naturally, this accusation of intolerance applies only to those who oppose pornography, not those who perpetuate it.

In other ways, the pro-pornography movement among women is more reactive than proactive. For years, women who fight for women's rights—and especially women who oppose pornography—have been accused of having no sense of humor. If they could just laugh it off, they would realize pornography is fine, their opponents argued. Many women have bought into this absurd proposition, accepting the idea that if you don't find porn funny or amusing or ironic, you just don't get it. Anti-pornography feminists have also been accused of perpetuating a culture of victimization: by pointing out that many women who participate in the production of pornography suffer sexual and emotional abuse, pornography opponents supposedly turn these women into victims. Shouldn't the real target of such accusations be the pornographers themselves?

Perhaps women who choose to participate in or consume pornography *are* making their own "choices." But rather than make choices based on a regressive male ideal of sexuality and limited options, they could make choices based on something beyond body parts and financial desperation. Indeed, hypocrisy reigns in the pro-porn feminist movement. Why insist that it is okay for women to exploit other women, but when men do so, it is harm, harassment, or sexual crime? Some pro-porn feminists remain opposed to prostitution, failing to see the thin line that separates the two forms of sex for sale. Others advocate prostitution as well as pornography, yet are opposed to other forms of human sale, arguing against the sex slavery trade and championing labor rights. In all likelihood, many of those who suggest that pornography is about sexual liberation have probably not seen the kind of pornography that many, perhaps most, men find alluring: the glorification of male promiscuity and adultery, the subordination of women, the sexualization of pain, and even hardcore depictions of female torture. In this context, pornography is not about desire and fantasy; it's about hostility and shame.

The pioneering feminists of the seventies anti-pornography movement were denounced as "radical" in their time; today, pro-porn feminists sometimes refer to their anti-porn counterparts as "conservative feminists." Have women really progressed so far as to make the changes advocated in the seventies somehow retrograde?

Today, the next generation seems all too ready to mock or reject arguments against pornography without giving them serious thought. The truth is, we have not moved forward or beyond those supposedly outdated ideas—we've merely resigned ourselves to them or rationalized them away. Women need to ask themselves, Is this progress or is it prurience? It's sad that ours is a culture where the inclusion of Olympic athletes in *Playboy* magazine is considered a leap forward. That female athletic achievement is reduced to a tool for male masturbatory pleasure is a sentiment scoffed at or ignored. The idea that women will do anything for a buck and a fleeting moment of fame not only still exists, women willingly propagate it. While pornography purports to value the female body above all, it devalues it substantially. Selling one's image online for paying customers doesn't exactly reflect a strong sense of self-respect.

One of the more insidious attacks against women who oppose pornography accuses them of being prudish and uncomfortable with their own sexuality, "insecure," and "jealous." Terrified of being labeled "anti-sex," "humorless," or "feminist," many women have neglected to stand up to pornography. Yet to be opposed to porn in no way means a person is opposed to sexuality in all of its healthy and positive forms. Women who are the most secure and confident, who have the temerity to stand up to such fallacious claims, are surely stronger than the women held in sway by the pornified culture's myths. Moreover, the idea that a woman can't "own" or "explore" her own sexuality without incorporating pornography into her life (as "sex-positive" pro-porn feminists would have it) is insulting, and an extraordinarily narrow and limiting view of sexuality.

The idea persists that people who dislike pornography are somehow repressed or wrestling under religious dogma or stymied by a conservative upbringing doesn't hold true. Interviewing women for this book, I repeatedly heard things like, "I don't mean to sound like a prude but . . ." bookending comments criticizing pornography, and sometimes chased down with the disclaimer, "And I'm liberal!" Sadly, women seem to have absorbed the message that to criticize pornography is to be uncool, unsexy, and reactionary. The reality is that women who are opposed to pornography or troubled by its effects on our society come from all walks of life and espouse a wide range of political ideologies. Many are attractive, happily single, sexually active, married, or fulfilled. They are strong, smart, opinionated women who, when it comes to articulating their feelings about pornography, feel silenced or fearful. They are reluctant to complain about pornography or to speak out about the subject. They are afraid to confront their boyfriends and husbands about it, nervous talking to their teenaged sons, cowed into accepting what they know in their hearts to be unacceptable.

Their reticence is understandable. It is tempting to acquiesce to the defensive cries of, "But it's just naked women! It's just sex!" For there is nothing wrong with naked women or sex. But pornography is not just naked women, and it is not sex. The sexual acts depicted in pornography are more about shame, humiliation, solitude, coldness, and degradation than they are about pleasure, intimacy, and love. The word *pornography* comes from the Greek *porne,* which means prostitute or whore, and *graphos,* which means depiction or writing. Pornography is, at its core, the commercialization of women, turning men into consumers and women into a product to be used and discarded. If pornography were truly just about sex and naked bodies, there would be nothing to get upset over, but those who know better, those who bother to think while they gaze or who stop averting their eyes for a moment and address what's on-screen in the cubicle behind them, should—and can—no longer be ignored.

The longer we ignore the problem of pornography, the worse it becomes. The dissemination and availability of pornography inevitably bring about increased individual and societal acceptance. Research shows that the more pornography one is exposed to, the more tolerant of pornography and indeed in favor of pornography one becomes.[7] What was once softcore pornography has become mainstream; magazines that were once considered pornographic are now filed under "men's lifestyle"; men's lifestyle magazines have in turn aspired toward the pornographic. As porn creeps into the mainstream press and into popular culture, it crowds out other, more positive forms of sexual expression. It also keeps raising the bar higher for "real" pornography, which stretches to surpass every imaginable ethical, humanistic, and societal limit. Pregnant women become pornified, their naked torsos wrested from personal Web sites onto "pregnant porn" Web sites, incest becomes fetishized, child pornography blends with adult pornography into an ageless "teen porn" middle ground. Any sense of taboo dissipates in a free-for-all porn world.

Not only does pornography viewing indulge and abet the pornographic culture, it also has policy implications. Studies have shown that those who view heavy doses of pornography are less likely to believe there's a need for restrictions on pornography for minors and are less likely to favor restrictions in broadcasting.[8] Passively accepting life in a pornified culture is helping pornography flourish, a fact of which the industry is well aware. Our eyes become blinded by porn.

Pornography is a moving target and it's time we catch up with it. For years, the pornography industry and the pornified culture have told both men and women who oppose pornography to shut up or turn a blind eye. They have accused anti-pornography activists, or even those who have dared question their profit equation, of being anti-sex and anti-freedom. They have done so while creating a forcefully anti-sex product that limits the freedom of men, women, and children. They have sold America on the idea of fantasy while inciting us to ignore reality. Those who have been silenced have only served to further legitimize pornography with their lack of censure. Those who are now quiet must speak out.

Notes

Introduction: A Pornified World

1. Jancee Dunn, "Rock-Porn Connection," Rolling Stone.com, August 3, 1999.

2. "The Making of Sex Hop," BET.com, July 31, 2003.

3. Lawrence Van Gelder, "Arts Briefing," *New York Times,* July 19, 2004.

4. Mark Caro, "The New Skin Trade," *Chicago Tribune,* September 19, 2004.

5. Richard Johnson, "Page Six," *New York Post,* May 4, 2004.

6. Johnny Maldaro, "Abu Gag!" Village Voice.com, August 6, 2004.

1. A Guy Thing: Why Men Look at Porn

1. Jake (anonymous), "Why Nice Guys Like Online Porn," *Glamour,* February 2004, p. 100.

2. John Schwartz, "Leisure Pursuits of Today's Young Man," *New York Times,* March 29, 2004

3. D. Zillmann, "Pornografie," in *Lehrbuch der Medienpsychologie,* ed. R. Mangold, P. Vorderer, and G. Bente (Göttingen, Germany: Hogrefe Verlag, 2004), pp. 565–85.

4. Jake (anonymous), "Jake's Guide to Talking Dirty," *Glamour,* May 2004, p. 124.

5. J. Michael Parker, "Sexual Healing: Ministries Help Men with Purity Struggle," *San Antonio Express-News,* January 31, 2004, p. 7B.

6. Bobby Ross, Jr., "Dallas Billboards Target Christians Addicted to Porn," Associated Press, February 21, 2004.

7. Ibid.

8. Beau Black, "Evangelical Churches Target Porn Addiction," *Orlando Sentinel,* February 21, 2004.

9. Burt Prelutsky, "Mortified and Mystified by This Business of Show," *Los Angeles Times,* February 2, 2004.

10. "Cerberian and SonicWALL Web Usage Survey Reveals 75% Accidentally See Porn at Work," Business Wire, June 23, 2004.

11. Julie Forster, "X-Rated Surfing Common at Work," *Saint Paul Pioneer Press,* February 14, 2004.

12. Associated Press, "State Ousts 23 Employees for Using Computers to Look at Porn," Frankfort, Ky., May 22, 2004.

13. Peter Bacque, "VDOT Computer Abuse Reported," *Richmond Times Dispatch,* February 4, 2004.

14. Forster, "X-Rated Surfing Common at Work."

15. Associated Press, "Report: FBI Reviewing Claims of Porn Web Site Viewing at UTHSC," February 3, 2004.

16. Michael Barron and Michael S. Kimmel, "Sexual Violence in Three Pornographic Media: Toward a Sociological Explanation," *Journal of Sex Research* 37 (May 2000): 6.

17. TalkAboutSupport.com, January 29, 2004.

18. Robert Jensen, "A Cruel Edge: The Painful Truth about Today's Pornography—and What Men Can Do About It," *Ms.,* Spring 2004, pp. 55–58.

2. How We Got Here: Life in the Porn Lane

1. David Mura, "A Male Grief: Notes on Pornography and Addiction," in *Men Confront Pornography,* ed. Michael S. Kimmel (New York: Crown Publishers, 1990), p. 137.

2. Larry Flynt, "Porn World's Sky Isn't Falling—It Doesn't Need a Condom Rule," *Los Angeles Times,* April 23, 2004.

3. Michael S. Kimmel, "'Insult' or 'Injury': Sex, Pornography and Sexism," in *Men Confront Pornography,* p. 317.

4. Michael Barron and Michael S. Kimmel, "Sexual Violence in Three

Pornographic Media: Toward a Sociological Explanation," *Journal of Sex Research* 37 (May 2000): 2.

5. Dennis McAlpine, interview, "American Porn," *Frontline,* PBS, August 2001.

6. John Motavalli, "Columbia House Plans Porn Club," *New York Post* online edition, January 10, 2005.

7. McAlpine, "American Porn."

8. CBSNews.com, "Porn in the U.S.A.," November 21, 2003.

9. McAlpine, "American Porn."

10. Chris Walsh, "Feeding on Flesh: Colorado Companies Are Making Millions in the Adult Entertainment Business," *Rocky Mountain News,* April 3, 2004.

11. McAlpine, "American Porn."

12. For example, a block of time watching standard Vivid Entertainment fare on the Playboy Channel might cost $5.95, while more hardcore material costs as much as $11.95.

13. Steve Donohue, "Playboy Takes a Soft Approach to Hard Content," *Multichannel News,* May 10, 2004, p. 30.

14. McAlpine, "American Porn."

15. Barron and Kimmel, "Sexual Violence in Three Pornographic Media," pp. 2–3.

16. Ibid., p. 5.

17. "Websense Research Shows Online Pornography Sites Continue Strong Growth," PRNewswire.com, April 4, 2004.

18. U.S. Government Accountability Office (GAO), "File-Sharing Programs: Peer-to-Peer Networks Provide Ready Access to Child Pornography" (Washington, D.C.: GAO, February 2003).

19. Frank Coggrave, "Bugwatch: The Perils of Peer-to-Peer," VNU Business Publications, March 31, 2004.

20. Elizabeth Armstrong, "America's New Cubicle Pirates Find Their Loot Online," *Christian Science Monitor,* March 19, 2004.

21. "Porn More Popular than Search," InternetWeek.com, June 4, 2004.

22. John Schwartz, "Google Protests Give Web Site an Audience," *New York Times,* February 2, 2004.

23. Jeffrey Selingo, "Entertaining Miss Daisy," *New York Times,* April 22, 2004.

24. Jennifer L. Schenker, "In Europe, Cellphone Profits Go Up as Clothes Come Off," *New York Times,* May 4, 2004.
25. "Porn Goes Portable," *Chicago Tribune,* February 26, 2003.
26. Mark Evans, "Porn Goes Wireless," *The National Post,* October 26, 2004.
27. Robert Yager, "The Trouble with Larry," *The Independent,* February 22, 2004.
28. Mireya Navarro, "Dancing in the Lap of Luxury," *New York Times,* May 12, 2004.
29. McAlpine, "American Porn."
30. CBSNews.com., "Porn in the U.S.A."
31. Reuters, "Janet Jackson's Bare Breast Tops Internet Searches," February 4, 2004.
32. *The O'Reilly Factor,* transcript, Fox News, February 9, 2004.
33. Rachel Lehmann-Haupt, "Does Sex Still Sell?" *Folio,* March 1, 2004.
34. "The Year in Sex: A Groping Governor, Nudity for Peace and Bennifer's Stripper," *Playboy,* February 2004, p. 66.

3. Me and My Porn: How Pornography Affects Men

1. J. Bryant and D. Zillmann, "Pornography: Models of Effects on Sexual Deviancy," in *Encyclopedia of Criminology and Deviant Behavior,* ed. C. D. Bryant (Philadelphia: Brunner-Routledge, 2001), pp. 241–44.
2. D. Zillmann, "Pornografie," in *Lehrbuch der Medienpsychologie,* ed. R. Mangold, P. Vorderer, and G. Bente (Göttingen, Germany: Hogrefe Verlag, 2004), pp. 565–85.
3. For a complete discussion of the study, see J. Bryant and D. Zillmann, "Pornography, Sexual Callousness and the Trivialization of Rape," *Journal of Communication* (Autumn 1982), pp. 10–21.
4. J. S. Lyons, R. L. Anderson, and D. Larsen, "A Systematic Review of the Effects of Aggressive and Nonaggressive Pornography," in *Media, Children and the Family: Social Scientific, Psychodynamic, and Clinical Perspectives,* ed. D. Zillmann, J. Bryant, and A. C. Huston (Hillsdale, N.J.: Erlbaum Associates, 1993), p. 305.
5. Paul Restivo, "Pass on the Porn," *Kansas State Collegian,* February 4, 2004.
6. Edward Donnerstein, Daniel Linz, and Steen Penrod, *The Question of Pornography: Research Findings and Policy Implications* (New York: Free Press, 1987), p. 29.

7. Robert Jensen, "A Cruel Edge: The Painful Truth About Today's Pornography—and What Men Can Do About It," *Ms.*, Spring 2004, pp. 55–58.
8. John Schwartz, "The Pornography Industry vs. Digital Pirates," *New York Times,* February 8, 2004.
9. Jensen, "A Cruel Edge," pp. 55–58.
10. "Young Women, Porn & Profits: Corporate America's Secret Affair," *Primetime Live,* ABC, Diane Sawyer, May 27, 2004.
11. D. Zillmann, "Pornografie," pp. 565–85. Author's emphasis.
12. Ryan J. Burns, "Male Internet Pornography Consumers' Perception of Women and Endorsement of Traditional Female Gender Roles" (Austin, Tex.: Department of Communication Studies, University of Texas, 2002), p. 11.

4. Porn Stars, Lovers, and Wives: How Women See Pornography

1. Beth Whiffen, "Confessions," *Cosmopolitan,* March 2004, p. 44.
2. Kenneth Turan, "Movie Review: A 'Girl Next Door' in Sheep's Clothing," *Los Angeles Times,* April 9, 2004.
3. Susan Dominus, "What Women Want to Watch," *New York Times,* Arts & Leisure section.
4. Mireya Navarro, "The Very Long Legs of 'Girls Gone Wild,' " *New York Times,* April 4, 2004.
5. Mireya Navarro, "Women Tailor Sex Industry to Their Eyes," *New York Times,* February 20, 2004.
6. Michael C. Harris, "Punk-Rock Pinups," *Chicago Tribune,* February 18, 2004.
7. Virginia Vitzthum, "Stripped of Our Senses," *Elle,* December 2003, p. 187.
8. Ben Flanagan, "Porn Debate Garners Huge Turnout at U. Alabama," *The Crimson White,* March 18, 2004.
9. Jennifer Harper, "At Harvard, All the Nudes Are Fit to Print," *Washington Times,* February 12, 2004.
10. Ebonie D. Hale, "Committee Approves Porn Magazine," *Harvard Crimson,* February 11, 2004.
11. Jenna Russell, "BU Students to Get Own Sex Magazine," *Boston Globe,* October 6, 2004.
12. Rebecca Rothbaum, "Harvard Lifts Vassar's Erotic Idea," *Poughkeepsie Journal,* February 17, 2004.

13. Tara Weiss, "Why Porn Is a Dirty Word at H Bomb," *Hartford Courant,* February 13, 2004.
14. Chris Freiberg, "Indiana U. Investigates New Dorm Porn," *Indiana Daily Student,* April 6, 2004.
15. Maegan Carberry, "Porn's Next Big Market: Women," *Chicago Tribune,* May 14, 2004.
16. Navarro, "The Very Long Legs of 'Girls Gone Wild.' "
17. Keith Olbermann, *Countdown,* MSNBC, February 23, 3004.
18. Navarro, "Women Tailor Sex Industry to Their Eyes."
19. Reuters, "To-Do List on Mind When Porn Plays?" May 22, 2004.
20. Anahad O'Connor, "In Sex, Brain Studies Show, 'La Differénce' Still Holds," *New York Times,* March 16, 2004.
21. Ibid.
22. Navarro, "Women Tailor Sex Industry to Their Eyes."
23. Robert Jensen, "A Cruel Edge: The Painful Truth About Today's Pornography—And What Men Can Do About It," *Sexual Assault Report,* January/February 2004, pp. 33–34, 45–48.
24. Laura Berman, "Women Warm to Female-Friendly Erotica," *Chicago Sun-Times,* April 26, 2004, p. 56.
25. Roberta Myers, "Editor's Page," *Elle,* February 2004.
26. Jane Stancill, "Playboy Visit Sparks UNC Protest," *Raleigh News & Observer,* April 6, 2004.
27. Marjorie Ingall, "31 Essential Sex & Love Experiences," *Glamour,* May 2004, p. 232.
28. Julie Polito, "Jump Start Your Sex Life," *Self,* March 2004, p. 135.
29. "The Help Desk," *New York,* April 19, 2004, p. 125.
30. Amy Dickinson, "Porn Viewing Draws Responses from Readers," *Chicago Tribune,* February 6, 2004.
31. Whiffen, "Confessions," p. 44.

5. You and Me and Pornography: How Porn Affects Relationships

1. *Pornified*/Harris poll, 2004.
2. Dr. Gail Saltz, interview, *The Today Show,* transcript, NBC, March 3, 2004.
3. *Pornified*/Harris poll, 2004.
4. E. Jean Carroll, "Ask E. Jean," *Elle,* March 2004, p. 148.

5. D. Zillmann, "Pornografie," in *Lehrbuch der Medienpsychologie,* ed. R. Mangold, P. Vorderer, and G. Bente (Göttingen, Germany: Hogrefe Verlag, 2004), pp. 565–85.

6. D. Zillmann, "Effects of Prolonged Consumption of Pornography," in *Pornography: Research Advances and Policy Considerations,* ed. D. Zillmann and J. Bryant (Hillsdale, N.J.: L. Erlbaum Associates, 1989), p. 155.

7. "Playboy Advisor," *Playboy,* March 2004, p. 50.

8. Ellie, "His Porn Habit Has Become a Hard-core Problem," *Toronto Star,* July 4, 2004.

9. Brenda Shoshanna, "Help! My Husband Is Addicted to Porn," iVillage.com, 2004.

10. Jennifer Schneider, "Effects of Cybersex Addiction on the Family," *Sexual Addiction and Compulsivity* 7 (2000): 31–58.

11. Susan Dominus, "Our Love/Hate Affair with Our Bodies," *Glamour,* May 2004, p. 219.

12. Jo Revill, "The New Nose Job: Designer Vaginas," *The Observer* (London), August 17, 2003.

13. TalkAboutSupport.com, January 29, 2004.

14. Schneider, "Effects of Cybersex Addiction on the Family."

15. Harlan Cohen, "Help Me, Harlan: Does Porn Have a Place in Their Lives?" *Saint Paul* (Minn.) *Pioneer Press,* April 20, 2004.

16. Lynn Harris, "Stop Him Before He Clicks Again!" Salon.com, April 15, 2004.

17. Women Online Worldwide, www.wowwomen.com.

18. "Dear Abby," *Contra Costa* (Calif.) *Times,* April 17, 2004, p. F4.

19. Ruth Westheimer, "Have I Been Replaced by Porn?" iVillage.com, 2004.

20. Patti Britton, "Porn: Fantasy or Filth?" iVillage.com, 2004.

6. Born into Porn: Kids in a Pornified Culture

1. Mark Prigg and Paul Sims, "Truth About Dangers of Net as Half of Children Are Exposed to Porn," *The Evening Standard* (London), September 3, 2004.

2. Of the 177 downloaded images, 61 were of adult pornography, 24 were cartoon pornography, 13 were child erotica, and 2 were child porn. U.S. Government Accountability Office, "File-Sharing Programs: Peer-to-Peer

Networks Provide Ready Access to Child Pornography" (Washington, D.C.: GAO, February 2003).

3. Diana Russell, "Children's Access to Child and Adult Pornography," work in progress.

4. Editorial, "Protecting Kids Online," *Washington Post,* July 1, 2004.

5. Stephen Jones, "Opinion—Young Voices: Libraries Should Put Permanent Blocks on Porn," *The Columbian* (Vancouver, Wa.), March 15, 2004.

6. Of those incidents, 472 involved children accessing pornography on the library's computers, 106 were situations in which adults exposed kids to pornography in the library, 23 were cases in which pornography was specifically left for children, and 113 instances occurred when pornography was left on the printer or computer screen. An additional 26 cases involved children accidentally viewing pornography at the library.

7. Associated Press, "High School Teacher Accused of Downloading Pornography, Assault," February 11, 2004.

8. Mel Melendez, "North High Math Teacher Faces Firing," *Arizona Republic,* March 6, 2004.

9. Associated Press, "Teacher Gets Seven Years for Showing Students Pornography," February 3, 2004.

10. Terry Webster, "Parents Say Porn Accessed in Class," *Fort Worth Star Telegram,* April 4, 2004.

11. Courtney C. Radsch, "Teenagers Sexual Activity Is Tied to Drugs and Drink," *New York Times,* August 30, 2004. In addition, a teenager with a majority of friends who do so is three times more likely to smoke, drink, or use illegal drugs than a teen who has no such friends.

12. National Center on Addiction and Substance Abuse, "National Survey of American Attitudes on Substance Abuse IX: Teen Dating Practices and Sexual Activity" (New York: Columbia University Press, 2004), p. 23.

13. Benoit Denizet-Lewis, "Friends, Friends with Benefits and the Benefits of the Local Mall," *The New York Times Magazine,* May 30, 2004, p. 30.

14. Tor Thorsen, "Take-Two, Sony, and Microsoft Sued Over 'The Guy Game,'" Gamespot.com, December 21, 2004.

15. Associated Press, "Boy Not Allowed to Bring Porn Star to Prom," June 7, 2004.

16. Klepal, Dan, "Two Students Accused of Selling Video Porn," *Cincinnati*

Enquirer, February 13, 2004; UPI, "Two 14-Year-Old Drunk Girls Videotaped," June 25, 2004.

17. Thomas Lake, "Stripper Pole in JU Dorm Draws Crowd," *Florida Times-Union,* September 23, 2004.

18. Joseph Ax, "Experts Say Culture, Technology to Blame," *Journal News* (Westchester County, N.Y.), June 25, 2004.

19. Strawberry Saroyan, "The XXX Files," *Los Angeles Times,* September 11, 2004.

20. Associated Press, "Closing Arguments Held for Orange County Teens Charged with Raping Unconscious Girl," June 23, 2004.

21. Lisa McPheron, "Porn Actresses May Testify in O.C. Rape Trial," *Inland Valley Daily Bulletin,* June 1, 2004.

22. R. Scott Moxley, "Hail Your Daughters," *OC* (Orange County) *Weekly,* May 7–13, 2004.

23. Deepa Bharath, "Adult Film Star Denied from Stand," *Los Angeles Times,* June 4, 2004.

24. Richard Jerome, "The Cyberporn Generation," *People,* April 26, 2004, p. 74.

25. Associated Press, "Student Suspended Over Tape of Herself and Classmates Having Sex," February 28, 2004.

26. Associated Press, "Teen Girl Charged with Posting Nude Photos on Internet," March 29, 2004.

27. Alison Pollet and Page Hurwitz, "Strip Till You Drop," *The Nation,* January 12, 2004, p. 20.

28. David K. Li, "Prince of Porn Hustling After Cable, NY Presence," *New York Post,* March 16, 2004.

29. Cynthia Littleton, "Hugh Hefner, Stan Lee to Hop to 'Superbunnies,'" *Reuters/Hollywood Reporter,* September 7, 2004.

30. Chris Morris, "Video Games Get Raunchy," CNNMoney.com, May 12, 2004.

31. Jerome, "The Cyberporn Generation," p. 72.

32. Susan Clairmont, "Porn Gave Kids Know-how to Assault Their Friends," *Hamilton Spectator* (Ontario), March 25, 2004.

33. Steve Sternberg and Anthony DeBarros, "Abstinence-Only Support Often Reflects State Politics," *USA Today,* June 29, 2004.

34. Russell, "Children's Access to Child and Adult Pornography."
35. David B. Caruso, "Internet Fuels Child Porn Trafficking," Associated Press, January 15, 2005. Cases went from 113 in fiscal 1996 to 2,645 in fiscal 2004.
36. PRNewswire.com, "Global Campaign Against Child Pornography Is Launched," April 22, 2004.
37. Bob Purvis, "Pedophiles Still Taking Internet Bait," *Milwaukee Journal Sentinel,* July 6, 2004.
38. GAO, "File-Sharing Programs."
39. Ibid.
40. Ibid.
41. PRNewswire.com, "Telenor and KRIPOS Introduce Internet Child Pornography Filter," September 21, 2004.
42. GAO, "File-Sharing Programs."
43. CTV News, June 15, 2004.
44. Tim Ross, and Ben Mitchell, "Disgraced Former Judge: I Downloaded Child Porn," Press Association News, June 16, 2004.
45. CP, "Kiddie-Porn Suspect Worked with Children," *Edmonton Sun,* May 26, 2004.
46. Frank Curreri, "Man's Arrest Surprises Neighbors," *Las Vegas Review-Journal,* February 18, 2004.
47. Mike Robinson, "Chicago School Principal Charged with Kiddie Porn," Associated Press, March 29, 2004.
48. Gail Gibson, "Jury Finds Man Guilty in Teen-Sex Sting Case," *Baltimore Sun,* March 24, 2004.
49. Peter Franceschina, "Ex-Youth Leader Receives 17½ Years for Child Porn," *Sun-Sentinel* (Fort Lauderdale), January 22, 2004.
50. Associated Press, "Former Christian Radio Employee Pleads Guilty in Child Porn Case," February 13, 2004.
51. Sheridan Lyons, "Halethorpe Man Charged in Child Pornography Case," *Baltimore Sun,* February 14, 2004.
52. Nicole Martin, "BT Blocks 20,000 Attempts a Day to Access Child Porn," *Daily Telegraph* (London), July 21, 2004.
53. Marc Hansen, "Imprisoned by the Internet," *Des Moines Register,* January 16, 2005.

54. Jonathan Athens, "Teen Admits to Downloading Child Porn," *Newark* (Ohio) *Advocate,* January 30, 2004.
55. Patrick Goodenough, "Online Porn Driving Sexually Aggressive Children," CNS News Web site, November 25, 2003.
56. Richard Oakley and Jan Battles, "Cork to Research Teen Porn Addicts," *Sunday Times* (London), January 25, 2004.
57. Martha Linden, "Parents Unaware of Children's Online Activities," Press Association News, July 21, 2004.
58. PRNewswire.com, "Global Campaign Against Child Pornography Is Launched."
59. *Pornified*/Harris poll.
60. Associated Press, "Couple Sues Blockbuster After Child Views Pornographic Images on Video," January 24, 2004.
61. T. M. Shultz, "Porn Replaces Youth Football Web Site," *Lansing* (Mich.) *State Journal,* July 26, 2004.
62. Pollet and Hurwitz, "Strip Till You Drop."
63. Editorial, "Chipping Away at Web Porn," *Los Angeles Times,* July 1, 2004.

7. Fantasy and Reality: Pornography Compulsion

1. Christopher S. Stewart, "God Loves Us All, Even You Sex Freaks," *GQ,* June 2004, p. 98.
2. Al Cooper, "In-Depth Study Outlines Reasons Men and Women Engage in Online Sexual Activities" (San Jose, Calif.: San Jose Marital and Sexuality Centre, n.d.).
3. www.pointlesswasteoftime.com/pornoff.html.
4. David Mura, "A Male Grief: Notes on Pornography and Addiction," in *Men Confront Pornography,* ed. Michael S. Kimmel (New York: Crown Publishers, 1990), p. 125.
5. D. Zillmann, "Pornografie," in *Lehrbuch der Medienpsychologie,* ed. R. Mangold, P. Vorderer, and G. Bente (Göttingen, Germany: Hogrefe Verlag, 2004), pp. 565–85.
6. Victor B. Cline, "Pornography's Effects on Adults and Children" (New York: Morality in Media, n.d.).
7. Jennifer Schneider, "Effects of Cybersex Addiction on the Family," *Sexual Addiction and Compulsivity* 7 (2000): 31–58.

8. The Truth about Pornography

1. www.extremeasssociates.com.

2. Anne Kingston, "Porn of Another Kind: To Sexually Humiliate Someone Is to Destroy His Sense of Self," *National Post* (Ontario), May 11, 2004.

3. Dan Savage, interviewed on CNN, *Paula Zahn Now,* transcript, March 4, 2004.

4. Amy Dickinson, "Porn Viewing Draws Responses from Readers," *Chicago Tribune,* February 6, 2004.

5. D. Zillmann, "Pornografie," in *Lehrbuch der Medienpsychologie,* ed. R. Mangold, P. Vorderer, and G. Bente (Göttingen, Germany: Hogrefe Verlag, 2004), pp. 565–85.

6. Christopher D. Hunter, "The Dangers of Pornography? A Review of the Effects Literature" (Ph.D. diss., Annenberg School for Communication, University of Pennsylvania Press, March 2000).

7. T. L. Stanley, "The Porno-ization of American Media and Marketing," AdAge.com, January 26, 2004.

8. Justin Vann, "Ashcroft Heading Anti-Porn Thrust," UniversityWire.com, April 14, 2004.

9. Stanley, "The Porno-ization of American Media and Marketing."

10. "Porn in the U.S.A.," CBSNews.com, September 5, 2004.

11. David Bowman, "Citizen Flynt," Salon.com, July 8, 2004.

12. Robert Yager, "The Trouble with Larry," *The Independent* (London), February 22, 2004.

13. Ibid.

14. David G. Savage, "Court Rejects Law Blocking Internet Porn," *Los Angeles Times,* June 30, 2004.

15. Wirthlin Worldwide March 2004 national telephone poll. Question was phrased:

> Since 1995, the World Wide Web has expanded rapidly and is now estimated to contain as many as 40 million Web sites. A large number of these Internet Web sites contain hardcore pornography. The Supreme Court has said that those who distribute hardcore pornography can be prosecuted under obscenity laws. In 1996, Congress expanded federal obscenity laws,

making it a crime to distribute obscene materials on the Internet. In your opinion should the federal laws against Internet obscenity be vigorously enforced?

16. General Social Survey of the National Opinion Research Center, 2000 and 2002.
17. Warren Richey, "Court Hears Case on Regulating the Web," *Christian Science Monitor,* March 2, 2004.
18. Andy Bull, "After the Fall," *The Times Magazine* (London), July 17, 2004, p. 39.
19. Anderson Cooper, *360 Degrees,* CNN, April 13, 2004.
20. Michael S. Kimmel, *Men Confront Pornography* (New York: Crown Publishers, 1990), p. 13. Author's emphasis.

Conclusion: The Censure-Not-Censor Solution

1. Dennis McAlpine, interview, "Porn America," *Frontline,* PBS, August 2001.
2. Jonathan A. Knee, "Is That Really Legal?" *New York Times,* May 2, 2004.
3. Jonathan Prynn, "Vodafone Restricts Sex Sites," *Evening Standard* (London), July 2, 2004.
4. Virginia Vitzthum, "Stripped of Our Senses," *Elle,* December 2003, p. 188.
5. Carina Chocano, "Scholars of Smut," Salon.com, October 5, 1998.
6. Neva Chonin, "Pretty in Porn: Alterna-Porn Is Challenging the Playboy Body Ideal," *San Francisco Chronicle,* July 25, 2004.
7. In the Zillmann-Bryant experiments, subjects were asked to evaluate a pornographic film following their six weeks of exposure (or nonexposure in the case of the control group) to pornographic movies. Among the high-exposure group, only 26 percent found the selected film to be offensive, compared with 75 percent of those who had not seen any pornographic films during the six-week period. Similarly, only 29 percent of those in the high-exposure group found the films to be pornographic while 70 percent of those in the control group considered the film pornographic.
8. Dolf Zillmann and Jennings Bryant, "Pornography, Sexual Callousness, and the Trivialization of Rape," *Journal of Communication* 32 (August 1982): 10–21.

Acknowledgments

First and foremost, I am indebted to all those men and women who agreed to spend hours talking to me for my interviews. For many, this was a private and sensitive topic, yet everyone was forthcoming and honest in ways I hardly could have imagined. Many thanks to all those anonymous individuals who gave so generously of their own free time.

I also would like to thank the sociologists, attorneys, psychologists, and other academics and professionals who answered my questions and allowed me to observe them at work. In particular, thanks to Robert Jensen, Bryant Jennings, Gary Brooks, Mark Schwartz, Aline Zoldbrod, Judith Coché, Michael Kimmel, and David Marcus.

Harris Interactive was a tremendous help to me. Thanks to Ria Ignacio, Robyn Bald, Nancy Wong, and, most especially, Humphrey Taylor at Harris. Humphrey, you said yes when you could have very easily said no. This book would not have been the same without your open-mindedness, willingness, and generosity. I cannot thank you enough.

This story began as an article for *Time* magazine, a publication any writer would dream of writing for, and to which this writer in particular is enormously grateful. This book would not have existed without "The Porn Factor" as impetus. I want to thank Steve Koepp, Priscilla

Painton, and Jan Simpson for encouraging me to write for *Time*. I especially would like to thank Claudia Wallis—without hyperbole, the ideal editor and a valuable mentor.

Many friends, fellow writers, and editors helped me both personally and practically with this book. Thanks to Alysia Abbott, Hilary Black, Victoria Camelio, Rachael Combe, Holly Gordon, Rachel Lehmann-Haupt, Ariel Levy, Mindy Lewis, Vanessa Mobley, Annie Murphy Paul, Pauline O'Connor, and Ericka Tullis for providing insight, assistance, and support. I would also like to thank Annie Paul and Alissa Quart as well as fellow members Stacy Sullivan, Heidi Postlewait, Sherri Fink, Susan Burton, Debbie Siegel, Paul Raeburn, Elizabeth DaVita-Raeburn, Rebecca Segall, Christine Kenneally, Abby Ellin, and Katie Orenstein, for our incredible authors' group.

Perhaps the smartest decision I made with this book was to publish with Times Books. Everyone there—Paul Golob, Christine Ball, Denise Cronin, Heather Florence, Chris O'Connell, Eva Diaz, Richard Rhorer, Maggie Richards, and especially my editor Robin Dennis—has been accommodating, generous and very, very smart about how this book should be handled. And of course, many thanks to the brilliant Lydia Wills, who led me there. I'm absolutely convinced I have the best agent there is.

Finally, I would like to thank those closest to me, my family—Mom, Dad, Carol, Roger, Brian and Suzanne, Nick, Erik and Debbie, and Kirsten—and the memory of my beloved late aunt Madelyn. Many thanks to my new family—Debra and David, Emily and Jeremy, Jessica and Sina. And to my own family, for now and forever, Michael and Beatrice. Michael, you know this book literally could not have been written without you. As I said on a certain special day in July, words cannot suffice. I'm just so glad you and Bee have been right here to keep me company along the way.

Index

About the Author

PAMELA PAUL is a contributor to *Time* magazine and the author of *The Starter Marriage and the Future of Matrimony*. Previously a senior editor at *American Demographics* and a correspondent for *The Economist,* she has written for such publications as *Psychology Today, Elle, Self, Marie Claire, Ladies' Home Journal,* and *The New York Times Book Review*.